D1383079

THE
PAPACY
IN
TRANSITION

THE
PAPACY
IN
TRANSITION

Patrick Granfield

Doubleday & Company, Inc., Garden City, New York

1980

Grateful acknowledgment is made to the following publishers for permission to quote from their published works:

Selections from *The Documents of Vatican II*, edited by W. M. Abbott, S.J., are reprinted with permission of America Press, Inc., 106 West 56th Street, New York, N.Y. 10019, © 1966. All rights reserved.

Selections from *The Teaching of the Church*, prepared by J. Neuner and H. Roos, edited by Karl Rahner, © 1967 by the Society of St. Paul are reprinted with permission of Alba House Publishers.

Selections from *Papal Primacy and the Universal Church* by P. C. Empie and T. A. Murphy, copyright © 1974, U.S.A. National Committee, Lutheran World Federation and Bishop's Committee for Ecumenical and Interreligious Affairs are reprinted with the permission of Augsburg Publishing House.

Selections from *The Resilient Church* by Avery Dulles, S.J., copyright © 1977 by Avery Dulles are reprinted with the permission of Doubleday & Company, Inc.

To My Mother

ISBN: 0-385-14327-3

Library of Congress Catalog Card Number 79-7049

CONTENTS

3

THE POPE AS MONARCH   34

4

THE POPE AS FELLOW BISHOP   62

5

THE POPE AS ECUMENICAL PASTOR   96

6

THE POPE AS ELECTED LEADER   124

7

THE LOSS OF THE PAPACY   151

8

THE POPE OF THE FUTURE   175

PREFACE

Seven years ago, I published *Ecclesial Cybernetics: A Study of Democracy in the Church* (Macmillan, 1973), convinced that cybernetics, the science of communication and control, could help the Church better understand its mission in the challenging last quarter of the twentieth century and that some form of participatory democracy, cybernetically and theologically sound, would make the Church more responsive and effective in realizing that goal. I still think so today and I am also sure that coresponsibility does not make papal leadership obsolete. On the contrary, this type of leadership is required more than ever before; the demands upon it, however, are the stringent demands of a radically new age. My purpose, then, is to examine in detail this multifaceted papacy in transition.

In one dramatic seventy-two-day period, during the writing of this book, two Popes died and two more were elected. Nothing like this had happened since 1605. Suddenly, all the world's focus was on Rome; John Paul I and John Paul II had revealed a papacy clearly in transition. For me, a scholarly research topic had become overnight front-page headlines. Yet as the memories of the inaugurations faded, there remained this new dimension, the profound change that had taken place symbolized perhaps by the absence of the tiara, the throne, the royal pageantry, but even more by the embracing warmth, the sophisticated intelligence, and the international rapport of the first non-Italian Pope in centuries—the papacy had entered the modern era. Christians everywhere began to look forward, more hopefully than ever before, to a deeper and wiser renewal of the papal office.

I try to foster this papal renewal, not by offering a complete theology of the papacy—I do not, for example, treat in detail the origins of the papacy in Scripture and tradition or the thorny problem of infallibility, two areas requiring much broader treatment than possible here—but by focusing specifically on the transitional aspects of the papacy. In doing so, I have had three goals: to delineate certain critical elements in the Petrine ministry today; to situate them in their historical contexts; and to suggest some reasonable directions for them in the future. My theological ground is the vision of the Church presented at Vatican II, with its emphasis on the pastoral quality of all Church ministry. Although I do write from a Catholic perspective, I am, nevertheless, sensitive to the significant ecumenical implications a renewed papacy has for all Christians.

This book is an attempt to see the full dimensions of the changing papacy. Today, the most radical transition is from a monarchical to a collegial self-understanding, and on this the other transitional aspects depend. But to understand what is happening currently, it is necessary to see what has happened historically. In the first chapter, therefore, I point out the crucial transitions of the papacy from the past up to the modern era. Since the papacy has had many enemies and critics, in the second chapter, I look over a cross section of these negative responses with the positive purpose of learning the basic objections to this, the oldest of institutions. In the third chapter, I confront squarely what has been at the root of much antipapal criticism, namely, the monarchical conception of the papacy, dominant in Catholic ecclesiology for over a millennium. I bring out the counterbalance to monarchy in the fourth chapter, which deals with the equally ancient episcopal and pastoral dimensions of the papal office. As an extension of this pastoral role, I try to assess in the fifth chapter the ecumenical aspects of the Petrine primacy as a means of bringing together all Christian churches. In the next two chapters, I examine areas ostensibly procedural but fraught with theological problems important to a renewed papacy: papal elections in the sixth chapter and papal resignation and deposition in the seventh. Finally, in the eighth chapter, I attempt a job description for an ideal modern Pope, evaluating the qualities needed if the successor of St. Peter is to communicate effectively the liberating spirit of the Gospel of Jesus Christ.

Before concluding, I want to express my thanks to the many who have helped me complete this work. First of all, I am deeply grateful to the two who first suggested that I write a book on the papacy: John A. Miles, Jr., then an editor at Doubleday, and Avery Dulles, S.J., my colleague at The Catholic University of America. To Father Dulles, I am additionally indebted for his careful reading of the manuscript and for his thoughtful and scholarly suggestions. My thanks also to John B. Breslin, S.J., present editor at Doubleday, for his patient co-operation; to Father Frederick R. McManus, another colleague, for sharing with me his canonical expertise; to Maureen Carroll, O.P., for her research assistance; to Carolyn Lee, David Gilson, and Shirley Pototsky of the Catholic University library staff; to Raymond Vandegrift, O.P., of the Dominican House of Studies library; to my students both at Catholic University and at St. Michael's College in Vermont who first heard some of these ideas; and to my many other unnamed friends. Finally, I want to note the special role of my brother, David Granfield, who at every stage was an unfailing source of help and encouragement.

I THE
PAPACY
IN
TRANSITION

> The papacy is the only institution
> that has existed continuously from the
> early Roman Empire. . . . There have
> been many great and saintly Popes,
> many nonentities and not a few worth-
> less or bad; but the office has always
> been greater than the man, and it sur-
> vives.
>
> DAVID KNOWLES[1]

The papacy, called by Toynbee "the greatest of all Western
institutions,"[2] is the most visible symbol of Catholic identity. Its
history, a tangle of complexities and contradictions, continues to
fascinate both believers and nonbelievers. A glance at papal history reveals a host of paradoxes. The papacy is esteemed for its
role in civilizing the barbarian nations and it is condemned for establishing the barbaric Inquisition. Portrayed as the conscience of
Europe, its own political activity has often been Machiavellian.
In the ninth century, Nicholas I (858–67) condemned torture as
against divine and human law; in the thirteenth century, Innocent IV (1243–54) allowed secular powers to torture heretics.

[1] Encyclopaedia Britannica (1965), 17:195.
[2] A Study of History (London: Oxford University Press, 1939),
IV: 512.

Traditionally, Popes have been revered as apostles of peace, yet some waged war. The Church has honored almost one hundred Popes as saints or blesseds, but some Popes, like John XII (955–64), elected when he was only eighteen, and Alexander VI (1492–1503), the "Spanish Bull," led scandalous lives. Finally, the Pope, the symbol of oneness, is, at the same time, a major obstacle to Christian reunion.

Many of the 263 Popes have found the office a high-risk occupation. Popes have met death by crucifixion, strangulation, poisoning, and beheading. Others have been imprisoned, exiled, and deposed. They have faced rival claimants, intense secular interference, heresies, mass defections, and schisms. The ninth and tenth centuries were especially difficult ones for the papacy. John X (914–28) and Benedict VI (973–74) were both smothered to death. For some there was no peace even after death. The corpse of John XIV (983–84), who died of hunger or poison in the prison of Castel Sant' Angelo, was skinned by a gang of ruffians and dragged through the streets of Rome. The most gruesome example of postmortem papal abuse was that directed against Formosus (891–96). He died a natural death, but nine months later his body was dug up. Clothed in pontifical garments and placed on a chair, the decaying body of the Pope was judged at a synod presided over by Stephen VI (896–97), with a trembling deacon as the defense attorney.

The papacy, however, has been able to endure this litany of horrors. As Geoffrey Barraclough notes: "Few institutions in the whole of history have shown an equal capacity for survival."[3] Although some may question whether longevity is an adequate theological reason for belief in the divine institution of the papacy, from a purely human standpoint it gives it remarkable credentials.

Roman Catholics believe that the papacy is more than a human reality, even a unique one. They believe that the papacy, the office of headship in the Roman Catholic Church, is the continuation of that ministry that was given by Christ in Peter and that is exercised by his successors in the historic Roman epis-

[3] *The Medieval Papacy* (New York: Harcourt, Brace & World, 1968), p. 10.

copate. The papacy is an essential and permanent element in the Church of Christ, because it is willed by Christ. It has both a human and a divine foundation, but it is the latter that guarantees its permanence.

Nevertheless, one should keep in mind two principles. First, to quote Avery Dulles: "The life of the Catholic Christian is by no means centered on the papacy; it ought, at least, to be centered on God and on Jesus Christ."[4] The papal office has to be seen in the perspective of the central Christian truths. Like all other ministries in the Church, the papacy is at the service of these realities and is spiritually meaningless isolated from them. Second, the papacy is not immutable; it is capable of change without losing its identity or its continuity with the past. In fact, it has to change if it is to respond to contemporary needs.

To see the present transitional crisis of the papacy, I shall discuss in this chapter some significant papal transitions of the past. This is a difficult task, since, as has been noted by Pollock and Maitland: "Such is the unity of all history that anyone who endeavours to tell a piece of it must feel that his first sentence tears a seamless web."[5] Yet it is possible to select from a history of nearly two thousand years a fair sampling of events that have manifestly changed the direction of the papacy. Even such a limited selection can provide some important insights into the twists and turns of papal development. The events themselves, of course, do not tell the whole story. But I have chosen these because they are watersheds—critical dividing lines that determined subsequent growth.

I consider the following to be decisive turning points in papal history. First, the religious toleration of Christians granted by the Edict of Milan; second, the beginning of the temporal

---

[4] *The Resilient Church* (Garden City, N.Y.: Doubleday & Company, 1977), p. 113. G. Alberigo makes a similar assertion: "The Roman papacy constitutes only one factor in the Church and certainly not the most decisive one" ("Pour une papauté rénovée au service de l'Église," in G. Alberigo et al., *Renouveau ecclésial et service papal à la fin du XXe siècle, Concilium* [French ed.], No. 108 [Paris: Beauchesne, 1975], 9).

[5] *History of English Law*, 2nd ed. (Cambridge: Cambridge University Press, 1899), I: 1.

power of the Pope with the Donation of Pepin; third, the institutional reform of the Church in the eleventh century; fourth, the split in papal leadership during the Great Western Schism; fifth, the split in Christian membership at the time of the Protestant Reformation; sixth, the centralization of the spiritual power of the papacy in Vatican I; seventh, the sharing of this power in Vatican II; and, finally, eighth, the present challenge of modernity.

I. Religious Toleration—
The Edict of Milan

For the first three hundred years the Church survived and grew strong despite the internal peril of heterodoxy and the external peril of persecution. In the fourth century, however, a radical change occurred. In 303, Diocletian launched the last and most fearful persecution of all: churches were burned, sacred books destroyed, and Christians who refused to offer sacrifices to pagan deities were maimed, exiled, or killed. Ten years later, the Church gained its liberty. By the so-called Edict of Milan (313), the co-emperors, Constantine and Licinius, abrogated laws prejudicial to Christians, returned confiscated Church property, and permitted Christians to form a legal corporation. The decree of toleration was one of the decisive events in world history. The Empire gave the Church its freedom and the Church in turn shared with the Empire its stability and its spiritual resources. It has been suggested that Constantine, who later became a Christian, saw toleration as primarily a matter of political expediency, since the State had come to realize the political value of its old enemy.[6] Whatever the motivation, the new policy toward Christians transformed Western civilization.

The results of the Edict of Milan were many: Church membership increased, new churches were built, and papal and episcopal prestige grew apace. Church government and law were modeled more and more after the Roman ideal, giving the

---

[6] According to Paul Johnson, Constantine "perceived that Christianity already possessed many of the characteristics of an imperial Church" (*A History of Christianity* [New York: Atheneum, 1977], p. 76).

Church a marked institutional development. Once Constantine moved the seat of the Empire to Constantinople around 330, the papacy began to exert a stronger influence in the West. By the end of the fourth century, not only had Christianity become the official religion of the State—under Theodosius I in 380—but already several Popes were slowly moving toward an explicit statement of papal primatial authority. The Edict of Milan, then, marks an important transitional date in the history of the papacy. When Christians were given equal status in the Empire, the Church soon went from being a persecuted sect to being an active participant in imperial politics. The groundwork was laid for that later development that saw Rome assert its claims as the *prima sedes*. It did this in the century between Popes Damasus I (366–84) and Leo I (440–61).

II. Temporal Power—
The Donation of Pepin

In 754, Stephen II (752–57) became the first Pope to cross the Alps. His mission was to meet with Pepin III, son of Charles Martel and King of the Franks and to plead with him, in the name of St. Peter, for help against the invading Lombards. Pepin agreed and promised to give to Stephen the Exarchate of Ravenna, some Byzantine territory in central Italy, and the duchies of Spoleto and Benevento. In gratitude, Stephen reconsecrated Pepin King of the Franks and gave him the added title of Patrician of the Romans. Pepin kept his word. He made several military expeditions against the Lombards and in 756 he deeded the captured cities to "St. Peter and the Roman Church."[7] Symbolically, the iron keys of the cities' gates were laid on the tomb of St. Peter.[8]

[7] For a description of the events surrounding the Donation of Pepin see L. Duchesne, ed., *Liber pontificalis* (Paris: E. Thorin, 1886), 1:445–56.

[8] The Donation of Pepin is different from the Donation of Constantine. The latter, a forged document that appeared about the same time, claimed that Constantine gave to Pope Sylvester I (314–35) "all provinces, localities, and towns in the Western Hemisphere." The author and place

The Donation of Pepin was an epoch-making event for several reasons. First, it was the beginning of the Papal States, which
lasted until 1870. With this donation, Stephen became the first of
a long line of Popes to be a temporal ruler—a tradition that
caused serious problems for the Church over the centuries.[9] Second, it initiated an alliance with the Frankish Kingdom, the foundation of which had been laid earlier, by Gregory I (590–604).
These links with the Franks were later to give the papacy of the
Middle Ages its unique character. Through his agreement with
Pepin, Stephen was able virtually to free the papacy from the
domination of Constantinople. It only remained for Leo III
(795–816) to crown Charlemagne, son of Pepin, Emperor of the
Romans in 800, to sever the last direct connection with Constantinople.

III. Institutional Reform—
The Hildebrandine Era

Another critical period of papal history was the eleventh-cen-
tury reform movement. It is usually dated from the election decree of 1059 of Nicholas II (1059–61)—whereby cardinal bishops
became papal electors—to the First Lateran Council in 1123,
which was convoked by Callistus II (1119–24). Although eight
Popes reigned during this time of renewal, it is commonly called
the Gregorian Reform after its most famous advocate, Gregory
VII (1073–85), surnamed Hildebrand. "This pontificate," wrote
Louis Duchesne, "realises the potential might of its religious and
moral power, and, with one vigorous stroke, rises above all the political considerations of the West."[10]

---

of composition are uncertain. It was not until the sixteenth century that it
was proven to be spurious. See S. Williams, "The Oldest Text of the *Con-
stitutum Constantini,*" *Traditio,* 20 (1964), 448–61.

[9] Two useful books on this subject are L. Duchesne, *The Beginnings
of the Temporal Sovereignty of the Popes,* A.D. 754–1073 (London: Kegan
Paul, Trench, Trübner, 1908) and P. Partner, *The Lands of St. Peter.
The Papal States in the Middle Ages and the Early Renaissance* (Berkeley
and Los Angeles: University of California Press, 1972).

[10] *The Beginnings of Temporal Sovereignty,* op. cit., p. 270.

The reform Popes concentrated their efforts in three principal areas. The first task was to restore prestige to the papacy in order to counteract the sorry state the papacy had descended to in the previous two centuries. In his letters and especially in the *Dictatus papae*, Gregory unambiguously identified himself with St. Peter (as Leo I had done before him); claimed universal authority over bishops, clerics, and councils; and asserted his right to make law, to render judgments beyond which there is no appeal, and even to depose the emperor. The second area of reform was directed against clerical corruption, in particular simony and incontinence. A series of severe measures sought to correct these abuses. The third area dealt with lay investiture—a custom that allowed feudal lords, princes, and emperors to select pastors, abbots, and bishops. Gregory's determination to root out this evil brought him into direct conflict with Emperor Henry IV, whom he finally excommunicated though later absolved in the famous wintry scene at Canossa in 1077.

Although the reform movement met fierce resistance and achieved only limited success, it is an important milestone in papal history. It was the first time that the extensive theoretical principles of papal authority were applied and tested in practice. From that time forward, the papacy exercised a new style of leadership; the Pope emerged not only as the undisputed head of the Church but also as the unifying force in medieval Europe. Toynbee may well be correct when he says that "Hildebrand and his successors succeeded in creating a master-institution of Western Christendom,"[11] but it was not until the twelfth and thirteenth centuries that the papacy reached the height of its influence in Europe. It peaked during the pontificate of Innocent III (1198–1216), but by the time of Boniface VIII (1294–1303), it was already in decline. From 1308 to 1378 the Popes resided in the French city of Avignon.

[11] *A Study of History*, op. cit., IV: 523.

IV.   Divided Leadership—
The Great Western Schism

No sooner had the papacy returned to Rome from Avignon when it faced another crisis. Urban VI was elected in 1378, but five months later, the cardinals, claiming coercion, rejected him and elected Clement VII, who took up residence in Avignon. Each Pope had his own curial staff and supporters. Even saints were confused: St. Catherine of Siena favored Urban, and St. Vincent Ferrer backed Clement. A Council was held at Pisa in 1409, but instead of resolving the dilemma only worsened it. A third papal claimant, Alexander V, entered the fray. Finally, a general Council that was held at Constance (1414–18) confronted the scandal of a three-headed papacy. Unity was restored with the election of Martin V in 1417.

What makes Constance, which brought to an end the Great Western Schism, a transitional date in the history of the papacy is the theological principle behind the action of the Council, namely conciliarism. In its decree *Haec sancta*, the Council affirmed that it was a general council representing the entire Church with the authority of Christ. It asserted that its authority was superior to that of any of the faithful, including the Pope himself. Although perhaps J. N. Figgis exaggerated when he called *Haec sancta* "the most revolutionary official document in the history of the world,"[12] it is undoubtedly extremely important. The theory of conciliarism had been widely discussed by canonists and theologians for two centuries before Constance. But at the Council it was put to the test and it was triumphant. It ended the schism.

After the Council of Constance, Rome considered conciliarism a threat to papal power, condemning it several times over the centuries. Nevertheless, the conciliarist idea did not die. It resurfaced again in seventeenth-century Gallicanism and in eighteenth-century Febronianism and Josephism. Vatican I resolutely

[12] *Studies in Political Thought from Gerson to Grotius: 1414–1625,* 2nd ed. (Cambridge: Cambridge University Press, 1916), p. 41.

rejected these movements. Since Vatican II, however, there has been a renewed historical and theological interest in conciliarism. The doctrine of collegiality and the possibility of some future heretical, insane, or immoral Pope again raises the question of whether some application of moderate conciliarism would yet be theologically feasible. I will return to this matter in later chapters.

V. Divided Membership—
The Protestant Reformation

The papacy in the early sixteenth century was severely weakened by excessive involvement in temporal matters, internal decay, and a general loss of its spiritual mission. These factors, coupled with a deep-seated religious, social, and economic unrest in Europe, set the stage for the Protestant Reformation. Rome had seriously misjudged the extent and intensity of antipapal sentiment. The Reformers—Luther, Calvin, Zwingli—repudiated all the principal papal claims; the papacy's control over the religious destiny of western Europe came to a dramatic end. By the end of the sixteenth century, millions of Catholics in Germany, Scandinavia, the Netherlands, Switzerland, and the British Isles had departed from the Roman communion. A new era in Church history had dawned.

The Church's answer to the Protestant Reformation was the Council of Trent (1545–63). In its twenty-five sessions, it discussed such major doctrinal issues as the authority of Scripture and tradition, original sin and justification, the sacraments, and sweeping reform legislation. It did not, strangely enough, elaborate a theology of the Church or the papal office. Nevertheless, zealous Popes for forty years after Trent implemented its decrees and strengthened papal leadership. Ecclesiology, long a neglected part of Catholic theology, became a favorite subject. Volumes, written in strong polemical language, multiplied. Unfortunately, the ecclesiology at that time was not only animated by a controversial spirit, but was concentrated almost exclusively on the juridical dimensions of the Church. The theology of the Church became a theology of the Pope and the bishops. This approach dominated ecclesiology for the next four hundred years.

VI. Centralized Spiritual Power— Vatican I

The next transitional period of the papacy, which I shall treat in detail in Chapter 3, is Vatican I (1869–70). This Council is remarkable for several reasons. First, it represents the most formal and most extensive doctrinal affirmation of papal prerogatives in the history of the Church. The dogmatic constitution *Pastor aeternus* defined papal primacy and infallibility. In emphasizing the spiritual and centralized sovereignty of the Pope, the Council employed a monarchical, juridical conception of the Church. It paid little attention to the bishops, to the faithful, and to the more spiritual aspects of ecclesial life. Second, the end of the Council also coincided with the end of the temporal sovereignty of the Pope. In September 1870, Italian troops invaded Rome, and a month later, Victor Emmanuel II announced the annexation of Rome and its environs. Thus ended the political life of the Papal States, which had survived for over a thousand years.

VII. Shared Spiritual Power— Vatican II

The Second Vatican Council (1962–65) and the efforts of John XXIII (1958–63) and Paul VI (1963–78) forced the Church to confront anew the world and its needs. These two Popes were truly transitional Popes. They radically changed the papacy by bringing the Church struggling into the twentieth-century world—a world it did not fully understand and with which it still has an uneasy alliance. This pastoral Council of reform and reunion left us with a rich heritage: a sacramental and ecumenical vision of the Church; a recognition of the need of broad lay participation; a doctrine of ministry based on service; and the need for the Church to heal a suffering humanity. Of special concern is its balanced approach to papal and episcopal authority. Through its doctrine of collegiality, it supplied what was lacking in Vatican I, and in so doing, it enabled the Church to grasp the meaning of spiritual leadership. Vatican II initiated a new phase in the Church's life, which profoundly affected the role of the Pope. Subsequent chapters in this book will attempt to explore some of the themes found in the Council.

The seven transitional events of the past I have treated above are but a few of the many critical factors that have influenced the development of the papacy. A fuller treatment would have to include the following: the fall of the Roman Empire; the break between Rome and the Eastern Church; the rise of Islam and the near disappearance of the African Church; the confrontation with the Ottoman Turks; the end of the Middle Ages, which saw the development of modern economy, the change from an agricultural to an urban society, and the formation of national states; the age of discoveries in Asia and the Americas; the Renaissance; the Enlightenment; the French Revolution; and the Industrial Revolution. In other words, the history of Western civilization and the history of the papacy are intertwined. Transition is a perennial quality of the papacy. Our next task is to examine the present transition of the papacy as it faces the challenge of modernity.

VIII. The Challenge of Modernity— The Present Era

The contemporary challenge facing the Church may not shake the Rock of Peter, but it does make it a slippery perch; for the papacy, as we have seen, has always been a salient in the transitional struggles of the Church. The present crisis is especially unsettling since it precipitates a twofold change: a doctrinal one based on the rise of theological pluralism within the Church itself; and a contextual one stemming from the jeopardy in which industrial technology has placed the entire world.

Although the critical stage has been reached only recently, the underlying forces have been at work for many years and, in some areas, for many centuries. But both of these transitional aspects have a common source. "Classical culture," explains Bernard Lonergan, "has given way to modern culture and, I would submit, that the crisis of our age is in no small measure the fact that modern culture has not yet reached its maturity."[13] The contemporary Pope thus finds himself in an awkwardly delicate position as the leader of a Church partially out of touch with a culture itself not yet mature. Faced with the instability that now characterizes the ecclesial and the secular arenas, the Pope has an awesome responsibility to both, in this the greatest of the Church's transitional phases. Let us briefly consider some aspects of this twofold problem.

The first of the two problems challenging the modern Pope is how to deal with the fact of theological pluralism—a radical change from 'the traditional unitary teaching of the Church.[14] A hundred years ago, in 1879, *Aeterni patris* of Leo XIII seemed to take for granted that Thomism would remain the sole ground for Catholic philosophy and theology. But this intellectual monopoly was not destined to last. Owing principally to the work of Joseph Maréchal and his many followers, post-Tridentine scholasticism was gradually forced to share its domain with others. The acceptance of the fact of philosophic pluralism helped justify the resultant theological pluralism, and with that comes the virtual end of the classical era of theology. The process is now in full swing, busily self-conscious, reflecting on the requisites of its new methodology.[15]

---

[13] *Collection. Papers by Bernard Lonergan, S.J.*, ed. F. E. Crowe (New York: Herder and Herder, 1967), p. 259.

[14] Cf. G. A. McCool, *Catholic Theology in the Nineteenth Century: The Quest for a Unitary Method* (New York: Seabury, 1977) and "Theology and Philosophy," *Proceedings of the Catholic Theological Society of America*, 32 (1977), 72–89, and responses by F. Lawrence and D. P. McCann, 90–101.

[15] Cf. Y. Congar, "Unité et pluralisme," in *Ministères et communion ecclésiale* (Paris: Cerf, 1971), pp. 229–58; R. Devettere, "Progress and Pluralism in Theology," *Theological Studies*, 35 (1974), 441–66; A. Dulles, *The Resilient Church*, op. cit., pp. 93–112; H. Fries, "Theological Reflections on the Problem of Pluralism," *Theological Studies*, 28 (1967), 3–26; B. Lonergan, *Doctrinal Pluralism* (Milwaukee: Marquette University, 1971); K. Rahner, "Pluralism in Theology and the Unity of the Creed in the Church," in *Theological Investigations* (New York: Seabury, 1974), 11:3–23; D. Tracy, *Blessed Rage for Order* (New York: Seabury, 1975).

To distinguish the classical and the modern mentality is important for an understanding of the papacy, for the theology of the Church has developed according to the classical mode. Catholics have been conditioned to view the papacy as absolute and immutable, almost as a metahistorical reality. This viewpoint characterizes not only the post-Tridentine ecclesiologies, but even most nineteenth-century histories of the papacy. This was a mentality formulated according to the spirit—and the letter—of Aristotle, Aquinas, and the later Scholastics; it sought the one truth, objective and nonhistorical, relying heavily on a deductive methodology.

The modern world looks at reality differently, focusing on the changing, the historical, the existential: it prefers induction to deduction.[16] Among Catholic theologians, however, this modern perspective does not amount to a denial that certain fundamental presuppositions exist or that abstract thought is possible. It is not necessarily relativistic. But it does force us to recognize the incarnational dimensions of the papacy as a concrete and developing reality, to realize that, like any other institutional structure, the papacy has its own share of anomalies, competing crosscurrents, misconceived actions, and underestimated obstacles. We learn that no simple linear papal progression can be drawn from Scripture and Church documents and extrapolated all the way to the Parousia. But if we use our historical consciousness aright in perceiving and evaluating the papacy, we will begin to see it—not necessarily more neatly and abstractly, but perhaps more honestly —for what it is and for what God intended it should be.

The second major problem facing the Pope today concerns the accelerating and threatening changes that industrialized civilization has brought upon itself and the rest of the world. When Kenneth Boulding wrote *The Meaning of the Twentieth Century*,[17] he described this century as "the great transition," a dangerously volatile stage in the shift from a civilized to a technological society. Deeply troubled about the future of mankind, he

[16] Cf. J. W. O'Malley, "Reform, Historical Consciousness, and Vatican II's Aggiornamento," *Theological Studies*, 32 (1971), 573–601.
[17] New York: Harper & Row, 1964.

warned of the "traps" that delay, and may even prevent, the full transition, and he enunciated his "dismal theories," suggesting the ultimate intractability of these obstacles to fulfillment.

Ten years after Boulding's book, another economist, Robert L. Heilbroner, faced the same problems in his ominously entitled book *An Inquiry into the Human Prospect*,[18] an examination of mankind's socioeconomic and political capabilities for survival. His prognosis was grim.[19] Both men are concerned about the global results of uncontrolled industrialization—as if industrialization were a monster with a destiny of its own acting in utter disregard of the good of mankind. The root of the danger, as Heilbroner notes, is obvious: an unprecedented population increase in a world of limited and diminishing resources. This imbalance presents the threat of starvation to great masses of people. In trying to avoid this disaster, the world finds itself facing a dilemma, for the very technology that caused the problem leaves it with two unacceptably lethal alternatives. If the attempt is made to fulfill societal needs by stepping up production in the industrialized nations as well as by industrializing the Third World, there is the very real probability of global environmental pollution of crippling dimensions, even before the eventual depletion of resources. On the other hand, if this attempt to increase production worldwide is not made, there arises the increasing threat of obliterative war. Heilbroner warns of nuclear terrorism: "Nuclear weaponry for the first time makes such action possible; and 'wars of redistribution' may be the only way by which the poor nations can hope to remedy their condition."[20]

Heilbroner, of course, recognizes a third alternative—attitudinal change—and yet he believes that the sense of assurance and control necessary for reversing the direction of events is lacking in modern man, caught up as he is in a process of his own making that sweeps him along inexorably. Whether the nation-

[18] New York: W. W. Norton, 1975.
[19] Thus: ". . . the answer to whether we can conceive of the future other than as a continuation of the darkness, cruelty, and disorder of the past seems to me to be no; and to the question of whether worse impends, yes" (ibid., p. 22).
[20] Ibid., p. 43.

states be capitalistic or communistic, they are equally in the grip
of the habits of industrialization. Most significant, then, on this
point, is John Paul II's first encyclical, *Redemptor hominis*
(1979), in which he advocates a redistribution of resources involving "the indispensable transformation of the structure of economic life."[21] Yet he clearly perceives that the core of this transformation is an attitudinal change, "a true conversion of mind,
will, and heart."[22]

To achieve this conversion, political control seems required.
In fact, Heilbroner finds a growing tendency toward the formation of military-socialist regimes. Phrased more generally, the
move seems to be in the direction of increased authority. "I not
only predict," he writes, "but I prescribe a centralization of power
as the only means by which our threatened and dangerous civilization will make way for its successor."[23] The reason is that "only
an authoritarian, or possibly only a revolutionary, regime will be
capable of mounting the immense task of social reorganization
needed to escape catastrophe."[24]

Does this worldwide socioeconomic crisis with its growing
political bias toward authoritarianism portend for the Church a
parallel emphasis on authority? If authoritarian regimes do tend to
characterize the nation-states of the technological era, will the papacy have much choice about its own political stance? For the
Church, as a human institution, does not exist in a vacuum, but
interacts with secular institutions. It is affected by current political myths and also affects both the creation and the transformation of these same myths. In fact, theological pluralism recognizes this interaction and works to develop its implications in
the manner most fruitful for both Church and state.

What specifically could this change in world politics mean
for the papacy? The rise of military-socialist states might well
threaten the independence of the Church, which in turn might
resort to a more centralized structure in self-defense. Moreover, if

---

21 *Origins* (Mar. 22, 1979), Vol. 8, No. 40, 636.
22 Ibid.
23 *An Inquiry into the Human Prospect,* op. cit., p. 165.
24 Ibid., p. 26.

people generally became accustomed to strong civil governments, they might expect, permit, and even demand a similar control from their ecclesial institutions. In other words, the state-model of institutions could once again become the norm among Christian churches.

The Church, as a consequence, especially the Pope, must be on guard, lest, following the lead of civil society, it gradually reverts to an unbalanced emphasis on authority, becoming more "papocentric" than collegial, more juridical than pastoral. Developmental constructs or futurist scenarios are risky; but, though they may fail as prophecies, they do serve as warning systems. Recognizing the temptation to ape the modern state, the papacy may react strenuously by asserting its role as a spiritual counterbalance to secular society, so that the very crisis that threatens the Church may sharpen the focus on shared responsibility with the Pope, symbolizing even more dramatically the Mystery that is the whole Christ, Head and members.

In conclusion, what I have attempted, in this chapter, is to identify some of the basic influences that condition the papacy as it moves from age to age, and especially as it moves from the classical to the modern world view. In subsequent chapters, I shall consider special areas of concern, structural as well as apostolic. Suffice it here to recognize the time-tested principle that the papacy must always function for a living constituency and to do so effectively must always be a papacy in transition.

2 THE CASE AGAINST THE PAPACY

All that—all that imperial paraphernalia. All that isolation of the Pope. All that medieval remoteness and inheritance that makes Europeans think that the Church is only Western. All that tightness that makes them fail to understand that young countries like mine want something different. They want simplicity. They want Jesus Christ. All that, all that must change.

JOSEPH CARDINAL MALULA[1]

The papacy is no stranger to criticism. From the very beginning, with Paul confronting Peter, Popes have attracted controversy and have continued to do so throughout history. Saints and rascals, theologians and historians, emperors and kings have leveled charges against the papacy in general as well as against individual Popes. From gentle scoldings to outrageous attacks, the pa-

---

[1] The cardinal from Zaire made these observations just before the conclave that elected John Paul II. They are quoted in *Time* (Oct. 30, 1978), p. 97.

pacy has received its share of disapproval. A few examples from
the past will show the intensity of this antipapal sentiment.[2]

In the third century, during the controversy over the baptism
of heretics, Firmilian, Bishop of Caesarea in Cappadocia, wrote
St. Cyprian. Firmilian attacked Pope Stephen I (254–57) for
"his audacity and pride" and was indignant over his "open and
manifest folly."[3] Gregory VII (1073–85), in a bitter exchange
with Henry IV on the subject of lay investiture, received a letter
from the emperor that began: "Henry, King not by usurpation
but by the pious ordination of God, to Hildebrand, now not Pope
but false monk."[4] It was in the sixteenth century, however, that
the art of papal criticism reached its apex in the polemical debates
between Protestants and Catholics. "Controversy," James Brodrick writes, "has never been a school for chivalry; in the sixteenth century it was a snake-pit."[5] Protestants wrote books on the
theme of the Pope as antichrist, and Catholics answered them. A
typical example is found in Luther: "I believe that the Pope is
the masked and incarnate devil because he is the antichrist. As
Christ is God incarnate, so the antichrist is the devil incarnate."[6]

    [2] For further examples see H. Thurston, *No Popery: Chapters on
Anti-Papal Prejudice* (New York: Longmans, Green, 1930) and E. R. Cham-
berlain, *The Bad Popes* (New York: Dial, 1969).
    [3] *Ep.* 75, 3 and 17. Text in *Corpus scriptorum ecclesiasticorum
latinorum*, ed. G. Hartel (Vienna: Apud C. Geroldi Filium, 1871), 3:811
and 821.
    [4] Translation from T. E. Mommsen and K. F. Morrison, *Imperial
Lives and Letters of the Eleventh Century*, ed. L. Benson (New York:
Columbia University Press, 1962), p. 150.
    [5] *Robert Bellarmine: Saint and Scholar*, rev. ed. (Westminster, Md.:
Newman, 1961), p. 81.
    [6] In *Luther's Works*, ed. and trans. T. G. Tappert (Philadelphia:
Fortress, 1967), Vol. 57, No. 4487, 346. The Lutheran confessional docu-
ments also call the Pope the antichrist. Thus the Smalcald Articles, Part II,
Art. IV, 10, 11, states: "This is a powerful demonstration that the pope is
the real Antichrist who has raised himself over and set himself against
Christ, for the pope will not permit Christians to be saved except by his
own power, which amounts to nothing since it is neither established nor
commanded by God" (in *The Book of Concord: The Confessions of the
Evangelical Lutheran Church*, ed. and trans. T. G. Tappert [Philadelphia:
Fortress, 1959], p. 300). Also see W. Lohff, "Would the Pope Still Have

Luther also referred to Clement VII (1523–34) as "the maddest tyrant of all."[7] Similar expression can be found in Calvin, who railed against the "impious superstitions and open idolatry" of Rome and called Paul III (1534–49) "truculent," Leo X (1513–21) "cruel," and Clement VII "blood-stained."

In England things were no different. Robert Abbot, the Protestant Bishop of Salisbury, called the Pope not only the antichrist but also "the man of sin, the harpy of Rome, the filthy harlot, the filthy and unnatural strumpet, the whore of Babylon."[8] King James I said of Paul V (1605–21) that "if the devil had studied a thousand years," he could not have worked more mischief than the Pope.[9] Dom Cuthbert Butler described Sixtus V (1585–90) as "that terrible old man, of whom Queen Elizabeth is reported to have said that he was the only man in Europe fit to be her husband."[10] Even the liturgy expressed antipathy toward the Pope. In the first English litany (1544) there is the petition: "From the tyrannye of the bishop of Rome and all his detestable enormities. . . . Good Lorde, deliver us."[11] John Henry Newman, when a boy, wrote in his dictionary "antichrist" next to the word "Pope."[12] Among others, Nathaniel Ward carried the English animosity toward the papacy to the New World. A Puritan

---

Been the Antichrist for Luther Today?" in H. Küng, ed., *Papal Ministry in the Church, Concilium*, Vol. 64 (New York: Herder and Herder, 1971), 68–74.

[7] *Luther's Works,* op. cit., Vol. 57, No. 1346, 141.

[8] From Brodrick, op. cit., p. 82.

[9] "An Apologie for the Oath of Allegiance. The Answere to the Second Breve," in C. H. McIlwain, *The Political Works of James I* (Cambridge: Harvard University Press, 1918), p. 81.

[10] *The Vatican Council 1869–1870,* ed. Christopher Butler (Westminster, Md.: Newman, 1962), p. 22.

[11] *The First and Second Prayer Books of King Edward the Sixth* (London: J. M. Dent & Sons, 1910), p. 232. See also W. P. Haugaard, "The English Liturgy from Henry to Elizabeth," *Anglican Theological Review,* 51 (1969), 177–203.

[12] For an excellent study on Newman's theology of the papacy see P. Misner, *Papacy and Development: Newman and the Primacy of the Pope* (Leiden: E. J. Brill, 1976).

dissenter and a minister in Aggawam (now Ipswich), Massachusetts, he had this to say about the Pope:

> No earthly man can be
> True Subject to this State;
> Who makes the Pope his Christ,
> An heretique his Mate.[13]

With such a background, it is no wonder that the present ecumenical dialogue is considered an almost miraculous event. Nevertheless, as Christianity approaches the end of its second millennium, criticism of the papacy, although appreciably less vitriolic than in the past, still perdures. What, then, is the current case against the papacy? Since no simple answer is possible, I have listed the following areas of concern. The papacy in transition will have to respond to these objections.

I.   The Papacy Is Nonscriptural

This is the classical Protestant objection that exists, with some variation, even today. The Protestant reformers rejected the papal claim of a primacy of jurisdiction on the grounds that it is not found in the Word of God, the decisive authority in Church doctrine. Since Scripture does not explicitly mention the papacy or the supreme role of the Bishop of Rome, the reformers dismissed papal claims according to the principle: *Quid non iubet, vetat* (What is not commanded, avoid). Protestants do not accept the Catholic teaching, found in Florence, Vatican I, and Vatican II, that the historic papacy is divinely willed and is an essential part of Church structure. The problem is not the idea or the possible value of a primatial office, but its lack of scriptural foundation. Anglican biblical scholar Frederick C. Grant argues

---

[13] Nathaniel Ward (1578–1652) wrote under the pseudonym Theodore de la Guard. The above passage appears in his *The Simple Cobler of Old Aggawam in America*, 4th ed. (London: John Dever and Robert Ibbitson for Stephen Botwell: At the Figure of the Bible in Popes Head Alley, 1647), p. 82.

that the major obstacle to reunion "is the violence done to the New Testament in every attempt to defend the primacy as an institution dating from the first century and founded by Christ himself."[14] The question of the divine character of the papacy has been seriously discussed in several recent ecumenical dialogues. I shall return to it in a later chapter.

Leaving aside the thorny question of the divine establishment of the papacy, many contemporary critics claim that the modern papacy does not adequately reflect the ideal of leadership found in the New Testament. Hans Küng, for example, says that "the Papacy as it is today depends in many respects not upon the original commission, but upon a very problematical historical development."[15] Others point to conciliar statements and theological commentaries that describe the papacy almost exclusively in terms of authority, jurisdiction, supremacy, obedience, and sanction. These ideas, they contend, reveal the papacy as an unfeeling, juridical institution that is unsympathetic to the real needs of suffering humanity. Where, they ask, is the freedom of the Gospel, the enlightening force of the Spirit, and the ideal of humble and caring service?

II.   The Papacy Is Anachronistic

The present papacy, according to some, is better suited to another time; it is chronologically out of place, a relic of the Middle Ages when Christendom and Western civilization were considered identical. The papacy may have worked well in an age with a homogeneous world-view, but today it more and more appears as anachronistically incapable of dealing with modern, technological, and pluralistic society. The papacy, in the words of

[14] *Rome and Reunion* (New York: Oxford University Press, 1965), p. 7. Stuart Louden, a Presbyterian scholar, makes a similar assertion: "The Bishop of Rome's office as Pope or Supreme Pontiff . . . obscures the sole Kingship or Headship of Jesus Christ in his church and is accordingly unbiblical and doctrinally misleading" (*The True Face of the Kirk* [London: Oxford University Press, 1963], p. 12).

[15] "Editorial," in *Papal Ministry i. the Church,* op. cit., 9.

Charles Davis, is "culturally estranged from the modern world"[16] and has not yet come to terms with the demands of modernity. It "belongs to the medieval cosmocentric world, for which the sacred was mediated by a permanent hierarchical order, cosmic and social, not subject to human questioning or meddling—a world without historical consciousness."[17] Can the Pope, who is entrusted with the pastoral ministry of the universal Church, deal responsibly and effectively with doctrinal and cultural diversity using outmoded theological and administrative concepts? At root, the issue is one of the self-understanding of the papacy and the necessity of responding to the "signs of the times." What is called for is a renewed papacy.

III.   The Papacy Is Imperialistic

Do Catholics deify the Pope? How can one man claim to be the Vicar of Christ on earth, the supreme and infallible teacher, the judge and ruler of all? How can he pretend to act, as some Tridentine theologians said, outside the law, above the law, and against the law? Throughout history many have found it difficult to deal with the imperial papacy. St. Catherine of Siena, for example, expressed her own frustration in a letter to Gregory XI (1370–78): "Do this so that I do not have to complain about you to Jesus crucified. There is no one else I can complain to, for you have no superior on earth."[18]

The papacy conveys to many the image of an absolute monarchy. They see the Pope as a monarch who treats his subjects as inferiors, jealously defends his prerogatives, grudgingly delegates authority, and is fearful of local autonomy. They also criticize papal style: the liturgical ceremonies reminiscent of the Byzantine court; the authoritarian tone of papal pronouncements; the formal and often obscurantist language in which they are

[16] "Questions for the Papacy Today," ibid., 12.
[17] Ibid., 16.
[18] N. Tommasseo and P. Misciattelli, eds., *Le lettere di S. Caterina da Siena*, 5th ed. (Siena: Giuntini and Bentivoglio, 1913), IV: 108.

couched; and the aloofness or inaccessibility of the Pope. Cornelius Ernst charges that "a violent, intolerant dominativeness has been a characteristic mode of papal utterance and behavior" and that "great, even saintly men have been the victims of a cruel, un-Christian system."[19]

The Vatican bureaucracy is often linked to the imperialistic conception of the papacy. The cumbersome machinery of the Roman Curia, despite recent improvements, is still far from efficient. Excessive paperwork—someone called it a *papierkrieg*—unreasonable delays, and a reluctance to recognize the principle of subsidiarity characterize the Church's central administration. These flaws are, of course, endemic to any large social organization, but in Rome, through centuries of practice, they have been honed to perfection.

IV.   The Papacy Is Too Italian

Lutheran theologian George A. Lindbeck sums it up: "Another objection is that the papacy is symbolically so Latin, Italian, and Western that it is not only unrealistic, but even positively harmful to try to make it the institutional focus of unity for the whole church with its Greek, African, and Asian dimensions."[20] Historically, the central government of the Church has been linked to the West, and the majority of the Popes have been Italian. To understand the full significance of this connection, it is necessary to note the relationship between the Church and the Roman Empire. The early Church paralleled in many ways the classical Roman system. As Thomas Hobbes said: "The papacy is no other than the Ghost of the deceased Roman Empire, sitting crowned upon the grave thereof."[21] Not only did the fledgling Church

[19] "The Primacy of Peter: Theology and Ideology—I," *New Black-friars*, 50 (1969), 349.

[20] "Lutherans and the Papacy," *Journal of Ecumenical Studies*, 13 (1976), 376. Also see G. Alberigo, "Influence de la situation italienne sur le comportement du saint-siège," *Lumière et vie*, 26 (1977), 5–17.

[21] *Leviathan*, ed. C. B. Macpherson (London: Penguin, 1968), Pt. IV, c. 47, p. 712.

adopt the Roman law as the model for its own legal system—
hence the expression *Ecclesia viget lege romana* (The Church
lives by Roman law)—but also, on a deeper level, it incorporated
the classical virtue of *romanitas*.[22] The secular *romanitas* had the
following characteristics: conservatism, resistance to innovation,
and a veneration of law, reason, stability, order, tradition, practi-
cality, and moderation. The papacy has never lost this distinctive
mark. It has always had a congenital affinity to these qualities and
saw them as providential means of spreading the Gospel message.

The contemporary devotion of the papacy to *romanitas* has
occasioned severe criticism. Some see it as a crippling influence
that has drained the papacy of any genuine creativity. It has
made the papacy a prisoner of the past and suspicious that any
change is a threat to stability and order. Although the survival of
Rome through periods of great upheaval may have been partly
due to its inbred conservatism—*Chi va piano, va lontano* (Who
travels slowly, travels a long way)—today it is often seen as an ex-
cuse for inaction, the path to stagnation, and a detriment to progressive leadership. An ultracautious papacy takes the safest route
but does not develop its charismatic potential.

Although for the first time in 455 years there is now a non-
Italian Pope in John Paul II, the Italian influence on the
Church's central administration will undoubtedly continue. Recent Popes have tried to broaden the geographic representation
in the Curia but, according to F. X. Murphy: "This attempt to in-
ternationalize the Curia has, in large part, backfired. Most of the
non-Italian cardinals were soon attempting to out-Roman the
Romans."[23] Frequently Vatican documents and regulations
reflect a European or Italian experience that makes application to
other countries difficult. Anglo-Saxons, for example, tend to interpret the law strictly; not so the Continentals. Perhaps the motto
current at the time of the Inquisition in Italy gives us a clue to
the Roman mentality: *Foris ut moris, intus ut libet* (Conform externally, but think what you want). A further element in under-

[22] This idea is developed by E. G. Weltin, *The Ancient Popes*
(Westminster, Md.: Newman, 1964), pp. 36 ff.
[23] "The Pope and Our Common Future," *Worldview*, 18 (1975), 24.

standing Vatican behavior is the importance of spectacle and symbol for the Italian mind. Luigi Barzini writes: "In other parts of the world substance always takes precedence and its external aspect is considered useful but secondary. Here [in Italy], on the other hand, the show is as important as, many times more important than, reality."[24]

V. The Papacy Is Remote

A common complaint is that the papacy is out of touch with the real needs of the Christian community. The Vatican seems to be so isolated from the daily lives of Christians that it is unable to recognize the urgency and the complexity of the problems they face. One sometimes gets the impression that the far-reaching cultural changes, the radical shifts in theological thinking, and the deep malaise on the part of many of the faithful has barely penetrated the immobile façade of Roman intransigence. Is Rome able to appreciate the agony of parents faced with the decision over birth control; the plight of divorced Catholics who desire remarriage and acceptance by the Church; the demands of women for ordination; the hopeless situation of the millions of economically poor and politically deprived people; and the pleas for greater participation in decision-making? In a word, does the papacy respond to the needs of the suffering Church with anything like the loving compassion of Jesus? Many today would answer in the negative.

G. Alberigo situates the problem of papal remoteness in the framework of self-sufficiency, which, he says, is a corollary to the idea of the Church as a "perfect society." He contends that for centuries there developed the view that the Pope is self-sufficient. He alone decides, he is the sole guardian of the faith, and he is isolated from the fraternity of believers. "Self-sufficiency," Alberigo writes, "each day becomes more a motif of isolation, of noncredibility, of refusal and is transformed into an obstacle rather than a help to communion and to the adherence to the

[24] *The Italians* (New York: Atheneum, 1965), p. 89.

faith."[25] What is needed is a Pope who has a greater personal contact with the faithful, who is willing to delegate authority and to implement subsidiarity, and who acts more as an inspirational leader than as a bureaucratic administrator.

A related problem is the way the Pope receives information about the state of the Church. A cybernetic analysis of papal decision-making is most helpful.[26] Cybernetically, the Church is an open system and its central administration can be considered as an informational processing unit. There is a continual interaction between input (information received from the system), output (information directed to the system in the form of authoritative decisions from the governing center), and feedback (information returned to the system in reaction to antecedent output). Today the feedback from the faithful is still sporadic. There is an insufficiency of regular and effective channels of information, and the laity, especially women, have only limited access to the decision-making process. Enlightened decision-making depends on three factors: the reception of information, the determination of the level and character of the demands and support that are received, and effective action based on a careful evaluation of what can and should be done to respond to the most pressing needs. Although it is true that the quantity of information received from representative sectors of the Church is no guarantee that Rome will take correct action, it is also true that without a sophisticated and sensitive evaluation of such information decisions tend to be made on insufficient grounds, with the margin of error increasing proportionately.

VI.   The Papacy Is Antitheological

In the minds of many, an antitheological bias is a regrettable characteristic of the papacy. In some sense, Rome has a clear am-

25 "Pour une papauté rénovée au service de l'Église," in G. Alberigo et al., *Renouveau ecclésial et service papal à la fin du XXe siècle, Concilium* (French ed.), No. 108 (Paris: Beauchesne, 1975), 12.

26 I have attempted to do this in *Ecclesial Cybernetics: A Study of Democracy in the Church* (New York: Macmillan, 1973).

bivalence toward theologians. On the one hand, Popes have recognized the invaluable contribution made by theologians in deep-
ening the understanding of the Christian heritage. They have
been architects of ecumenical councils; advisers to the Popes;
stanch defenders of the faith and the Holy See; authors of
influential books; and teachers of great merit. On the other hand,
Rome has often been suspicious of theologians and feared that
they substitute reason for revelation and human logic for faith.
Theologians have been historically linked to any number of heresies and schisms. It is hard to think of any other single group in
the Church that has been more of a constant thorn in the side of
Rome than the theologians. They have received their share of
monita, suspensions, and interdicts. Their writings filled the
pages of the now defunct *Index librorum prohibitorum*, which
was described by Fra Paolo Sarpi (d. 1623), Servite theologian
and enemy of the Roman Curia, as "the finest secret device ever
invented for applying religion to the purpose of making men
stupid."[27]

Despite the often chilling effect of papal supervision, theologians will continue to exercise an important function in the
Church. The traditional distinction between the *ecclesia docens*
and the *ecclesia discens*—between the teaching Church and the
learning Church—is now being reinterpreted. Myles M. Bourke,
for example, says that the charism of teaching (1 Co. 12:28) is
possessed by both the hierarchy and the theologians. He writes:
"If the 'whole church' is to have a part in the making of decisions, particularly in the making of decisions which bear upon the
content of the faith, the proper authority of the theologians must
be given more weight than is often the case in the present func-
tioning of the church."[28]

Concretely, this means there has to be a closer working relationship between the theologians and the magisterium—the
Church's teaching authority. This issue has been a touchy one

[27] *Istoria del Concilio Tridentino* (Florence: G. C. Sansoni, 1966),
II: 598. This book, published originally in 1619, was immediately placed
on the *Index*.

[28] "Collegial Decision-Making in the New Testament," *The Jurist*,
31 (1971), 13.

since Vatican II, and it is not yet resolved. Mutual criticism has increased. Rome has shown extreme displeasure over certain theological tendencies in the postconciliar Church and has rebuked several theologians for their teachings. On their part, theologians have criticized the magisterium for its juridical tone, its appeal to its own authority (rather than to convincing reasons), and its claim that it is the sole interpreter of doctrinal truth.[29] What is needed is a greater collaboration among all levels of the Church and a recognition that both the magisterium and the theologians are at the service of Scripture and tradition. A papal magisterium that is overused becomes ineffective. Ideally, it should show an awareness of the complexity of truth, engage in broad consultation before speaking out on controversial issues, and function sensitively in relation to the entire Church. Avery Dulles has put the matter well:

> The proper balance of authority demands that theologians should not be merely apologists for what the pastoral leaders decide, nor mere consultors to the pastors (though they may well be this *also*), but that they have a recognized voice in the Church, with a certain relative autonomy to develop their own positions by their own methodology and to seek to gain acceptance for these positions by the pastoral magisterium.[30]

The touchstone of orthodoxy for Rome is the apostolic teaching

[29] The doctrine of infallibility has come under severe attack during the last decade. Thus, Brian Tierney writes: "The doctrine of infallibility no longer serves anyone's convenience—least of all the pope's. The papacy adopted the doctrine out of weakness. Perhaps one day the church will feel strong enough to renounce it" (*Origins of Papal Infallibility 1150–1350* [Leiden: E. J. Brill, 1972], p. 281). Also see F. Simmons, *Infallibility and the Evidence* (Springfield, Ill.: Templegate, 1968) and H. Küng, *Infallible? An Inquiry* (Garden City, N.Y.: Doubleday & Company, 1971).

[30] *The Resilient Church* (Garden City, N.Y.: Doubleday & Company, 1977), p. 106. Dulles also discusses this problem in *The Survival of Dogma* (Garden City, N.Y.: Doubleday & Company, 1971), Chap. 5–7. Also see K. Rahner, "The Teaching Office in the Church in the Present-day Crisis of Authority," in *Theological Investigations* (New York: Seabury, 1974), 12:3–30 and International Theological Commission, *Theses on the Relationship between the Ecclesiastical Magisterium and Theology* (Washington: USCC, 1977).

found in Scripture and tradition. Anything that deviates from what has been handed down is considered a dangerous novelty and its proponent a *novator*. The problem arises when the concept of tradition is extended beyond the strict deposit of faith to include all previous papal decisions. Every new Pope is sensitive to what his predecessors have done, and he stresses continuity with them. Tradition in this sense can easily imprison a Pope and make reform painfully slow. It does not favor risk-taking or creative progress. *Humanae vitae* can perhaps be partially explained in this context. Its controversial assertion that "every conjugal act must be open to the transmission of life"[31] is due in part to the reluctance of Paul VI to depart from the teaching of his predecessors.

VII. The Papacy Is Discriminatory

Vatican II declared: "With respect to the fundamental rights of the person, every type of discrimination, whether social or cultural, whether based on sex, race, color, social condition, language, or religion, is to be overcome and eradicated as contrary to God's intent."[32] Several critics have accused Rome of failing to honor its own words. More pointedly, they argue that the Church under the direction of the Pope is guilty of discrimination. The two principal areas of controversy involve women and minorities.

First of all, there are many who feel that the Church has not implemented the Pauline charter that "there are no more distinctions between Jew and Greek, slave and free, male and female, but all of you are one in Christ Jesus" (Ga. 3:28). They contend that not only are women excluded from the ordained ministry but also that in the governance of the Roman Catholic Church women have no significant role in the decision-making. The Church, then, is seen as a bastion of male clericalism, one of the

---

[31] No. 11, *Acta apostolicae sedis*, 60 (1968), 488.
[32] *Pastoral Constitution on the Church in the Modern World* (*Gaudium et spes*), Art. 29. Unless otherwise noted, I use the English translation of the documents of Vatican II from W. M. Abbott, ed., *The Documents of Vatican II* (New York: America Press, 1966).

few institutions in the modern world that refuses to recognize the
full equality of women. Celibate men make moral decisions and
issue disciplinary regulations that affect the lives of millions of
women. The 1976 Vatican declaration, which reaffirmed the exclusion of women from the ministerial priesthood, unleashed a
new wave of opposition. It has been criticized for its insensitivity
to women, its faulty methodology and theological argumentation,
and its failure to employ broad consultation. Margaret A. Farley
reflects the opinion of many: "We are left with clear inequality
of opportunity, an inequality that is not justified by morally relevant factors. This is to say that we are left with sexual discrimination, the violation of rights, and an overall unjust order in
the Church."[33]

Second, the Church has been accused of discriminating
against minorities—racial, ethnic, and religious. In the United
States, for example, where an estimated 30 per cent of the Catholic population is Hispanic and 4 per cent black, there is some animosity against Church leadership. The minority spokesmen point
out that they are underrepresented in the episcopate and in the
priesthood. They question the colonial attitude of the Roman
Church and ask for a greater recognition of ethnic and racial
differences with restructured seminary programs and a plurality
of liturgical celebrations. A similar situation exists between Rome
and Eastern Catholics. There are about one million of the latter
in the United States. Some of them resent the romanization of
their Church and plead for greater autonomy and a return to
some of their cherished traditions, which would include a married
clergy.

VIII. The Papacy Is Too Liberal

"We refuse and have always refused to follow the Rome of
neo-Modernist and neo-Protestant tendencies, which clearly man-

[33] "Discrimination or Equality? The Old Order or the New?" in
L. Swidler and A. Swidler, eds., *Women Priests—A Catholic Commentary
on the Vatican Declaration* (New York: Paulist, 1977), p. 314.

ifested themselves in the Second Vatican Council and after the Council in all the reforms which issued from it."[34] These are the words of French Archbishop Marcel Lefebvre, who became in the early 1970s a central figure among extreme conservative Catholics. He has thousands of followers in Europe and North America and has been an embarrassment to the Holy See and to the Church at large. On the grounds that the Pope and the Church have violated sacred tradition through their liberalism, Lefebvre rejects Vatican II, and especially its liturgical reforms, as heretical. In defiance of the wishes of Rome, he has illicitly ordained priests, established a seminary, and persisted in celebrating the Latin Tridentine Mass of Pius V.

Another conservative group is the Catholic Traditionalist Movement, which was established in 1965 by Father Gommar A. De Pauw. Its purpose is to defend the traditional doctrines and practices of the Roman Catholic Church, with special emphasis on maintaining completely unchanged the Latin Mass of Pius V. De Pauw disavows any connection with Lefebvre. De Pauw claims to speak for 90 per cent of U.S. Catholics, although there are only an estimated ten thousand active members in his organization.

There are other Catholics who belong to neither of the above groups but who are uneasy with what they consider the liberal direction of the Roman Catholic Church. Their complaints are many: the dress and life-style of priests and religious; the avantgarde teachings of theologians and biblical scholars; the failure of the Pope to act more authoritatively; and the ecumenical movement as a betrayal of Catholic tradition.

IX. The Papacy Is Not Credible

There has been a palpable decrease in the level of confidence and respect toward the papacy since the close of Vatican II. The

---

[34] From the "Profession of Faith" of Marcel Lefebvre (Nov. 21, 1974). Found in Y. Congar, *Challenge to the Church—The Case of Archbishop Lefebvre* (Huntington, Ind.: Our Sunday Visitor, 1976), p. 77.

overused expression "credibility gap" describes the present relationship between the Pope and many of the faithful. It may be
part of a broader cultural crisis and it may exist more in the West
than in the East, but the fact remains that the papacy does not
enjoy the prestige it once did. Millions may watch papal funerals
and inaugurations on television, but there is a decisive change in
the legendary Catholic loyalty to the Pope. The traditional *Roma
locuta est, causa finita est* (Rome has spoken, the case is closed)
has been replaced by "Rome has spoken, the case has just begun."
Papal pronouncements are often met with open criticism or
dismissed as unconvincing.

Many theologians contend that a critical factor adversely
affecting the present papacy is its failure to implement adequately
the doctrine of collegiality found in Vatican II. Since the Council, Rome has shown great reluctance to share the decision-making process with the episcopal college. The Synod of Bishops,
which has immense potential, has so far been largely ineffective.
The Roman Curia has clung stubbornly to the monarchical ideal.
"Vatican bureaucracies," notes Richard P. McBrien, "try to play
by the 'old rules,' whether in attempting to put over the revised
Code of Canon Law or in correcting 'abuses' or 'distortions' in
American Catholic pastoral practice."[35] The reformed papacy has
to be more collegial.

There are many reasons, as we have seen in the previous
pages, for the decrease in papal credibility. The list is not exhaustive, but it clearly reveals a deep-seated conflict with Church authority. William C. McCready, for example, in examining the
marked drop in Sunday Mass attendance, found that the major
causes were *Humanae vitae*, the Church's teaching on divorce
and remarriage, and the authority of the Pope.[36] Some Catholics
have agreed with Charles Davis that "the Roman Catholic

[35] "The Roman Catholic Church: Can It Transcend the Crisis?"
The Christian Century (Jan. 17, 1979), p. 44.
[36] *Changing Attitudes of American Catholics Toward the Liturgy:
A National Survey 1974* (Chicago: National Opinion Research Center,
1975), pp. 10–11.

Church is not a zone of truth but, rather, of untruth,"[37] and, like him, they have left it. Although there has been no mass departure from the Church, many Catholics are disturbed about the papacy. It is accused of being conservative or liberal, authoritarian or permissive, enlightened or misdirected. Some support collegiality but others feel it would be destructive of papal stability. Whatever the complaint, there is a consensus that all is not well in Rome. Even discounting much of the rhetoric, there is still a deep malaise.

In conclusion, the case against the papacy reveals that the papacy is not what it once was. It is in the process of transition. There is a widespread feeling among many Christians today that the papacy needs to be reformed. The following chapters will attempt to indicate some of the directions this reform may take.[38] In the next chapter I shall examine the starting point of this transformation—the monarchical conception of the papacy.

[37] *A Question of Conscience* (New York: Harper & Row, 1967), p. 77.

[38] Although I do not use a strict "models approach," some dominant images of the papacy will be evident. See A. Dulles, *Models of the Church* (Garden City, N.Y.: Doubleday & Company, 1974); B. Carra de Vaux, "Les images de la papauté au cours des siècles," *Lumière et vie*, 26 (1977), 37–69; K. McDonnell, "Papal Primacy: Development, Centralization, and Changing Styles," in P. C. Empie and T. A. Murphy, eds., *Papal Primacy and the Universal Church* (Minneapolis: Augsburg, 1974), pp. 173–93; T. F. O'Meara, "Philosophical Models in Ecclesiology," *Theological Studies*, 39 (1978), 3–21; B. Tierney, "Modèles historiques de la papauté," in G. Alberigo et al., *Renouveau ecclésial et service papal à la fin du XXe siècle*, op. cit., 65–74; and J. Theisen, "Models of Papal Ministry and Reliability," *American Benedictine Review*, 27 (1976), 270–84.

3 THE POPE AS MONARCH

The only great elective monarchy in
the world is the Papacy, and the results
have not been wholly satisfactory.

SIR FREDERICK POLLOCK[1]

The doctrinal apogee of papal monarchism was reached in the
fourth session of the First Vatican Council on July 18, 1870. The
scene, more dramatic than any Roman publicist could invent, is
described by one of its participants, the English Benedictine
Bishop of Birmingham, William Bernard Ullathorne.

> The great Session is over. The decree was voted by 533
> "placets" to 2 "non placets" amidst a great storm. The
> lightning flashed into the aula, thunder rolled over the
> roof, and glass was broken by the tempest in a window
> nearly over the pontifical throne and came rattling down.
> After the votes were given the Pope confirmed it at once,
> and immediately there was a great cheering and clapping
> from the bishops and cheers in the body of St. Peter's.

[1] In a letter to Justice Oliver Wendell Holmes, Jr. (Aug. 22, 1925).
M. DeWolfe Howe, ed., *Holmes-Pollock Letters,* 2nd ed. (Cambridge:
Belknap Press of Harvard University Press, 1961), II: 167.

Then the "Te Deum" began, the thunder forming the
diapason.[2]

By a nearly unanimous vote the Council approved the Constitution on the Church, *Pastor aeternus*. The two dissenters, who
later submitted, were Bishop Luigi Riccio of Caiazzo of the Kingdom of Naples and Bishop Edward Fitzgerald of Little Rock, Ar-
kansas. The Council taught that the Roman Pontiff is the successor of St. Peter, possessor of full and supreme power of
jurisdiction over the entire Church, and infallible, under certain
conditions, when defining a matter of faith or morals. Although
the overwhelming majority of the Catholic faithful throughout
the world accepted the Vatican dogmas, there were some who did
not. Many German priests and laity persistently opposed the
Council's teaching on papal primacy and infallibility. Among
their number were scholars like J. J. I. von Döllinger, Franz
Reusch, Johann Friedrich, and Johann von Schulte, who were
very influential in the formation of the schismatic group called
Old Catholics.

Vatican I unequivocally defined papal primacy and did so in
monarchical terms. The Council, however, was the culmination
of a nearly two-thousand-year development. In this chapter, I
shall treat historically and theologically the gradual emergence of
the monarchical papacy. My concern is not the scriptural and
early patristic data on which there is an abundance of recent
scholarly studies.[3] Rather, I shall deal with three main historical

2 Quoted in C. Butler, *The Vatican Council 1869–1870*, ed. Christopher Butler (Westminster, Md.: Newman, 1962), p. 416.
3 For a bibliography on the scriptural evidence see R. E. Brown,
K. P. Donfried, and J. Reumann, *Peter in the New Testament* (Minneapolis: Augsburg, 1973), pp. 169–77. The basic patristic documentation
can be found in E. Giles, ed., *Documents Illustrating Papal Authority*
A.D. 96–454 (London: SPCK, 1952) and J. T. Shotwell and L. R. Loomis,
The See of Peter (New York: Columbia University Press, 1927). The following studies examine the papacy in the early Church: P. Batiffol, *Cathedra
Petri. Études d'histoire ancienne de l'Église* (Paris: Cerf, 1938); L. Duchesne, *Early History of the Christian Church from Its Foundation to the
End of the Third Century*, 4th ed. (New York: Longmans, Green & Todd,
1909); C. Hofstetter, "La primauté dans l'Église dans la perspective de
l'histoire du salut," *Istina*, 8 (1961–62), 333–58; T. G. Jalland, *The
Church and the Papacy* (London: SPCK, 1944); J. F. McCue, "Roman

periods: first, the early period from the fourth to the tenth century, which saw the political establishment of the primacy; second, the medieval period from the tenth to the fourteenth century, in which the temporal dimension of the papacy developed; and third, the nineteenth and twentieth centuries, during which the doctrinal high point of papal claims was reached. This division is, of course, not meant to be rigidly understood, since in all periods there was a mixture of the political, the temporal, and the doctrinal.

I. The Historical Background

The Christian churches for the first three hundred years were not unified internationally, but rather made up of a loose *communio* or network of local churches whose common identity was allegiance to the apostolic tradition. Customs and structures were diverse, and any organizational unity that did exist was largely on a regional basis. Rome, Antioch, Alexandria, and Carthage, as major urban centers, dominated the life of the Church around them. Nevertheless, almost from its first-century beginnings, the Church of Rome was accorded a pre-eminent position, and understandably so. Rome was the only apostolic see in the West; it was the place where Peter and Paul were martyred; and it was, of course, the capital city of the Empire. Ignatius of Antioch called it the Church "presiding in love," and Irenaeus referred to its "more important prominence." In the fourth century, Rome gained further strength and prestige when the persecutions ended and Christians were granted religious freedom. Both orthodox and heterodox teachers came to Rome for confirmation of their views.

Primacy in the Second Century and the Problem of the Development of Dogma," *Theological Studies,* 25 (1964), 161–96, and "The Roman Primacy in the Patristic Era: The Beginnings Through Nicaea," in P. C. Empie and T. A. Murphy, eds., *Papal Primacy and the Universal Church* (Minneapolis: Augsburg, 1974), pp. 44–72; A. C. Piepkorn, "The Roman Primacy in the Patristic Era: From Nicaea to Leo the Great," in Empie and Murphy, pp. 73–97; and H. von Campenhausen, *Ecclesiastical Authority and Spiritual Power in the Church of the First Three Centuries* (Stanford: Stanford University Press, 1969).

More and more, it was the Bishop of Rome who settled the doctrinal and disciplinary disputes between the other churches. At the end of the fourth century, Rome began to assert her primatial claims.

A. The Early Period

The critical period in the doctrinal systematization of papal primacy took place in the years between Damasus I (366–84) and Leo I (440–61). In a little less than a century, the basic structure of the monarchical papacy was set. During that period, nine Popes insisted on Rome's supremacy. For them, the Pope was the head of the universal Church, he had special authority rooted in Peter, his rulings were normative for all the churches, and his decisions were above review. Rome was *the* apostolic see, and the Bishop of Rome was the leader of all the bishops. Thus the bishops of the province of Arles wrote Leo: "Through the most blessed Peter, chief of the Apostles, the holy Roman Church holds the primacy over all the churches of the whole world."[4]

According to Walter Ullmann, "the fixation of papal primacy was the achievement of Leo I."[5] T. G. Jalland calls him "a master builder" of the papacy, and although other Popes had prepared the way, "it was due to his genius that the Papacy emerged from the trials of his pontificate stronger and, if it be possible, more impregnable than ever before."[6] Leo was a remarkable Pope: diplomat, theologian, orator, administrator, and saint. A man of deep pastoral and spiritual sensitivity, and yet a "Roman of the Romans" in spirit, he was the first Pope to take the title *"pontifex maximus,"* which the emperors no longer used, and the first Pope to claim the *"plenitudo potestatis."* He governed the Church during a tumultuous period of barbarian invasions and internal Church disputes. Throughout it all, he de-

---

[4] *Ep.* 65 (J.-P. Migne, *Patrologia latina,* 54:879). Hereafter cited as PL or PG (*Patrologia graeca*).

[5] "Leo I and the Theme of Papal Primacy," *The Journal of Theological Studies,* N.S. 11 (1960), 25.

[6] *The Church and the Papacy,* op. cit., p. 302.

fended the rights of the Roman see, and one of his principal arguments was the continuity and identity that existed between himself and St. Peter.

Leo the Great was not the first Pope to stress the relationship between Peter and the Bishop of Rome. Earlier, Damasus had said that it was Peter who directed him, and Innocent I (401–17) said that he spoke "by the apostolic mouth."[7] Moreover, Siricius (384–99) wrote graphically: "We bear the burdens of all who are heavy laden, or rather the blessed apostle Peter bears them in us, who in all things, as we trust, protects and defends those who are heirs of his government."[8] What Leo did was to elaborate this theme and make it a foundational argument in favor of Roman primacy. In so doing, he identified himself with Peter. He was "Peter in Peter's see,"[9] and the representative of Peter (*cuius vice fungimur*).[10] In one of his famous sermons given on the anniversary of his episcopal consecration, he said:

> Now he [Peter] performs the duties entrusted to him with wider scope and greater power, and executes all parts of his obligations and responsibilities in and with that person [Leo himself] through whom he has been honoured. Hence if a right action is done by us or a right decision made, if anything is obtained from God in His mercy by daily prayers, it is a consequence of his good works and merits, whose power still survives and whose authority redounds in his see.[11]

Leo taught that the Pope, as the successor of Peter, possesses the plenitude of power that Christ gave to Peter. Peter, then, acts, speaks, judges, and continues to live in and through the Pope. Leo referred to himself as an "unworthy heir"[12] of Peter but one who, like him, is responsible for all the Christian churches. For Leo, each Pope was seen as a direct successor of Peter and not of

---

[7] *Ep.* 17 (PL 20:536).
[8] *Ep.* I, Letter to Himerius, Bishop of Tarragona (PL 13:1133).
[9] *Ser.* 2, 2 (PL 54:143).
[10] *Ser.* 3, 4 (PL 54:147).
[11] *Ser.* 3, 3 (PL 54:146). Translation from T. Jalland, *The Life and Times of St. Leo the Great* (London: SPCK, 1941), p. 70.
[12] *Ser.* 3, 4 (PL 54:147).

his immediate predecessor: the Pope receives the power to bind and to loose through Peter. If Peter is the fountainhead of all graces in the sense that "nothing has passed to others without his participation,"[13] so too all graces flow from the See of Peter to the rest of the Church.

There are two principal interpretations, one juridical and the other sacramental, of Leo's Petrine-papal concept. The first is found in Ullmann, who argues that Leo drew upon Roman jurisprudence to construct a legal framework for the papacy and to establish the identity between Peter and the reigning Pope. In so doing, "the concept of monarchy has found its highest possible expression."[14] Leo used the classical Roman-law principle that "the heir continues the deceased"—the heir takes the place of the deceased and receives all his assets and liabilities. The Pope, then, is the heir of Peter and possesses all the powers that Peter possessed. The juridical powers but not the personal qualities of Peter are transmitted. Although a particular Pope may be sinful, the papacy as an institution retains its Petrine character. This distinction between person and office has enabled the papacy to survive many major crises. According to Ullmann, Leo's explanation of the identity between Peter and the Pope is completely juridical and in no way sacramental or charismatic. Leo established "on a purely juridical basis, the continuity of the Petrine office on the Pope."[15]

The other interpretation is illustrated by Cornelius Ernst, who rejects the exclusive juridical view of Ullmann. Ernst argues that Leo sacramentally linked his own episcopal consecration to the event at which Christ gave Peter a special office in the Church. Both actions can be called "sacraments." The papal office, therefore, becomes the symbolic representation of the one faith that exists between Christ and Peter and also between Christ and Christians. He writes: "The continuance of Peter's profession of faith and its associated participation in Christ is seen

---

13 *Ser.* 4, 2 (*PL* 54:149).
14 "Leo I and the Theme of Papal Primacy," op. cit., 45.
15 Ibid., 33.

by Leo as a 'sacramental' identity of Peter and his successors."[16] According to Ernst, this sacramental conception of the papacy was lost and "led to a jurisdictional or 'political' theology of the primacy, which was to find its most balanced expression in Vatican I."[17]

These two interpretations reveal two aspects of the papacy that are present in Leo's writing. What is needed today, however, is a recovery of the sacramental dimension of the papacy. Such a view offers a better perspective in which to evaluate papal reform and it lends itself to a valuable symbolic understanding of the papacy in the context of the Church. A sacramental interpretation, properly understood, presents a necessary corrective to an overly juridical view of the papacy. It does not eliminate the juridical elements of the Petrine office, but it does situate them according to a more balanced ecclesiological idea.

The Peter-Pope identity has survived from Leo to the present. The Fathers at Chalcedon (451) accepted the *Tome* of Leo with the cry: "Peter has spoken through Leo."[18] When Paul VI visited the headquarters of the World Council of Churches in 1969, he said: "I am Peter." More recently, John Paul II made a similar reference in his inaugural address on October 17, 1978. Speaking of the magisterium, he said: "It is obvious that fidelity also demands adherence to the teaching of Peter, especially in the field of doctrine."[19]

Although Leo I laid the theoretical foundation of papal primacy, it was many centuries before it was accepted. Papal monarchy developed slowly and painfully over the next six hundred years. That period, approximately from the fall of the Roman Empire (476) to the Norman Conquest (1066), is commonly re-

---

[16] "The Primacy of Peter: Theology and Ideology—I," *New Black-friars*, 50 (1969), 354. Y. Congar discusses this same idea in *L'ecclésiologie du haut Moyen-Age* (Paris: Cerf, 1968).

[17] Ibid., 355.

[18] See F. X. Murphy, *Peter Speaks Through Leo: The Council of Chalcedon A.D. 451* (Washington: The Catholic University of America Press, 1953). In the papal feudal contracts made in the Middle Ages, St. Peter, acting through the Pope, had the role of the feudal lord with the obligation of protecting his vassals.

[19] *Origins* (Oct. 26, 1978), Vol. 8, No. 19, 293.

ferred to as the Dark Ages. A more optimistic view is given by Christopher Dawson, who calls them "ages of dawn, for they witnessed the conversion of the West, the foundation of Christian civilization, and the creation of Christian art and Catholic liturgy."[20] Nevertheless, it was a troublesome time for the Church, which had to face the barbarian invasions, disputes with the East, constant secular interference, and several unworthy Popes. The papacy, however, continued steadily to defend its rights and to extend its control over the various churches.

Several Popes shared the conviction of Leo that the duty of Peter's successors was "the care of all the churches."[21] Leo had strongly exercised jurisdiction over Christian communities in Italy, Africa, and Gaul, and demanded respect for the Apostolic See. Other Popes continued this tradition.

Gelasius I (492–96), for example, vigorously applied Leo's principles and defended papal primacy and the independence of the Church from the state. He insisted that the Roman See had supreme jurisdiction, which included the "right to loose what has been bound by the sentence of any bishop, because it has the authority to judge all the churches but can be judged by none."[22] Gregory I (590–604) likewise affirmed the authority of Rome, while respecting the rights of the local bishops: "I desire to honor my fellow bishops in everything and strive to uphold the honor of each, provided there is no conflict of rights between them."[23] His support of missionary efforts in Gaul and Britain also strengthened papal authority.

In the eighth century two important events took place that increased Rome's primatial role. First, Stephen II (752–57) became the first temporal ruler among the Popes through the Donation of Pepin, and second, the Islamic conquests destroyed the

[20] *The Making of Europe: An Introduction to the History of European Unity* (New York: New American Library, Meridian Books, 1956), p. 17.

[21] *Ser.* 3, 4 (*PL* 54:152).

[22] *Ep.* 10, 5 (P. Jaffé and F. Kaltenbrunner, *Regesta pontificum romanorum*, reprint (Graz: Akademische Druck-u. Verlagsanstalt, 1956), I: 622.

[23] *Ep.* 2, 52 (Jaffé, I: 1199).

Church in North Africa and ended the strong influence of the patriarchates of Alexandria, Antioch, and Jerusalem. Rome was able more and more to extend its administrative control. By the middle of the ninth century, Nicholas I (858–67) was able to act as the supreme judge and lawmaker for the entire Church. He resisted Carolingian interference in Church affairs and dealt severely with recalcitrant archbishops.[24]

B. The Medieval Period

The Popes of the tenth century, as we saw in Chapter 1, did little to enhance the See of Peter. A new era, however, began with the election of Leo IX (1049–54).[25] A reform movement

[24] Nicholas I deposed several archbishops and overruled the decisions of others. A major figure at this time was Archbishop Hincmar of Rheims (d. 882). Although a defender of the rights of the Church against state control, he also advocated greater power for metropolitans. Both Rome and the local bishops had difficulty with this idea. Cf. Hincmar's *De iure metropolitanorum* (PL 126:189–210) and M. Andrieu, "Le sacre épiscopal d'après Hincmar de Reims," *Revue d'histoire ecclésiastique*, 48 (1953), 22–73.

[25] In writing this section, I have found the following works especially useful: G. Barraclough, *The Medieval Papacy* (New York: Harcourt, Brace & World, 1968); A. Black, "The Influence of the Conception of Absolute Monarchy upon the Understanding and Practice of Papal Authority," in G. Alberigo and A. Weiler, eds., *Election and Consensus in the Church*, *Concilium*, Vol. 77 (New York: Herder and Herder, 1972), 103–12; Y. Congar, *L'ecclésiologie du haut Moyen-Age*, op. cit.; J. E. Lynch, "The History of Centralization: Papal Reservations," in J. A. Coriden, ed., *The Once and Future Church: A Communion of Freedom* (Staten Island, N.Y.: Alba House, 1971), pp. 57–109; R. Markus and E. John, *Pastors or Princes: A New Look at the Papacy and Hierarchy* (Washington: Corpus, 1969); M. Pacaut, *La théocratie, L'Église, et le pouvoir au Moyen-Age* (Paris: Aubier, 1957); A. Stacpoole, "The Institutionalisation of the Church in the Middle Ages," *The Ampleforth Journal*, 73 (1968), 337–52; B. Tierney, *Foundations of the Conciliar Theory* (Cambridge: Cambridge University Press, 1955); G. Tellenbach, *Church, State, and Christian Society at the Time of the Investiture Struggle* (Oxford: Blackwell, 1940); W. Ullmann, *Medieval Papalism: The Political Theories of the Medieval Canonists* (London: Methuen, 1949) and *The Growth of Papal Government in the Middle Ages*, 3rd ed. (London: Methuen, 1970); J. A. Watt, *The Theory of Papal Monarchy in the Thirteenth Century: The Contribution of the Canonists* (London: Burns & Oates, 1966); and M. J. Wilks, *The Problem of Sov-*

was organized around the idea of a strong monarchical foundation. Henceforward, until the pontificate of John XXII
(1313–34), the Roman bureaucracy had its most rapid period of
development. "At this point," writes John E. Lynch, "the papacy
controlled appointments to almost every significant post in the
Western Church along with the most minute aspects of ecclesiastical development."[26]

Gregory VII (1073–85) was a major figure in the reform
movement. An extraordinarily gifted and industrious individual,
he took resolute steps to curb the abuses of clerical immorality,
simony, and lay investiture. Although many of his biographers
portray him as a saintly and exemplary Pontiff, others refer to his
ruthless manner and ambition. St. Peter Damian, his contemporary, called him "My holy Satan," and, recently, Eric John referred to him as "the triumphalist's hero."[27] Gregory acted on the
principle that a reformed Church required a powerful papacy.
Thus Geoffrey Barraclough writes:

> To secure the "liberty" of the church, the church itself
> and society had to be reorganized on monarchical lines,
> ecclesiastical administration streamlined in the direction
> of centralized control, kings and rulers reduced, like the
> bishops, to the position of executors of the pope's will.[28]

Gregory VII's views on the papacy are principally contained
in the *Dictatus papae*—a list of twenty-seven propositions that
may have originally been chapter headings for a canonical treatise
that has been lost.[29] The following selection reveals his definite
monarchical conception of the papal office: (2) "That the Roman

---

ereignty in the Later Middle Ages (Cambridge: Cambridge University
Press, 1963).

[26] "The History of Centralization," op. cit., p. 60.

[27] *Pastors or Princes*, op. cit., p. 63.

[28] *The Medieval Papacy*, op. cit., p. 86.

[29] Latin text in E. Caspar, ed., *Das Register Gregors VII*, in *Monumenta germaniae historica, Epistolae Selectae*, II: 55 a, 201–8. English
translation from S. Z. Ehler and J. B. Morall, *Church and State Through
the Centuries* (Westminster, Md.: Newman, 1954), pp. 43–44.

Pontiff alone is rightly to be called universal."[30] (9) "That the Pope is the only one whose feet are to be kissed by all princes."[31] (12) "That he may depose Emperors."[32] (19) "That he himself can be judged by no one." (23) "That the Roman Pontiff, if canonically ordained, is undoubtedly sanctified by the merits of St. Peter." (25) "That without convening a synod he can depose and reinstate bishops."

Within a hundred years of the death of Gregory VII, the Popes became the effective heads of Western Christendom. During the pontificate of Innocent III (1198–1216), one of the most brilliant of all the Popes, the papacy reached the summit of universal power and controlled the religious, social, and political life of the West. Many of the greatest Popes were canonists and proclaimed a pontifical world monarchy. The Pope was not only the Vicar of Peter or the Vicar of Christ, he was also, according to Innocent III, the Vicar of God on earth.[33] To resist the commands of the Pope was to resist God, and no restrictions could be put on papal power. As Panormitanus (d. 1453) put it: "Whatever God can do, the Pope can do."[34] Yet Guilemus de Monte Lauduno (d. 1343) admitted that not even the Pope could turn black into white.[35] Innocent III declared that the Pope was "the meeting point between God and man . . . who can judge all things and be judged by no one."[36] For Johannes Andreae (d. 1348), the Pope "is neither God nor man, but somewhere be-

[30] Compare this with the refusal of Gregory I to be called "universal Pontiff." He felt it was a "proud title" and preferred the title "servant of the servants of God." Cf. *Ep.* 30 (PL 77:933).

[31] The kissing of the Pope's slipper was later reserved for liturgical functions. Relics of the saints were enclosed in the top of the slipper.

[32] This was not idle speculation. Gregory VII, in fact, deposed Henry IV. There have been other notable depositions: Zachary (741–52) of Childeric III, the last Merovingian King; Innocent III (1198–1216) of Otto IV; Innocent IV (1243–54) of Frederick II; and Pius V (1566–72), albeit futilely, of Queen Elizabeth I.

[33] Text in *Decretalium D. Gregorii Papae IV*, Lib. I, Tit. vii, c. 3 in *Corpus iuris canonici*, 2nd ed. Leipzig, A. Friedberg, ed. repr. (Graz: Akademische Druck-u. Verlagsanstalt, 1959), col. 99.

[34] Abbatis Panormitani (Nicholaus de Tudeschis), *Commentaria decretalium librum* (Venice: Iuntas, 1588), Lvi, 34.

[35] Referred to by Tierney in *Foundations of the Conciliar Theory*, op. cit., p. 200, n. 3.

[36] *Ser.* 2 (PL 217:658).

tween the two."[37] Furthermore, the canonists used several scriptural passages as literally applicable to the Pope in a political sense: "Look, today I am setting you over nations and kingdoms" (Jr. 1:10); "To Yahweh belong earth and all it holds, the world and all who live in it" (Ps. 24:1); and "All authority in heaven and on earth has been given to me" (Mt. 28:18).

On the basis of such claims, it was logical that papal power would be extended even over non-Christians. For Innocent IV (1243–54), "every creature is subject to the vicar of the creator."[38] The Pope, he felt, could interfere in any country that at any time had been under the rule of Christian princes. The Pope was viewed as a quasi-emperor in non-Christian areas, because "both infidel and faithful are the sheep of Christ through their creation."[39] This idea of a world monarchy was part of the theological and political justification for the Crusades.

Boniface VIII (1294–1303) reiterated the claims of papal sovereignty but was ultimately a failure. Boniface, who had become Pope ten days after the resignation of Celestine V, was an arrogant and ill-tempered person. The words of the holy Celestine to Boniface proved true: "You have entered like a fox. You will reign like a lion—and you will die like a dog." In his long controversy with Philip the Fair, King of France, he stanchly affirmed papal claims. He wrote to Philip: "Let no one persuade you that you have no superior and that you are not subject to the supreme hierarchy of the Church."[40] Philip often replied to such papal admonitions in the following manner: "To Boniface, who calls himself Pope, little or no greeting. Let your stupendous fatuity know that in temporal matters we are subject to no man."[41] In his dogmatic bull *Unam sanctam*, Boniface solemnly announced: "We declare, state, define, and pronounce that it is altogether necessary to salvation for every human creature to be subject to the Roman

[37] *Clementis papae quinti constitutiones* (Paris, 1601), Gloss. *Proemium*, s.v. *papa.*

[38] *Com. ad Extra*, I, ii, I.

[39] *Com. in Decretales*, III, xxxiv, 8.

[40] *Les registres de Boniface VIII*, eds. G. Digard et al. (Paris: E. De Boccard, 1939), Vol. III, No. 4424, col. 329.

[41] In P. Dupuy, *Histoire du différend d'entre le pape Boniface VIII et Philippe le Bel* (Paris, 1655), p. 44.

Pontiff."[42] In September 1303, William Nogaret, an agent of King Philip, and Sciarra Colonna, an old enemy, imprisoned Boniface in the papal palace at Anagni. After three days he was released and returned to Rome. Within a month he died—a broken man and the last of the Emperor-Popes.

The death of Boniface marked the end of the grandiose idea of a theocratic world order with all power, temporal and spiritual, emanating from the Pope. Five years later, the Popes took up residence in Avignon and remained there for seventy years. Although the experiment—to construct a Christian commonwealth under the headship of the Pope—failed, one must judge it in context. The Popes themselves were caught up in a bitter Church-State debate, and both parties resorted to various devices, rhetorical and otherwise, to protect their independence. The issue was further complicated by the status of the Popes as temporal rulers. They were monarchs who owned vast land holdings, collected taxes, had feudal vassals, organized armies, and resorted to devious political machinations. The medieval papacy surrounded itself with monarchical symbols: the coronation ceremony, the tiara, and the scarlet mantle, shoes, and stockings in imitation of the imperial garments. The Pope's spiritual role was intertwined with his temporal. Although Ullmann notes that "there is no statement by any medieval pope that justified papal jurisdiction on grounds that were or could be considered temporal,"[43] it is also true that this regrettable linking of the spiritual and the temporal harmed the papacy. As Dante said in his criticism of Boniface VIII: "The Church of Rome commingling in herself two ruling powers, falls into the mud and soils herself and her task."[44]

In evaluating the medieval papacy, it should be remembered that Europe at the time was a mosaic of feudal territories. Nations, as we know them today, were only in the process of formation. It was a period of violence, intrigue, and constant feuds—in

[42] In H. Denzinger and A. Schönmetzer, *Enchiridion symbolorum definitionum et declarationum de rebus fidei et morum,* 36th ed. (Freiburg: Herder, 1976), 875. Hereafter cited as Denzinger-Schönmetzer.

[43] "Papacy," in the New Catholic Encyclopedia, 10:956.

[44] *The Divine Comedy,* trans. L. Biancolli (New York: Washington Square Press, 1966), Purgatorio, Canto XVI, 127–29, p. 67.

short, a turbulent and unstable time.[45] The emergence of the monarchical papacy is closely related to the secular development of Europe at that time.[46] Moreover, in the Middle Ages, the papacy was the only institution in the West that had the authority and the influence to provide for order and unity. At times it went to excess, but medieval Europe owed it a considerable debt.

C. The Modern Period

Pius IX (1846–78), who has been called "the creator of the modern papacy,"[47] convoked the First Vatican Council. It began on December 8, 1869, and held its last general congregation meeting on September 1, 1870. Its dogmatic constitution *Pastor aeternus* defined papal primacy and infallibility. Although it did not use the term "monarchy,"[48] it presented the most formal and detailed magisterial statement we have of a monarchical conception of the papacy.[49] The following three canons speak for themselves:

[45] Life in the papal court itself was also turbulent. Joannes Monachus (d. 1313), a cardinal and a canonist, complained to Boniface VIII about his roughshod treatment of the cardinals: "I told the Pope that he would do well to obey himself the laws he made for others." On another occasion, Boniface is reported to have said to him: "Pig-head from Picardy, I want no advice from asses like you." Quoted in Tierney, *Foundations of the Conciliar Theory*, op. cit., pp. 181–82.

[46] Cf. R. A. Markus, "Papal Primacy: Light from the Early Middle Ages," *The Month*, 229 (1970), 352–61.

[47] E. E. Y. Hales, *Pio Nono: A Study in European Politics and Religion in the Nineteenth Century* (New York: Kenedy & Sons, 1954), p. xiii.

[48] The terms "monarchy" or "monarch" have been rarely used in official Church documents to describe the Church. An exceptional usage is found in the address of Pius X to the archbishops of the Near East in 1910. He urged them to condemn those who hold "that the Catholic Church in the first centuries was not the principate of one sole man, that is to say a monarchy, or that the primacy of the Roman Church rests on no valid ground" (Denzinger-Schönmetzer, 3555).

[49] Papal primacy was also taught at the Council of Florence. The Decree for the Greeks (1439) declared: "We decree that the Holy Apostolic See and the Roman Pontiff have primacy in the whole world, and that this Roman Pontiff is the successor of blessed Peter, Prince of the Apostles, and true vicar of Christ, head of the whole Church and father and teacher of

If any one, therefore, shall say that Blessed Peter the Apostle was not appointed the Prince of all the Apostles and the visible Head of the whole Church Militant; or that he directly and immediately received from the same our Lord Jesus Christ a primacy of honour only, and not of true and proper jurisdiction—*anathema sit*.[50]

If, then, any one shall say that it is not by the institution of Christ the Lord, or by divine right, that Blessed Peter should have a perpetual line of successors in the primacy over the Universal Church; or that the Roman Pontiff is not the successor of Blessed Peter in this primacy—*anathema sit*.[51]

If, then, any one shall say that the Roman Pontiff has the office merely of inspection or direction, but not full and supreme power and jurisdiction over the Universal Church, not only in things pertaining to faith and morals, but also in those things that relate to the discipline and government of the Church spread throughout the world; or that he possesses merely the principal part, and not all the fulness of this supreme power; or that this power which he enjoys is not ordinary and immediate, both over each and all the Churches and all the pastors and the faithful—*anathema sit*.[52]

Finally, the Council defined the doctrine of papal infallibility as a divinely revealed dogma.

We teach and define that it is a dogma divinely revealed: that the Roman Pontiff, when he speaks *ex cathedra*, that is, when in discharge of the office of Pastor and Doctor of all Christians, by virtue of his supreme apostolic authority he defines a doctrine regarding faith or morals to be held by the Universal Church, by the divine assistance promised him in Blessed Peter, is pos-

---

all Christians; that to him in blessed Peter was given by our Lord Jesus Christ the full power of feeding, ruling, and governing the universal Church as it is contained in the acts of the ecumenical Councils and in the sacred canons" (Denzinger-Schönmetzer, 1307). Translations of this passage and of subsequent passages from Vatican I are taken from *The Teaching of the Catholic Church*, prepared by J. Neuner and H. Roos and edited by K. Rahner (Staten Island, N.Y.: Alba House, 1967).

[50] Denzinger-Schönmetzer, 3055.

[51] Ibid., 3058.

[52] Ibid., 3064.

> sessed of that infallibility with which the Divine Re-
> deemer willed that his Church should be endowed for
> defining doctrine regarding faith or morals: and that
> therefore such definitions of the Roman Pontiff are ir-
> reformable of themselves, and not from the consent of
> the Church.[53]

In addition to the above, the Council also affirmed that the
Pope has the right to communicate freely with the bishops and
the faithful without being subject to secular interference[54] and
that the faithful have the right of recourse to the Pope as supreme judge "whose authority is unsurpassed" and "is not subject
to review by anyone."[55] The Council further stated that the jurisdiction of the Pope is "truly episcopal" as well as being ordinary
and immediate.[56]

What prompted the definition of papal primacy at Vatican I?
Several reasons have been suggested.[57] The remote occasion was
apparently the conciliarist errors of Gallicanism, Febronianism,
and Josephism, whose centers were respectively in France, Germany, and the Austro-Hungarian Empire. These three movements had two things in common: a strong nationalistic feeling
and a vigorous antipapal bias. They resented Roman centralism,
urged greater autonomy for national churches, and encouraged
state interference in ecclesiastical affairs. It is somewhat paradox-
ical that the conciliar debates focused so much on these errors,
since by the middle of the nineteenth century they posed no
major threat. The Church had weathered their assaults and they
are reflected in the Council more because of Rome's long memory
than because of any imminent danger.

[53] Ibid., 3074.
[54] Ibid., 3062.
[55] Ibid., 3063.
[56] Ibid., 3060.
[57] Cf. V. Conzemius, "Why Was the Primacy of the Pope Defined
in 1870?" in H. Küng, ed., *Papal Ministry in the Church, Concilium,* Vol.
64 (New York: Herder and Herder, 1971), pp. 75–83; K.-H. Ohlig, *Why
We Need the Pope. The Necessity and Limitation of Papal Primacy* (St.
Meinrad, Ind.: Abbey Press, 1975); H. J. Pottmeyer, *Unfehlbarkeit und
Souveränität* (Mainz: M. Grünewald, 1975); and G. H. Williams, "*Omnium
Christianorum Pastor et Doctor:* Vatican I et l'Angleterre victorienne,"
Nouvelle revue théologique, 96 (1974), 113–46, 337–65.

The more proximate occasion of the primacy definition may be found in the sociopolitical sphere. Rome had not fully adjusted to the upheavals caused by the French Revolution; and the papacy, held in such low esteem by Napoleon and other rulers, had lost much of its influence in European politics. Many bishops in the Catholic world who would benefit from a strong papacy urged a forthright proclamation of papal authority. Bishops in France, Belgium, and some of the German-speaking countries were uneasy about state interference; the Church in Italy and in Spain needed Rome's help against the forces of nationalism; and the Catholic minorities in England, Holland, North America, and Asia looked to Rome for support. For many Catholics the papacy represented the only viable source of moral authority against the evils of liberalism, materialism, and secularism. Rome itself, conscious of its declining prestige and the deterioration of its temporal authority in the Papal States, also felt that a forceful affirmation of its primacy was needed. To all these constituencies, *Pastor aeternus* was seen as an appropriate response.

Vatican I relied heavily on a juridical vocabulary to describe the papal office. It used such terms as "jurisdiction," "primacy," "full and supreme power," "plenitude of power," "discipline," "government," and "binding force." The resulting picture was that of a monarchy with the Pope as the King and the faithful as loyal and obedient subjects. The Church was portrayed more as a legal corporation than as a worshiping community directed by the Spirit.[58]

Pastor aeternus described papal jurisdiction as ordinary, immediate, and truly episcopal. The meaning of these terms is garnered not so much from the final text but from the conciliar debate that preceded it. Some of the Fathers felt that these terms should be omitted altogether, not because they were not true, but because they would be easily misunderstood. But the terms re-

[58] For further information on the preparation of Vatican I's *Pastor aeternus,* see R. Aubert, *Vatican I* (Paris: L'Orante, 1964); U. Betti, *La costituzione dommatica "Pastor aeternus" del concilio Vaticano I* (Rome: Antonianum, 1961); and W. F. Dewan, "Preparation of the Vatican Council's Schema on the Power and Nature of the Primacy," *Ephemerides theologicae lovanienses,* 36 (1960), 23–56.

mained and their meaning was clear. The term *ordinary* was used
in the canonical sense of a power that is not delegated but belongs to an office by reason of its function.[59] The Fathers agreed
that the Pope could use his authority at any time, but they rejected the implication that ordinary meant daily, habitual, or con-
tinuous. They argued also that the bishops, too, have ordinary
and immediate power in their own dioceses; that they are not
mere representatives of the Pope; and that the Pope does not take
the place of a bishop in his own diocese. Next, the term *immediate* meant that the Pope can exercise his authority directly over all
the faithful everywhere without any intermediary. Finally, the
term *episcopal* meant that the Pope has the pastoral authority to
teach, to sanctify, and to rule, and that his authority over the entire Church is the same as a bishop's authority in his own diocese.
This was not an invitation for constant meddling, for the episcopal power of the Pope "implies neither a necessity nor an implicit invitation to the Roman authority to be constantly involving
itself in local affairs."[60]

Two major problems were left unresolved by Vatican I: the
relationship between the papacy and the episcopacy, and the limitations of papal authority. The first question was discussed several
times in the debates, and many Fathers wanted a text that would
balance the Pope's authority and the unique role of the bishops.
Pastor aeternus, in response to these suggestions, did assert that
there was no conflict between the Pope and the bishops[61] but, unfortunately, this line of thought was not developed further. Although a schema on the episcopate had been prepared, the Coun-

[59] Cf. G. Thils, "Postestas ordinaria," in Y. Congar and B.-D. Dupuy,
eds., *L'épiscopat et l'Église universelle, Unam Sanctam,* 39 (Paris: Cerf,
1962), 689–707.

[60] W. F. Dewan, " 'Potestas vere episcopalis' au premier concile du
Vatican," in ibid., 683–84.

[61] "But so far is this power of the Supreme Pontiff from being any
prejudice to the ordinary and immediate power of episcopal jurisdiction, by
which bishops, who have been set by the Holy Spirit to succeed and hold
the place of the Apostles, feed and govern, each his own flock, as true
pastors, that this their episcopal authority is really asserted, strengthened
and protected by the supreme and universal pastor" (Denzinger-Schönmetzer,
3061).

cil's abrupt termination prevented its being discussed.[62] The second question, the limitation of papal primacy, was likewise debated. Bishop Federico Zinelli of Treviso, for example, asserted in the name of the Deputation on the Faith that the Pope's plenary power can only be restricted by natural and divine law but that neither the Pope nor an ecumenical council could suppress the episcopate or other things that were of divine origin.[63] It is regrettable that the traditional criteria for papal intervention, such as necessity and clear usefulness, were not included in the final text.[64] Much confusion could have been avoided.

Vatican I discussed the fact of papal sovereignty but not its exercise. As a result, many have incorrectly concluded that papal authority is absolute and arbitrary and that the law of the Church depends on the whim of the Pope. Some critics felt that the Council marked a return to the thinking of the Middle Ages.[65] Thus W. E. Gladstone, the Prime Minister of England, wrote: "Rome has refurbished and paraded anew every rusty tool she was fondly thought to have disused."[66] One of the strongest criticisms of the Council came from Bismarck, the German imperial Chancellor, who, with obvious political intent, issued a circular in

[62] Cf. G. Dejaifve, "Primauté et collegialité au premier concile du Vatican," in L'épiscopat et l'Église universelle, op. cit., 639–60; J.-P. Torrell, La théologie de l'épiscopat au premier concile du Vatican (Paris: Cerf, 1961); and W. Kasper, "Primat und Episkopat nach dem Vatikanum I," Theologische Quartalschrift, 142 (1962), 47–83.

[63] J. Mansi, Sacrorum conciliorum nova et amplissima collectio (Arnhem and Leipzig: Welter, 1927), 52:1114. Hereafter cited as Mansi.

[64] On this point see G. Thils, "The Theology of the Papacy: Towards a Revision," One in Christ, 10 (1974), 24–26 and Y. Congar, "Quelques expressions traditionnelles du service chrétien," in L'épiscopat et l'Église universelle, op. cit., 101–32, esp. 106–23.

[65] The reaction to Vatican I in the American secular press was often alarmist. The Buffalo Advertiser, for example, felt that the Council opposed everything that the United States stood for (cf. J. Ryan Beiser, American Secular Newspapers and the Vatican Council [Washington: The Catholic University of America, 1941], p. 211). A correspondent for the New York Times wrote: "I know you, old Roman spy of the Inquisition, and see you now, peering with your cunning, merciless eyes through your fingers—those fingers, bony, raw, and red with the stains of blood and itching for the blood of new victims" (ibid., p. 34).

[66] The Vatican Decrees in Their Bearing on Civil Allegiance: A Political Expostulation (New York: D. Appleton, 1875), p. 16.

1874. He claimed that as a result of Vatican I papal jurisdiction had absorbed episcopal jurisdiction; that the Pope had replaced in principle each local bishop; and that bishops were only functionaries of the Pope—agents of a foreign sovereign who was more of an absolute monarch than any other in the world. The German bishops forcefully answered Bismarck and, using Vatican I, denied his assertions. Pius IX praised the bishops for having explained "the true meaning of the Vatican decrees" in a way that "leaves nothing to be desired."[67]

Pastor aeternus dealt almost exclusively with papal prerogatives. However, it failed to situate the papacy in the broader context of the Church and its references to the episcopate are minimal. We have, in fact, what Gustave Thils called an "ecclesiological disequilibrium."[68] But history cannot be rewritten, and almost a hundred years were to pass before Vatican II was to redress this imbalance.

The year 1870 saw the Pope firmly established as the universal spiritual leader of the Roman Catholic Church, but it also marked the end of his position as the temporal ruler of the Papal States—the oldest sovereignty in Europe, which had existed for over a millennium. For the next sixty years the Popes remained as voluntary prisoners in the Vatican until the Lateran Pacts of 1929 created Vatican City. It is the smallest state in the world, with a territory of some 109 acres, and the Pope is its absolute sovereign.[69]

Between Vatican I and Vatican II, the papacy reinforced its primatial role, now almost exclusively spiritual. This was done in several ways. First, the Code of Canon Law, which was promul-

[67] The text of this declaration and the subsequent papal approval can be found in Denzinger-Schönmetzer, 3112–16. Also see O. Rousseau, "Le vrai valeur de l'épiscopat dans l'Église d'après d'importants documents de 1875," in *L'épiscopat et l'Église universelle,* op. cit., 709–36.

[68] "The Theology of the Papacy: Towards a Revision," op. cit., 19. See also by same author *La primauté pontificale. La doctrine de Vatican I. Les voies d'une révision* (Gembloux: Duculot, 1972).

[69] For an ecumenical discussion of the Pope as a head of state see L. Vischer, "The Holy See, the Vatican State, and the Church's Common Witness: A Neglected Ecumenical Problem," *Journal of Ecumenical Studies,* 11 (1974), 617–36.

gated in 1917 and went into effect a year later, stressed the Pope's supreme authority and provided a legal structure for detailed implementation.[70] Second, Church control became much more centralized and bureaucratized, and the Roman Curia increased its power. Third, Popes from the time of Leo XIII (1878–1903) widely exercised their teaching authority and issued a multitude of statements on doctrinal, disciplinary, moral, and political subjects. The prodigious output of magisterial pronouncements of Pius XII (1939–58) is unmatched. These three factors contributed to the prestige of the papal office, which was conceived of in monarchical terms, albeit a spiritual monarchy.

II. The Theological Background

The imperial analogy, as we have seen above, played an important role in the development of the papal office. From the fourth century, the Popes, later supported by canonical scholarship, constructed a legal and political theory that related the papacy to the model of the Roman imperial structure.[71] The Pope, as the successor of Peter, was the final court of appeal and possessed the fullness of legislative, executive, and judicial power. Vatican I raised this conception to the level of dogma. To see this development more fully, however, it is necessary to consider some of the theological argumentation relevant to papal monarchism. In this section, therefore, I shall discuss first some of the major theological reasons favoring ecclesial monarchy, and second, some dissenting views.

---

[70] F. Heiler considers the Code of Canon Law to be the final element in the development of papal centralization (*Altkirchliche Autonomie und päpstlicher Zentralismus* [Munich: E. Reinhardt, 1941], pp. 356 ff.).

[71] This tendency is also seen in some of the titles applied to the Pope, especially *Pontifex Maximus* and *Summus Pontifex*. See Y. Congar, "Titres donnés au pape," in G. Alberigo et al., *Renouveau ecclésial et service papal à la fin du XXe siècle*, *Concilium* (French ed.), No. 108 (Paris: Beauchesne, 1975), 55–64; H. Burn-Murdoch, *The Development of the Papacy* (New York: Praeger, 1954), pp. 73–79, and "Titles of the Roman See," *Church Quarterly Review*, 159 (1958), 257–364.

A.   Proponents of Papal Monarchy

From John of Torquemada (d. 1468) to the Fathers of Vatican II, Roman Catholic theologians have asked the question:
What form of government applies most suitably to the Church?
They distinguished three principal forms: monarchy (the rule of
one); aristocracy (the rule of a few); and democracy (the rule of
many). First, they rejected democracy, because authority does not
reside in the Christian community as a whole which, in Cajetan's
(d. 1534) lapidary expression, "is born to obey, not to command."[72] Unlike the secular state, the People of God do not possess ruling power and, therefore, cannot transmit it to someone
who would represent them.[73] The Pope, it was argued, is the
Vicar of Christ and not the Vicar of the Church. The Pope may
be designated by community but he receives his authority directly
from God—the only example of government by divine right. Next,
the theologians rejected aristocracy, because Christ immediately
and directly appointed Peter (and not some or all of the Apostles)
as the head of the Church. Since the Pope is the successor of
Peter, then there is no possibility that an elite group (the bishops)
could govern the Church. Finally, most theologians concluded
that the Church most closely resembled a monarchy in which one
person—the Pope—had universal sovereignty. The assertion of
Franz Hettinger (d. 1890), one of the redactors of the schema on
papal primacy at Vatican I, is typical: "The Church is essentially
a monarchy, since there is one person in it who constitutes in himself the plenitude of power, who commands all, and whom all
obey."[74]

Robert Bellarmine (d. 1621), brilliant controversialist during

[72] *Scripta theologica*, Vol. I, *De comparatione auctoritatis papae et
concilii cum apologia eiusdem tractatus*, ed. V. Pollet (Rome: Angelicum,
1936), No. 452, p. 205.

[73] On the problem of the vesting of ecclesial authority see P. Granfield, *Ecclesial Cybernetics: A Study of Democracy in the Church* (New
York: Macmillan, 1973), pp. 179–87.

[74] *Apologie du christianisme*, 2nd ed. (Bar-le-Duc: L. Guérin,
1869), V: 17.

the Counter Reformation and Doctor of the Church, has given us the most detailed theological exposition of papal monarchy. It is found in his *De controversiis*, a theological compendium of two million words that influenced theological thought for centuries.[75] Acknowledging his debt to St. Thomas Aquinas (d. 1274), to John of Torquemada and his *Summa de ecclesia*, and to English controversialist Nicholas Sander (d. 1581), Bellarmine argued that Christ deliberately chose the monarchical form of government for his Church, because it was the best and the most useful. Bellarmine listed the following advantages of monarchical rule.[76] First, it better preserves order, because there is a clear distinction between the ruler and his subjects, between superiors and inferiors. This is not true in an aristocracy or in a democracy. Second, a monarchy better fosters unity and peace, because there exists a strong bond when all the members of a society depend on one person. A natural unity results and it is less easily disturbed by factions. Thus St. Thomas noted that "one person is a more fitting basis of unity than many persons would be."[77] Third, it makes for a stronger body politic, since the monarch can channel the energies of his people into a productive unity. Fourth, it provides greater stability and longevity for a society, because it is easier to govern monarchically and, unlike democracies and aristocracies, it is less subject to contention, ambition, and intrigue.

In fairness to Bellarmine and the theologians who followed him, it should be pointed out that they were aware of the unique character of Church government. Bellarmine, for example, recognized that the Church is fundamentally a spiritual and not a political entity.[78] He insisted that Christ alone is "the absolute and

[75] *Opera omnia, De controversiis christianae fidei*, I, *De romano pontifice*, Liber I (Naples: J. Giuliano, 1856).

[76] Ibid., Liber I, cap. 2.

[77] *Summa contra gentiles*, Lib. IV, cap. 76. Also see *Summa theologiae*, I, Q. 103, art. 3.

[78] Bellarmine admitted only indirect temporal jurisdiction for the Pope. This position so displeased Pope Sixtus V (1585–90) that he put the first volume of the *De controversiis* on the Index. But Sixtus V died before this was carried out, and his successor, Urban VII (1590), who reigned only twelve days, had his name immediately removed. According to J. C. Murray, Bellarmine "effected a doctrinal advance within the Church herself, by

free king of the entire Church"[79] and that all in the Church are, in St. Paul's words, "Christ's servants, stewards entrusted with the mysteries of God" (1 Co. 4:1). Although Bellarmine considered a pure monarchy to be the ideal form of government, he concluded realistically that "because of the corruption of human nature,"[80] a mixed monarchy, with elements of aristocracy and democracy, is preferable. In relating this to the Church, he pointed out that the bishops form a kind of aristocracy and that "they are true princes and pastors and not vicars of the Pope."[81] He also said that there is a democratic quality in Church government, since "there is no one from the entire Christian multitude who is not able to be called to the episcopate, if he is found worthy of the task."[82]

In the final analysis, then, according to the traditional opinion, the Church may be called a monarchy, but, as Charles Journet warned, it must be applied "with precautions."[83] Similarly, Louis Billot, whose ecclesiology was indeed monarchically centered, doubted whether any term could be found to describe the uniqueness of ecclesiastical government. The Church, he maintained, is a monarchy but *"omnino sui generis."*[84] Because the Church is a mystery, we can only analogously and, therefore, only partially describe it by using terms taken from secular society. "The government of the Church," said Bishop Krementz at Vatican I, "cannot be adequately compared to a monarchy, whether absolute or mixed, or to an aristocracy or any such thing."[85]

---

finally disposing of the confusions and exaggerations of the hierocrats" ("St. Robert Bellarmine on the Indirect Power," *Theological Studies,* 9 [1948], 532).

[79] Bellarmine, op. cit., Liber I, cap. 5, 317.

[80] Ibid., cap. 1, 311.

[81] Ibid., cap. 3, 316.

[82] Ibid.

[83] *The Church of the Word Incarnate* (London: Sheed and Ward, 1955), 1:422.

[84] *Tractatus de ecclesia Christi,* 5th ed. (Rome: Gregoriana, 1927), 1:535.

[85] Mansi, 52:683.

B. Some Dissenting Views

There are many modern Catholic ecclesiologists who have difficulty with the traditional monarchical emphasis on the papacy. Their uneasiness centers not on the essence of the papacy but on its exercise. They agree that "the papacy belongs to the binding content of our faith,"[86] but they insist that a "reform through creative interaction"[87] is needed. It is not, therefore, a question of denying the unique leadership of the Pope in the Catholic communion but rather of doubting the appropriateness of the monarchical conception of that leadership. The following three passages from Karl Rahner, Richard McBrien, and Karl-Heinz Ohlig illustrate this concern.

> To define the Church as a monarchy is to fail to throw into relief the scope which, as history shows, here remains for the play of the charismatic and unexpected qualities of the Church's character, her perennial youthfulness, her vigor.[88]

> The present system exemplifies numerous qualities of monarchical absolutism: Pope and bishops remain for all practical purposes the exclusive rulers in the Church, combining the legislative, executive, and judicial powers in one hand.[89]

> Papal primacy as presently exercised, constitutes a block both to further development of the ecumenical movement and to reform movements with the Catholic Church.[90]

[86] K. Rahner, *The Shape of the Church to Come* (New York: Seabury, 1974), p. 53.

[87] A term used by A. Dulles in *The Resilient Church* (Garden City, N.Y.: Doubleday & Company, 1977), p. 29.

[88] K. Rahner, *The Episcopate and the Primacy* (New York: Herder and Herder, 1962), p. 15.

[89] R. P. McBrien, *The Remaking of the Church* (New York: Harper & Row, 1973), p. 86.

[90] K.-H. Ohlig, *Why We Need the Pope,* op. cit., p. ix.

An initial problem in calling the Church a monarchy is to determine what kind of monarchy is meant.[91] First, it is not a hered-
itary monarchy, whereby a blood relationship dictates who will be
the Pope. Although there have been at least two instances where
Popes have been the sons of Popes,[92] historically, elevation to the
papacy has always entailed some kind of election, designation, or
approbation. Second, the Church is not an absolute monarchy in
the sense that the duly elected Pope has unlimited authority over
Church polity, belief, and discipline. The Pope is bound by certain doctrinal and structural restraints. He cannot (and still remain Pope) publicly repudiate what has been revealed or what
has been proposed as the core of the Christian faith. Furthermore,
although the Pope may remove one or several bishops, he cannot
suppress the entire episcopate, because it is of divine origin.
Third, the Church is a constitutional monarchy, not in a strict political sense but analogously, since at present there is no juridi-
cally constituted body that can sanction the actions of the Pope.
The Pope is not, as Rahner remarks, "merely a representative
commissioned by the college of bishops and the executor of the
collegiate will."[93] Although the legitimate head of the Church,
enjoying a primatial status in the Christian community, the Pope
is, nevertheless, bound by some divinely established elements
rooted in revelation. The Pope has to operate within the context
of the faith community to which he belongs and whose leader he
is.

   Many, since Vatican I, have felt that the papacy has devel-

   [91] K. Rahner discusses this in *The Episcopate and the Primacy*, op.
cit., pp. 14–19.
   [92] Pope St. Silverius (536–37) was the son of Pope St. Hormisdas
(514–23), and Pope John XI (931–35) is alleged to be the illegitimate son
of Pope Sergius III (904–11).
   [93] "Church: Constitution of the Church," in *Sacramentum Mundi:
An Encyclopedia of Theology*, ed. K. Rahner, C. Ernst, and K. Smyth (New
York: Herder and Herder, 1968), 1:327. Rahner says further that even
though there is no written constitution of the Church, "Catholic ecclesiology
does not hesitate to use the analogy between Church and State, despite the
radical differences between them" (ibid., 328). For an interesting collection
of articles on ecclesial constitutionalism see J. A. Coriden, ed., *We, the
People of God . . . : A Study of Constitutional Government for the Church*
(Huntington, Ind.: Our Sunday Visitor, 1968).

oped more as an absolute than as a constitutional monarchy. They point to a juridical ecclesiology that lent itself to unilateralism in decision-making, triumphalism in papal style, and isolationism in regard to the believing community and to the College of Bishops. Anglican theologian Eric Mascall, for example, could write shortly before Vatican II that "the Pope [is] in effect not a member of the Church at all, but an external authority to which the Church is subjected."[94] Despite the corrective interpretations found in the debates at Vatican I, the papacy itself conveyed the impression that the Pope exists in solitary isolation from the rest of the Church. The increased centralization of Church authority and the influence of the Roman Curia only served to reinforce that view.

Between the two Vatican councils an exaggerated understanding of papal primacy and infallibility developed. A monarchical "one-man rule" and a kind of "creeping infallibility" were all too evident during the last hundred years. It was erroneously assumed that because the Pope on occasion could intervene in the life of the local Church, personally settle disputed questions without consultation, teach infallibly, and reserve to himself certain decisions, then he must always act in this manner.[95] As a result, papal prerogatives expanded and unilateralism became normative. Rome almost alone spoke authoritatively on such controversial issues as social justice, biblical studies, Modernism, war and peace, and contraception. Armed with the mandate of Vatican I, the Popes generally saw no need for regular collaboration with the bishops in the exercise of the teaching office. The papal magisterium became inflated and the bishops were expected only to communicate papal teaching faithfully to their flocks.

A new ecclesiological consciousness emerged at Vatican II. Prepared for by an earlier renaissance in scriptural, patristic, and liturgical studies, the Church itself, in the process of its own self-

[94] *The Recovery of Unity* (London: Longmans, Green, 1958), p. 210.

[95] G. Thils develops this idea in "Primacy and Collegiality," in J. de Broucker, *The Suenens Dossier: The Case for Collegiality* (Notre Dame, Ind.: Fides, 1970), pp. 150–52.

understanding, realized that a creative reform was necessary if it was to function as an effective sacrament of Christ on earth. In this perspective, the renewal of the papal office must be situated. The papacy should recover its deep pastoral character and eliminate those legalistic qualities that limit its effectiveness. What is needed, then, is a transition from a monarchical papacy to a collegial one. The next chapter will deal with that issue.

4 THE POPE AS FELLOW BISHOP

> A Pope of our time must be a true fellow bishop. He should be confident enough of his own office to risk sharing power with the other bishops, conducting himself not as a master over his servants but as a brother among his brethren.
>
> A COMMITTEE OF THEOLOGIANS[1]

Perhaps the single most important aspect of the papacy in transition, one that determines whether the Pope will be a monarch or a pastor, is the relationship between the Pope and the bishops. Vatican II gave the Church a charter for a pastoral papacy with its doctrine of collegiality.[2] In doing so, the Council stressed the unity and collaboration that should exist between the papal and episcopal offices; it described the corporate responsibility of the

[1] From a statement published shortly after the death of Paul VI and signed by ten theologians: G. Alberigo; M. D. Chenu; Y. Congar; C. Geffré; A. Greeley; N. Greinacher; J. Grootaers; G. Gutierrez; H. Küng; and E. Schillebeeckx (*Time* [Aug. 21, 1978], p. 71).

[2] The term "collegiality" was not used in the official documents of Vatican II. It became part of the theological vocabulary through the efforts of Y. Congar, who first used it in the 1950s in the context of the theology of the laity. It was later applied to the relationship between the Pope and the College of Bishops.

College of Bishops for the universal Church. For collegiality rests on the ancient idea of the Church as *communio*—a united people participating in God's saving grace in Christ and celebrating his presence most visibly at the Eucharist. The universal Church is a *communio ecclesiarum*, a fraternity of local communities joined together by the one Spirit.

Communio is not an ad hoc political expedient; it is found in Scripture and is evidenced in the early Church.[3] *Communio* is grounded in a twofold relationship: one that exists between the individual bishop and the members of the local church, and the other, which is a binding together of the local churches and their bishops into a larger unity. We must always keep in mind that the local church is not simply a part of a greater reality; it is the real Church, embodying the mystery of Christ's salvific presence and sustained by the sacramental graces, especially the Lord's Supper, the preaching of the Gospel, and the gifts of the Holy Spirit.[4] Accordingly, Ludwig Hertling defines *communio* in the early Church as "the bond that united the bishops and the faithful, the bishops among themselves and the faithful among them-

[3] On this subject see: L.-M. Dewailly, "Communio-Communicatio," *Revue des sciences philosophiques et théologiques*, 54–63; L. Hertling, *Communio: Church and Papacy in Early Christianity* (Chicago: Loyola University Press, 1972); O. Saier, *"Communio" in des Lehre des zweiten Vatikanischen Konzils* (Munich: Hueber, 1973); J. M. McDermott, "The Biblical Doctrine of Koinonia," *Biblische Zeitschrift*, 19 (1975), 64–77 and 219–33; E. Lanne, "Le service de communion entre les Églises catholiques romaines," in G. Alberigo et al., *Renouveau ecclesial et service papal à la fin du XXe siècle*, *Concilium* (French ed.), No. 108 (Paris: Beauchesne, 1975), 87–104; and the entire issue of *The Jurist*, 36 (1976) is devoted to this theme.

[4] The *Constitution on the Church (Lumen gentium)* stated: "The Church of Christ is truly present in all legitimate local congregations of the faithful which, united with their pastors, are themselves called churches in the New Testament" (Article 26). On the theology of the local church see B. Neunheuser, "Église universelle et Église locale," in G. Barauna, ed., *L'Église de Vatican II* (Paris: Cerf, 1966), II: 607–38; E. Lanne, "L'Église locale et l'Église universelle," *Irenikon*, 43 (1970), 481–511; A. Tessarolo, *La chiesa locale* (Bologna: Dehoniane, 1970); H. de Lubac, *Les Églises particulières dans l'Église universelle* (Paris: Aubier, 1971); and H.-M. Legrand, "The Revaluation of Local Churches: Some Theological Implications," in E. Schillebeeckx, ed., *The Unifying Role of the Bishop, Concilium*, Vol. 71 (New York: Herder and Herder, 1972), 53–64.

selves, a bond that was both effected and at the same time made manifest by eucharistic communion."[5] Precisely because of this bond, the various local churches were joined to the primatial Church of Rome. The concept of *communio* protects the unity of the universal Church as well as the individuality of the local church—thus revealing both apostolicity and catholicity. The entire Church is the creation of the Spirit, which manifests a diversity but also a unity of faith and sacrament.

The idea of *communio* is necessary for a full understanding of primacy and collegiality, for as Joseph Ratzinger, former professor of dogmatic theology at the University of Regensburg and now Cardinal Archbishop of Munich, says, the papal primacy is "a primacy of communion in the midst of the Church as a community and understanding itself as such."[6] Both the Pope and the bishops are essential to the Church; the doctrine of collegiality helps us to balance the complex relationships that exist between the local churches and the universal Church and between the episcopal and papal functions. Although collegiality is an involved theological, pastoral, and canonical issue with serious ecumenical ramifications, it is, nevertheless, a decisive element in comprehending the papacy in transition.

In this chapter I shall discuss collegiality from the perspective of the papacy and try to suggest some concrete ways in which this ideal can be realized. I shall be dealing with a transition that has already begun and one that must be further implemented, if executive reform is to be complete. In simple terms, the question is: How can the Pope be less a monarch and more a fellow bishop? The answer involves collegiality at two levels: a sound understanding of it, rooted in faith; and a prudent carrying out of it, guided by charity.[7]

[5] *Communio: Church and Papacy,* op. cit., p. 6.

[6] "Pastoral Implications of Episcopal Collegiality," in E. Schillebeeckx, ed., *The Church and Mankind, Concilium,* Vol. 1 (Glen Rock, N.J.: Paulist, 1965), 52.

[7] Much has been written on collegiality. Still one of the best speculative analyses is that of K. Rahner and J. Ratzinger, *The Episcopate and the Primacy* (New York: Herder and Herder, 1962). An updated version of Rahner's ideas can be found in his "On the Relationship Between the Pope and the College of Bishops," in *Theological Investigations* (New York: Seabury, 1977), 10:50–70. A good overview with bibliography is R. Mc-

I. The Collegial Ideal

It is axiomatic that every conciliar statement is to some extent a compromise. After several unsatisfactory drafts, the final text more or less successfully integrates the various suggestions made by the participants, yet necessarily reflects their diverse points of view. Ambiguity, therefore, is almost inevitable. Vatican II proved no exception. Take, for example, Chapter 3 of the *Constitution on the Church* (*Lumen gentium*), Articles 18 to 29, which describes the papal and episcopal ministries. There are at least two ecclesiologies present in that section: One begins with the universal Church and adopts a juridical approach; the other begins with the local church and favors a sacramental approach.[8] Keeping in mind, then, that there are two compatible but different approaches at work here, we must be careful in our interpretation of this conciliar teaching.

A. The Co-operation of Pope and Bishops

The Council's express aim was to elaborate a doctrine about the bishops, the successors of the apostles, "who together with the successor of Peter, the Vicar of Christ and the visible head of the

---

Brien, "Collegiality: The State of the Question," in J. A. Coriden, ed., *The Once and Future Church: A Communion of Freedom* (Staten Island, N.Y.: Alba House, 1971), pp. 1–24. Other studies I have found helpful in preparing this section are: Y. Congar, *La collégialité épiscopale. Histoire et théologie, Unam Sanctam,* 52 (Paris: Cerf, 1965); Y. Congar and B.-D. Dupuy, eds., *L'épiscopat et l'Église universelle, Unam Sanctam,* 39 (Paris: Cerf, 1962); Y. Congar, *Ministères et communion ecclésiale* (Paris: Cerf, 1971); Groupe des Dombes, *Le ministère épiscopal* (Taizé: Presses de Taizé, 1976); C. Butler, *The Theology of Vatican II* (London: Darton, Longman, & Todd, 1967); Sacred Congregation for Bishops, *Dictionary on the Pastoral Ministry of Bishops* (Ottawa: Canadian Catholic Conference, 1974); A. Ganoczy, "Ministry, Episcopacy, Primacy," *One in Christ,* 6 (1970), 348–85 and "How Can We Evaluate Collegiality vis-à-vis Papal Primacy?" in H. Küng, ed., *Papal Ministry in the Church, Concilium,* Vol. 64 (New York: Herder and Herder, 1971), 84–94.

[8] See A. Acerbi, *Due ecclesiologie. Ecclesiologia giuridica ed ecclesiologia di communione nella "Lumen Gentium"* (Bologna: Dehoniane, 1975).

whole Church, govern the house of the living God."[9] It began by stating that Christ instituted in the Church a permanent and stable college that was originally called "the Twelve." The apostolic college, with Peter as its head, continues in the Church today under the headship of Peter's successor, the Roman Pontiff. A parallel continuity exists between these two groups.[10] One becomes a member of the College of Bishops through episcopal consecration, which confers the tasks (munera) of sanctifying, teaching, and governing. These tasks, however, can only be exercised in communion with the head and with the other members of the episcopal college.[11]

Prior to Vatican II, there was a long-standing controversy concerning episcopal powers. It originated in the twelfth century, when a distinction was made between the power of order (potestas ordinis) and the power of jurisdiction (potestas jurisdictionis).[12] An ordained bishop, so went the theory, derived from his consecration the power to ordain and to perform sacramental rites but received directly from the Pope the power to teach and to govern.[13] This same theory was applied to the College of Bishops when they acted together in an ecumenical council. Vatican II approached this problem in a different way and made two far-reaching revisions: First, it used the term "task" or "function"

[9] Lumen gentium, Art. 18.

[10] The following authors discuss this idea: J. Colson, L'épiscopat catholique: Collégialité et primauté dans les trois premiers siècles de l'Église (Paris: Cerf, 1963); J. Lecuyer, Études sur la collégialité épiscopale (Le Puy and Lyons: Mappus, 1964); D. M. Stanley, "The New Testament Basis for the Concept of Collegiality," Theological Studies, 25 (1964), 197–216; M.-J. Guillou, "Le parallelisme entre le collège apostolique et le collège épiscopal," Istina, 10 (1964), 103–10; and A. Lemaire, Les ministères aux origines de l'Église (Paris: Cerf, 1971).

[11] In order to avoid the impression that the term collegium referred to a group of equals, the Council also used the terms ordo, coetus, and corpus.

[12] See G. Alberigo, Lo sviluppo della dottrina sui poteri nella chiesa universale (Rome: Herder, 1964).

[13] Charles Journet gives us a good example of this approach: "When the Supreme Pontiff . . . invests bishops, the proper jurisdiction they receive does not come directly from God, it comes directly from the Supreme Pontiff to whom Christ gives it in a plenary manner" (The Church of the Word Incarnate [New York: Sheed and Ward, 1955]), 1:405.

(*munus*) rather than "power" (*potestas*); and second, in accord
with this terminology, it replaced a juridical emphasis with a sacramental one. It taught in effect that the authority of a bishop to
sanctify, teach, and govern is fundamentally one—derived from
Christ through episcopal consecration.[14]

The doctrine of collegiality was intended to unite the Pope
and the bishops. It is not a question, therefore, of the Pope on
one hand and the bishops on the other, but, rather, of the College
of Bishops as one entity, with the Pope as its head. Both the papacy and the episcopate are of divine right and both have their
own legitimate authority. The Pope cannot, for example, abolish
the episcopate, nor can the bishops function without the Pope.
Together they form one communion, although they have distinct
responsibilities. The Pope, as the Bishop of Rome, is the head of
the primatial see and also exercises leadership in the college. This
does not mean that the bishops are simply agents of the Pope.
Lumen gentium declared: "Nor are they [the bishops] to be
regarded as vicars of the Roman Pontiff, for they exercise an authority which is proper to them, and they are quite correctly
called 'prelates,' heads of the people they govern. Their power,
therefore, is not destroyed by the supreme and universal power."[15]
To speak of the College of Bishops is to include the Pope, who is
both member and head. As Richard McBrien sums it up: "The
college is nothing without the Pope and the Pope is nothing without the college."[16]

In *Lumen gentium*, however, there appears to be a theological dilemma concerning the precise roles of the Pope and the college. The problem arises primarily in the interpretation of the following passage from Article 22.

> The Roman Pontiff has, in relation to the Church, by
> virtue of his office as Vicar of Christ and pastor of the

[14] Christopher Butler writes: "There is no hint in the Constitution
that the powers of the college are derived from the Pope. On the contrary,
there is reason to think that they derive from the sacrament of Order" (*The
Theology of Vatican II*, op. cit., p. 103).

[15] Art. 27.

[16] "Collegiality: The State of the Question," op. cit., p. 18.

> whole Church, full, supreme, and universal power, which
> he can always freely exercise. . . . Together with its
> head, the Roman Pontiff, and never without this head,
> the episcopal order is the subject of supreme and full
> power in relation to the universal Church. But this
> power can be exercised only with the consent of the
> Roman Pontiff.[17]

This passage attempted to reconcile the definition of primacy at
Vatican I with the doctrine of collegiality. It left us, however,
with several questions. Who is the subject of supreme authority
in the Church? Is it the Pope as Vicar of Christ and head of the
Church or is it the College of Bishops under the leadership of the
Pope? Or is it both? Two theological opinions have been proposed.

One school of thought holds that there are two supreme subjects of authority in the Church, which are inadequately distinct:
the Pope as head of the Church, and the Pope with the episcopal
college.[18] This position, held today by only a few theologians, rests
its case on Vatican I and on the teaching of Vatican II, especially
"The Prefatory Note of Explanation."[19] According to this view,
the Pope, as supreme pastor of the universal Church, has the
fullness of power and he can freely decide how best to serve the
Church, either personally or collegially. Furthermore, the Pope is
the head of the college and "he alone can perform certain acts
which in no wise belong to the bishops, for example, the convok-

[17] The phrase "in relation to the (universal) Church" is a translation
of "in (universam) ecclesiam." I follow here the translation of Bishop Butler,
who prefers this rendition to the more usual "over the (universal) Church,"
in order to avoid the idea that the Pope is "above and outside the Church"
(Theology of Vatican II, op. cit., pp. 101-2).

[18] Cf. W. F. Bertrams, "De subjecto supremae potestatis ecclesiae,"
Periodica de re morali, canonica, liturgica, 54 (1965), 173-232, and
M. Browne, "Il collegio episcopale soggetto di potestà suprema di governo
della Chiesa Cattolica e la 'nota explicativa praevia,'" Divinitas, 9 (1965),
379-84.

[19] The "Nota explicativa praevia," issued by the Theological Commission on the order of Paul VI, served as an interpretative norm for Chapter
3 of Lumen gentium. It was neither debated nor voted on at the Council.
An English translation of it is in W. M. Abbott, ed., The Documents of
Vatican II (New York: America Press, 1966), pp. 98-101.

ing and directing of the college, approving the norms of action, etc."[20]

A second school of thought, which is shared by the majority of theologians today, affirms that there is only one subject of supreme authority in the Church: the episcopal college with papal leadership. Karl Rahner, for example, calls the two-power theory a "metaphysical absurdity"[21] that is "obscure and imprecise in the extreme"[22] and that would break the essential unity of the Church. He argues that just as Peter and the apostolic college formed one ontological entity, so too do the Pope and the College of Bishops. The supreme authority in the Church, therefore, is always collegial, because the Pope belongs to the college. This is true even when he acts alone. Yves Congar frequently refers to "the supreme power that is always collegial."[23] Cardinal Suenens makes the same point: "The word 'alone' never means 'separately' or 'in isolation.' Even when the Pope acts without the formal collaboration of the bishops—as he has the legal right to do—he is still acting as their leader."[24] Therefore there is only one subject of authority in the Church, but it can operate in two different ways: through a collegial act in the strict sense or through a personal act of the Pope as head of the college.

The papal-episcopal relationship seen as a function of *communio* protects both the rights of the Pope and the college. "Together," as Vatican II declared, "they represent the entire Church joined in the bond of peace, love, and unity."[25] The Pope, then, is not simply the spokesman of the college nor is the college

[20] "Prefatory Note," No. 3.

[21] *The Episcopate and the Primacy,* op. cit., p. 93.

[22] "On the Relationship Between the Pope and the College of Bishops," op. cit., 61.

[23] *Ministères et communion ecclésiale,* op. cit., pp. 179 and 202. This interpretation is also held by O. Semmelroth, "Die Lehre von der kollegialen Hirtengewalt über die Gesamtkirche unter Berücksichtigung der angefügten Erklärungen," *Scholastik,* 40 (1965), 161–79; R. McBrien, "Collegiality: The State of the Question," op. cit.; C. Butler, *The Theology of Vatican II,* op. cit.; and G. Philips, *L'Église et son mystère au IIe Concile du Vatican* (Paris: Desclée, 1967–68).

[24] In J. de Broucker, *The Suenens Dossier: The Case for Collegiality* (Notre Dame, Ind.: Fides, 1970), p. 12.

[25] *Lumen gentium,* Art. 23.

merely his agent. Both serve the Church under the divine mandate to preserve unity, to foster faith, and to make Christ present in the world. Collegiality—coresponsibility of Pope and bishops—means that the bishops share with the Pope the tasks of teaching and policy-making within the universal Church.

B.   The Legal Limits of Primacy

Cardinal Suenens pointed out a "serious omission" in Vatican II's doctrine of collegiality, "since nothing was said of the consequences of collegiality for the Pope in his relationship to the other bishops."[26] Cardinal Suenens felt that Vatican II proposed the theory of collegiality but did not indicate how it would affect the function of the Pope. This raises several intriguing questions: Should there be canonical restrictions limiting the Pope's exercise of his primacy? Should the Pope be canonically bound to act always in consultation with the bishops? Must the Pope respect the coresponsibility of the episcopal college?

Vatican I and Vatican II did not deal with this issue, yet they both acknowledged the existence of *moral* norms governing papal action. They also agreed that the Pope's power is not absolute, since he is bound by revelation and prior dogmatic decrees. During Vatican II, Paul VI suggested the addition of a phrase that the Pope "is answerable to the Lord alone," but the Theological Commission rejected that proposal, arguing that "the Roman Pontiff is also bound to revelation itself, to the fundamental structure of the Church, to the definitions of earlier councils, and other obligations too numerous to mention."[27] Furthermore, Vatican II stated that the Pope and the bishops should use "appropriate means to inquire into that revelation and to give apt expression to its contents."[28] Concretely, for the Pope, this would involve collaboration and consultation with the bishops. It means that the bishops should be consulted before Rome issues a statement affecting the whole Church.

26 *The Suenens Dossier*, op. cit., pp. 11–12.
27 Quoted in H. Vorgrimler, ed., *Commentary on the Documents of Vatican II* (New York: Herder and Herder, 1967), 1:202.
28 *Lumen gentium*, Art. 25.

Nevertheless, the Council did not say that a failure to engage in broad consultation with the bishops would invalidate the Pope's action. Theoretically, it would seem, a Pope could refuse any form of collaboration with his fellow bishops. The Pope, as the Council noted, can always freely exercise his supreme and full authority. Although such action might incur the wrath of the bishops and diminish papal credibility, at present it is subject to no canonical prohibition. A Pope might sin gravely by totally disregarding the bishops, but he would not be breaking the law.

The question is, then, whether the moral norms of collegiality should be made into canonical laws. Many theologians feel that this is theoretically possible. Gregory Baum, for example, argues that if there are moral limits to papal primacy, there can also be minimal legal limits. "Human morality," he writes, "is always sufficiently objective to find some suitable legal norm expressing and protecting it."[29] He concludes that it is possible to have some kind of constitutional guarantee for papal and episcopal action. Using *Haec sancta* of the Council of Constance as a precedent, he believes that "papal primacy is not intrinsically irreconcilable with canonical norms limiting its exercise."[30]

Other theologians, however, without denying the possibility of establishing canonical norms, doubt the wisdom of framing collegiality in legal terms. They do not see the value of drawing up statutes that would bind the Pope to follow specific procedures in the practice of collegiality. Nevertheless, conceivably an autocratic Pope, acting independently, might habitually ignore the bishops in his deliberations. To this situation Rahner responds: "The simple answer is that he 'can' do so, but he will not. The Catholic mind does not demand a juridical norm by which the Pope could be impeached; he relies on the power of the grace of God and the Holy Spirit in the Church."[31]

As a matter of fact, every dogmatic definition of the last century has been made either in an ecumenical council (infallibility) or after wide consultation (Mary's Assumption). But before we

29 "Suenens Crying in the Wilderness," *The Catholic World* (Dec. 1969), p. 107.
30 Ibid.
31 In *Commentary on the Documents of Vatican II*, op. cit., 1:203.

subscribe to Rahner's conclusion, we should note two things: first, in the past there have been unilateral papal actions with disastrous results; and second, curial activity, less dramatic but important and extensive, generally operates with only limited consultation. It would seem, then, that more attention should be paid to the establishment of canonical guidelines in order to insure thoroughness and efficiency in all ecclesial decision-making. Of course, such norms might well be largely declaratory, for the Pope would not be bound by the purely canonical specifications, but they would formulate what is expected of him in furtherance of the collegial ideal. Thus Carl Peter, aware of the potential abuse of papal power but without trying to minimize papal authority, suggests "something akin to a constitution or at least a bill of rights for the Roman Catholic Church."[32]

In the final analysis, however, collegiality cannot be fully realized through legal prescriptions. It is, like the Church itself, ultimately under the guidance of the Holy Spirit. There have been, and undoubtedly there will be in the future, tensions between the Pope and the College of Bishops. These will not be resolved by law but by a generous response to God's will and a deep concern for the welfare of the People of God. Bishop Butler's observation is timely: "In the end the Church lives by conscientious charity rather than by law."[33]

C. The Possibility of a Plural Primacy

A fundamental question about collegiality, one pregnant with untold theological and political implications, is whether or not the head of the Church must be an individual person. In other words, is it possible for a group to hold a primatial position in the Church? "In theory," according to Avery Dulles, "the Petrine function could be performed either by a single individual presiding over the whole Church or by some kind of committee,

---

[32] "Papal Primacy: Ecumenical Considerations," *Proceedings of the Catholic Theological Society of America*, 31 (1976), 138–39.
[33] *The Theology of Vatican II*, op. cit., p. 105.

board, synod, or parliament—possibly with a 'division of powers' into judicial, legislative, administrative, and the like."[34]

The historical evidence for group governance in the Church of Rome, at least in the Church's early years, has long been a subject of controversy.[35] Today it is considered more probable, although the evidence is scanty and often obscure, that through the first century the Church at Rome was governed not by one bishop but by a college of presbyter-bishops. The letter of Clement to the Corinthians (c. 93–97) seems to suggest this. Furthermore, Ignatius of Antioch, who died during the reign of Trajan, 97–117, makes no reference to the Bishop of Rome in his letter to that Church, despite his preoccupation with the monarchical episcopate. Finally, the Shepherd of Hermas (c. 120) refers to the elders presiding over the Roman Church but does not indicate that one bishop among them either rules or presides. It may be presumed, therefore, that the early Church of Rome was ruled by several bishops. Nevertheless, by the middle of the second century, Rome clearly had a monarchical episcopate.

If there is considerable agreement among contemporary scholars that the early Church was governed collegially, there is no such consensus concerning how this collegial body was structured. Some would hold that within the college there was one

[34] *The Resilient Church* (Garden City, N.Y.: Doubleday & Company, 1977), pp. 118–19.

[35] Several recent studies discuss the evidence for a collegial papacy in the early Church. See P. Burke, "The Monarchical Episcopate at the End of the First Century," *Journal of Ecumenical Studies*, 7 (1970), 499–518; J. E. Lynch, "Coresponsibility in the First Three Centuries: Presbyterial Colleges and the Election of Bishops," *The Jurist*, 31 (1971), 14–53; J. Fuellenbach, *An Evaluation of the Recent Theological Discussion of First Clement. The Question of the Primacy of Rome. Studies in Sacred Theology*, Second Series No. 267 (Washington, D.C.: The Catholic University of America, 1977), esp. pp. 338–41 and 395–98; and three articles by J. F. McCue: "The Roman Primacy in the Second Century and the Problem of the Development of Dogma," *Theological Studies*, 25 (1964), 161–96; "Roman Primacy in the First Three Centuries," in H. Küng, *Papal Ministry in the Church, Concilium*, Vol. 64 (New York: Herder and Herder, 1971), 36–53; and "The Roman Primacy in the Patristic Era: The Beginnings Through Nicaea," in P. C. Empie and T. A. Murphy, eds., *Papal Primacy and the Universal Church* (Minneapolis: Augsburg, 1974), pp. 44–72.

bishop who had certain presidential prerogatives. Thus Louis Duchesne, on the basis that there was one presiding bishop, could accept the idea of an early collegiate episcopate at Rome, since "between this president and the one monarchical bishop of succeeding centuries, there is no difference in principle."[36] Such an interpretation may solve the doctrinal problem of a single primate, but it appears to be based on weak grounds; we simply do not possess sufficient evidence to know how the college operated and what role, if any, was enjoyed by the presiding bishop. Other scholars argue that the Roman Church at the end of the first century was ruled by an episcopal college of equals. This view raises problems, in addition to that of insufficient evidence, when we attempt to apply it to the modern papacy. First there is the question of determining whether the later development and its connection with one individual—the Bishop of Rome—is in fact part of the divinely willed structure of the Church. The consistent teaching of the Church, including Vatican I and Vatican II, asserts that only one individual is Peter's legitimate successor, apparently ruling out the possibility of a plural primacy. Second, there is the matter of practical feasibility. Historically, rule by committee or by a triumvirate has proved an ineffectual way to govern a large social organization. Plural leadership of the Church would present major organizational difficulties with limited benefits.

Although the notion of a plural papacy may never be realized, there is an underlying issue here that has ecumenical significance. The doctrine of collegiality may be a partial response to the objections of the Orthodox Christians to the form and function of the traditional papacy. The Orthodox acknowledge that Rome has a primacy of witnessing and caring for the universal Church, but they reject any kind of juridical supremacy. Yet, since all bishops are fundamentally equal, they would be willing to assign to the Bishop of Rome the title "first among equals" (*primus inter pares*). A problem arises here, because Vatican I taught that the Bishop of Rome possesses both a primacy of honor and of jurisdiction.

[36] *Early History of the Christian Church from Its Foundation to the End of the Third Century*, 4th ed. (New York: Longmans, Green & Todd, 1909), 1:70.

In an attempt to reconcile these two views, Pierre Duprey points out that Eastern theology recognizes both a primatial and a collegial authority; the axiom "first among equals" historically included jurisdictional as well as honorary authority. Orthodox theologian Nicolas Afanassieff illustrates this idea when he writes that the conciliar ideal presupposes primacy and that "equality is really a difficult claim, when the patriarch possesses rights of which the other bishops are deprived."[37] Duprey feels that it is possible, on the basis of the sacramental nature of collegiality, to understand the formula "first among equals" in the context of Roman Catholic theology. He argues that the primatial and collegial exercise of authority are interdependent; every honor in the Church must be seen as a service. The critical question regarding primatial authority is not "the juridical standing of the exercise of this authority—several are possible—but of the spirit, which inspires the way in which those endowed with this authority carry out their work."[38]

In examining the collegial ideal, we have seen first the need for co-operation between the Pope and the bishops; second, the practical legal formulation of this interaction; and third, the theoretical possibility of a shared primatial authority. The collegial ideal, however, should never be the occasion of a conflict between the Pope and the bishops but a way of recovering the unity of ecclesial authority. Both the papacy and the episcopacy are of divine origin and both, therefore, are permanent elements in the Church. To affirm that there is one subject of supreme authority in the Church—the episcopal college under the leadership of the Pope—is to emphasize a collaborative, not a divisive dimension. Papal prerogatives are not rejected but, seen in their proper perspective, are preserved and fostered.

[37] "The Church Which Presides in Love," in J. Meyendorff et al., *The Primacy of Peter in the Orthodox Church* (Leighton Buzzard, Bedfordshire: The Faith Press, 1963), p. 69.

[38] "Brief Reflections on the Title 'Primus inter Pares,'" *One in Christ*, 10 (1974), 11. Also see G. Dejaifve, "First Among Bishops," *Eastern Churches Quarterly*, 14 (1961), 2–25.

II. The Implementation of Collegiality

It is no secret that the collegial ideal taught by Vatican II has
not yet been fully implemented. The adage, "Authority never exercised is no authority at all," may apply in some sense to the present College of Bishops. Despite some efforts toward coresponsibility, Rome has been reluctant to share its power with the
bishops. "Collegiality," according to Cardinal Suenens, "is an art
that must be learned in common or not at all."[39] Without the support of the Holy See, collegiality will not be realized, for Roman
traditions die slowly. Yet, if there is to be a reformed papacy,
collegiality must be more than a pious ideal. The complexity of
the problems facing the Church make it imperative that collegiality be exercised. No Pope, no matter how brilliant or creative he
may be, can govern the Church single-handedly. He needs regular and sustained co-operation and consultation with the College
of Bishops and others. The Pope should make no major decision
affecting the entire Church until he has engaged in broad consultation.

To see how papal structures are to be renewed, we must first
see how collegiality interacts with two other principles, as the
Lutheran-Roman Catholic Dialogue suggests in giving three principles for papal reform.[40] Let us, then, see how two of them, legitimate diversity and subsidiarity, relate to the third, our area of
major concern, collegiality.

The first principle, legitimate diversity, is based on the variety of gifts given to the Church of Christ by the Spirit. It is a call
for Church authority to discern these gifts as they are manifested
in different peoples and cultures and result in different thought
patterns, theologies, ecclesial structures, and liturgical practices.
The papacy in transition has to take these factors into account
and allow for legitimate diversity that is in accord with the unity
of the faith. The papacy should respect this diversity, foster unity

[39] *The Suenens Dossier,* op. cit., p. 36.
[40] *Papal Primacy and the Universal Church,* op. cit., Nos. 23–25,
pp. 19–20. For an excellent evaluation of the Dialogue see A. Dulles, "The
Papacy: Bond or Barrier?" *Origins* (May 2, 1974), Vol. 3, No. 45, 705–12.

without demanding stringent uniformity, and be willing to renew itself. In the words of the Dialogue: "Even the exercise of the Petrine function should evolve with the changing times, in keeping with a legitimate diversity of ecclesial types within the church."[41]

The second principle, subsidiarity, is described by Pius XI: "That which individual men can accomplish by their own initiative and by their own industry cannot be taken from them and assigned to the community; in the same way, that which minor communities can do should not be assigned to a greater or higher community."[42] Pius XII said that subsidiarity "is valid for social life in all its organizations and also for the life of the Church."[43] Vatican II supported this idea and based it on both the radical sacramental equality among Christians and the integrity of the local church. At the papal level it means that Rome should not interfere when smaller units of the Church can adequately manage their own affairs. When Rome does act, in times of necessity but not as a regular occurrence, it should be in the spirit of assistance and not of domination. Concretely, this means that the Pope should encourage shared responsibility and participatory decision-making in the national episcopal conferences, diocesan pastoral councils, and parish councils.[44] In a word, he should decentralize the authority of Rome and allow, as far as possible, local churches to govern themselves. Greater decentralization in the Church would not go against the nature of the papacy, for, as Killian McDonnell notes: "Historically it would be impossible to assert centralism as an essential element in papal primacy."[45]

One very visible way the Pope could manifest the principle

[41] *Papal Primacy and the Universal Church*, op. cit., p. 20.

[42] *Acta apostolicae sedis*, 23 (1931), 203.

[43] Ibid., 38 (1946), 145. Cf. also J. S. George, *The Principle of Subsidiarity with Special Reference to Its Role in Papal and Episcopal Relations in the Light of Lumen Gentium. Canon Law Studies*, No. 463 (Washington, D.C.: The Catholic University of America, 1968) and W. W. Bassett, "Subsidiarity, Order and Freedom in the Church," in J. A. Coriden, ed., *The Once and Future Church*, op. cit., pp. 205–65.

[44] I have analyzed the theological and historical arguments for greater lay participation in the Church with a plea for the election of bishops by the community in *Ecclesial Cybernetics: A Study of Democracy in the Church* (New York: Macmillan, 1973).

[45] "Papal Primacy: Development, Centralization, and Changing Styles," in *Papal Primacy and the Universal Church*, op. cit., p. 183.

of subsidiarity would be to change the present method of selecting bishops and to make it a community decision. Popular election of bishops was the custom for nearly a thousand years, and
the Pope did not nominate bishops for specific sees.[46] What is
now needed is the involvement of all segments of the Christian
community in this important decision. Bishops, priests, religious,
and laity should all have a voice. A bishop, then, could be nomi-
nated by an elected committee after wide consultation and the
names submitted to the national episcopal conference and to the
Pope for final approval. Such a procedure would bring greater
credibility and accountability to the episcopal office.

These two principles form the framework within which collegiality can effectively operate. In the following pages I shall
explore in greater detail, with specific recommendations, how the
Pope can function collegially, both as fellow bishop and head of
the Church. I shall discuss the conciliar and symbolic aspects of
collegiality.

A. The Conciliar Approach

The most ancient way that Popes have exercised collegiality
has been through councils and synods.[47] From the time of the so-

[46] On this point G. Philips writes: "During the first ten centuries,
there was no formal intervention by the pope in the nomination of bishops,
except for those in his immediate entourage, or later in the wider Western
world. During all this time, the *communio* was still maintained even with
the African and Oriental bishops. The theological system, according to which
the pope conferred jurisdiction, could not have arisen before early scholasticism had elaborated a sufficiently clear distinction between the power of
order and the power of jurisdiction. Of the granting of jurisdiction by the
pope to the ancient patriarchates, there is not the slightest historical trace"
(*L'Église et son mystère au IIe Concile du Vatican*, op. cit., 1:278). Translation from G. Thils, "The Theology of the Primacy: Towards a Revision,"
One in Christ, 10 (1974), 22–23. Yet in this century, F. X. Wernz could
write: "The personal right of instituting bishops belongs by nature to the
Roman Pontiff" (*Ius canonicum* [Rome: Gregoriana, 1943]), I, No. 578,
725.

[47] An indispensable source for the study of Church councils is C. J.
Hefele and H. Leclercq, *Histoire des conciles d'après des documents
originaux* (Paris: Letouzey et Ané, 1907–21). For more modern studies

called Council of Jerusalem (Ac. 15), Church leaders in both East and West have assembled to resolve pressing problems, to decide doctrinal and disciplinary questions, and to discern the direction in which the Spirit was leading the Church. As early as the second century, bishops of a province assembled at the death of a fellow bishop to participate in the election of his successor. These meetings may have been the beginning of organized episcopal assemblies. By the end of the second century, the bishops, with the clergy and the laity, held regular councils. Collegiality was most effectively exercised in relationship to the universal Church through general councils, so we will restrict our observations to its two major forms: the traditional ecumenical council and the recently established World Synod of Bishops.

1. The Ecumenical Council

An ecumenical or general council refers, according to current usage, to that assembly of bishops and major prelates throughout the world convoked by the Pope for the purpose of dealing with matters that affect the entire Church. In all there have been twenty-one ecumenical councils—from Nicaea (325) to Vatican II (1962–65). The first eight councils were held in eastern Europe or Asia Minor, with Greek as the official language; and the rest in western Europe (Italy, France, and Germany), with Latin being used.[48] The first eight councils were convoked by civil authorities,

see Y. Congar, "The Council as an Assembly and the Church as Essentially Conciliar," in H. Vorgrimler, ed., One, Holy, Catholic and Apostolic (London: Sheed and Ward, 1968), pp. 44–88; E. Lanne, "L'origine des synodes," Theologische Zeitschrift, 27 (1971), 201–22; P. J. Burns, "Communion, Councils, and Collegiality," in Papal Primacy and the Universal Church, op. cit., pp. 151–72; P. L'Huiller, "Le concile oecumenique comme autorité suprême de l'Église," Analekta, 24 (1975), 78–102; and R. Eno, "Pope and Council: The Patristic Origins," Science et esprit, 28 (1976), 183–211.

[48] There is a controversy among Roman Catholic scholars over the ecumenicity of Constantinople IV (869–70). F. Dvornik, for example, makes a strong case that this council is not ecumenical, since its acts were annulled by Pope John VIII (872–82). See Dvornik, The Photian Schism: History and Legend (Cambridge: Cambridge University Press, 1948). V. Grumel, however, presents an opposing view in "La lettre du pape Étienne

by emperors, or, in the case of Nicaea II (787), by the Empress Irene. Ecumenical councils are a rare phenomenon; they have usually been held to confront some serious crisis threatening the Church. Not all the councils had a lasting impact on the Church; some spent much of their time on relatively trivial matters. Others, like Nicaea I, Ephesus, Chalcedon, Florence, Trent, Vatican I, and Vatican II, dealt with major doctrinal issues and were responsible for significant disciplinary and pastoral reform.

An ecumenical council is the most solemn assembly in the Church; its authority is traditionally said to be divine.[49] Thus Gregory the Great declared: "I confess that I accept and honor the four councils as I do the four books of the Holy Gospel."[50] According to Canon Law, "an ecumenical council possesses supreme power over the universal Church" (Canon 228, 1),[51] but Canons 222–29 state clearly that it is the Roman Pontiff who convokes and presides over the council and who confirms its acts. Although the Pope is not obliged, either by divine or ecclesiastical law, to call a council, there may be a moral obligation to do so in view of grave problems facing the Church. Finally, it is not permitted to appeal a decision of the Pope to an ecumenical council (Canon 228, 2).

This last canonical prescription reflects a long-standing theological controversy—conciliarism, or the doctrine of the supremacy of a general council over the Pope. The conciliarist theory, as we saw earlier, was applied at the Council of Constance (1414–18)

V à l'empereur Basile Ier," *Revue des études byzantines*, 11 (1953), 129–55. The Orthodox Church recognizes only the first seven councils as genuinely ecumenical. See W. de Vries, *Orient et occident. Les structures ecclésiales vues dans l'histoire des sept premiers conciles oecuméniques* (Paris: Cerf, 1971); P. Duprey, "The Synodal Structure of the Church in Eastern Theology," *One in Christ*, 7 (1971), 152–82; and Y. Congar, "Church Structures and Councils in the Relations between East and West," *One in Christ*, 11 (1975), 224–65.

[49] See H. Bacht, "Sind die Lehrentscheidung der ökumenische Konzilien göttlich inspiriert?" *Catholica*, 13 (1959), 128–39.

[50] A synodal letter of February 591 (*Monumenta germaniae historica, Epp.* I, 36).

[51] This canon is discussed by W. de Vries, "Das ökumenische Konzil und das Petrusamt," *Theologische-Praktische Quartalschrift*, 124 (1976), 27–40.

and ended the Great Western Schism. The decree *Haec sancta* stated:

> This holy synod of Constance . . . declares that, being legitimately assembled in the Holy Spirit, constituting a general council and representing the militant Catholic Church, it has its power immediately from Christ and that every person of whatsoever state or dignity, even the papal, is bound to obey it in those matters which pertain to the faith, the rooting out of the said schism, and the general reform of the said Church in head and members.[52]

Historians and theologians agree that Constance resolved a scandalous situation—there were three claimants to the papacy—but differ in interpreting the dogmatic force of *Haec sancta*. Some reject its dogmatic validity;[53] others ascribe to it a limited power in an exceptional situation;[54] and still others accept its conciliar principle as binding and permanent.[55] Paul de Vooght, for example, sees no conflict between the conciliar theory of Con-

---

[52] Latin text in G. Alberigo et al., eds., *Conciliorum oecumenicorum decreta* (Freiburg: Herder, 1962), p. 385. On the origins and development of medieval conciliarism see B. Tierney, *Foundations of the Conciliar Theory* (Cambridge: Cambridge University Press, 1955); "Roots of Western Constitutionalism in the Church's Own Tradition," in J. A. Coriden, ed., *We, the People of God* (Huntington, Ind.: Our Sunday Visitor, 1968), pp. 113–28; W. Ullmann, *The Origins of the Great Schism* (London: Burns, Oates, and Washbourne, 1948); and A. Franzen and W. Müller, eds., *Das Konzil von Konstanz* (Freiburg: Herder, 1964).

[53] Cf. J. Gill, "The Fifth Session of the Council of Constance," *Heythrop Journal*, 5 (1964), 131–43.

[54] Cf. H. Jedin, *Bischöfliches Konzil oder Kirchenparlament? Ein Beitrag zur Ekklesiologie der Konzilien von Konstanz und Basel* (Basel: Helbing and Lichtenzahn, 1963).

[55] Cf. H. Küng, *Structures of the Church* (New York: Thomas Nelson, 1964), pp. 268–319; P. de Vooght, *Les pouvoirs du concile et l'autorité du pape au concile de Constance*, Unam Sanctam, 56 (Paris: Cerf, 1965); "Les controverses récentes sur les pouvoirs du concile et l'autorité du pape au concile de Constance," *Revue théologique de Louvain*, 1 (1970), 45–75; "The Results of Recent Historical Research on Conciliarism," in *Papal Ministry in the Church*, op. cit., 148–57; and F. Oakley, *Council over Pope?* (New York: Herder and Herder, 1969); "The 'New Conciliarism' and Its Implications: A Problem of History and Hermeneutics," *Journal of Ecumenical Studies*, 8 (1971), 815–40.

stance and the definition of primacy at Vatican I. He believes
that *Haec sancta* did not make an ecumenical council superior to
the Pope, but that "it allows the council to impose its will and
save the Church in such a situation as obtained in 1415, when a
pope defaults gravely in matters of faith, unity, and the pastoral
virtues."[56] One may agree with de Vooght that a heretical or
schismatic Pope could be judged by an ecumenical council, but
grave failure in "the pastoral virtues" is a much more ambiguous
category.

The actual role the Pope plays during an ecumenical council
has varied over the centuries.[57] Sylvester I (314–35) did not attend Nicaea and apparently set a precedent, for Popes did not
personally attend the next seven councils in the East but only
sent legates as their representatives. E. G. Weltin mentions the
psychological advantage the Popes gained from nonattendance:
"Instinctively they felt that their dignity would be the surer, the
less it was soiled by competition in the arena of debate."[58] Later
Popes presided over the Western councils, but their participation
was often far from active. Most recently, Pope Paul VI opened
and closed the sessions of Vatican II taking place during his
pontificate and occasionally made a ceremonial appearance at
some of the public sessions. But he did not participate in the regular working sessions. Occasionally he made written interventions
and he was kept abreast of the proceedings through closed-circuit
television. Most Popes have been unwilling to engage in the
sometimes heated conciliar debates; they preferred to review the
deliberations of the council in a quieter atmosphere. Pius IX
said: "A council always passes through three phases. First there is
that of the devil; then comes that of men, finally that of God."[59]
Popes have generally awaited the third stage before getting fully
involved.

[56] "The Results of Recent Historical Research on Conciliarism,"
op. cit., 115.
[57] Cf. G. Schwaiger, *Päpstlicher Primat und Autorität der Allgemeinen Konzilien im Spiegel der Geschichte* (Paderborn: F. Schöning,
1977).
[58] *The Ancient Popes* (Westminster, Md.: Newman, 1964), p. 173.
[59] Cited in F. Mourret, *Le concile du Vatican* (Paris, 1919), p. 129.

Two technical problems about future ecumenical councils face the papacy: their membership and their frequency. First, in regard to membership, the Code of Canon Law (Can. 223) decrees that the following are entitled to be invited to an ecumenical council: all residential bishops, cardinals, patriarchs, primates, archbishops, abbots and prelates *nullius,* the abbot primate, abbots who are superiors of monastic congregations, and superiors general of major religious congregations. Titular bishops may be invited. All of the above were invited to Vatican II and had a determinative or decisive vote. The canonists and theologians in attendance had only a consultative vote. Although Christians from other denominations were present as observers, they did not have the right to vote or to speak at the Council. They were, however, permitted to attend both the public sessions and the general congregations; they could communicate their reactions to the various drafts of conciliar documents through the Secretariat for Promoting Christian Unity.

Under the present law, the membership profile of an ecumenical council is male, clerical, and Roman Catholic. Should this not be changed? First of all, one may argue that an ecumenical council is incomplete unless it includes representatives (both men and women) from the laity. If all believers share sacramentally in the priesthood of Christ, why should the laity be excluded from the council? There is no convincing theological reason, no mandate from divine law or Scripture that supports this prohibition. Historically, in fact, there is evidence of the laity with voting rights participating in past councils.[60] The next ecumenical council should revive this tradition. If nonbishops (abbots and major superiors) are given a deliberative vote, should not selected lay representatives be given equal treatment? Second is the more difficult question concerning the possibility of inviting non-Roman Catholic Christians to participate in the council. On the one hand, the teaching of Vatican II—that other Christian churches and ecclesial communities possess a genuine ecclesial character—would support the inclusion of voting representatives

[60] Discussed by H. Küng, *Structures of the Church,* op. cit., pp. 74–105.

from these groups. The Orthodox Christians would clearly have a special claim here. On the other hand, does the fact of the present incomplete unity between Rome and other Christian bodies and the existence of doctrinal differences automatically exclude non-Catholic participation at an ecumenical council?[61]

A second question for the papacy deals with the frequency of ecumenical councils. Twenty-one general councils in nearly two thousand years can hardly be called an excessive use of the conciliar approach. Moreover, the frequency rate has been uneven. In some centuries several ecumenical councils were held: two in each of the third, fourth, fourteenth, and fifteenth centuries, and three in each of the eleventh and twelfth centuries. Yet in the last four hundred years—from Trent to Vatican II— there have been only three councils.

Should ecumenical councils be held on a regular basis? This goal was established by the Council of Constance in the decree *Frequens* (October 9, 1414), which declared that "the frequent celebration of general councils is the best of all methods for tilling the Lord's field and for rooting out the weeds and thorns of heresy, schisms, and errors."[62] It further legislated that a council should be held five years after the end of Constance, another seven years later, and then regularly every ten years. In accord with these provisions, a council was convened at Siena-Pavia (1423–24) but was finally dissolved. Seven years later, another was held at Basel-Ferrara-Florence (1431–45). But the next ecumenical council, Lateran V (1512–17), did not take place until almost a century had passed. Granting the unique circumstances of *Frequens*, this decree may still contain a valid idea for contemporary consideration. Should an ecumenical council be held every

---

[61] The following studies treat this problem: L. Vischer, "Christian Councils: Instruments of Ecclesial Communion," *Ecumenical Review*, 24 (1972), 72–78; H. Mühlen, "Modelle der Einigung, auf dem Weg zu einem universalem Konzil aller Christen," *Catholica*, 27 (1973), 111–34; *Morgen wird Einheit sein. Das kommende Konzil aller Christen: Ziel der getrennten Kirchen* (Paderborn: F. Schöningh, 1974); G. Alberigo, "For a Christian Ecumenical Council," in D. Tracy, H. Küng, and J. B. Metz, eds. *Toward Vatican III: The Work that Needs to be Done* (New York: Seabury, 1978), pp. 57–66.

[62] G. Alberigo, *Conciliorum oecumenicorum decreta*, op. cit., p. 414.

ten years, according to *Frequens,* or even every twenty years, as
with provincial episcopal councils (Canon 283)?

There are arguments both for and against this proposal.
Some see it as an unwise expenditure of time, money, and energy;
as a needless undertaking in view of the Synod of Bishops; as an
unsettling influence in the Church; and as a threat to papal autonomy. Others, more positively, see an ecumenical council at regular intervals as a creative protection against complacency; as a
powerful symbolic act of universal solidarity and co-operation in
the Church; as a valuable opportunity to assess performance and
to establish priorities; and as a strengthening of papal ministry.
The reasons on both sides deserve serious consideration. There
does not seem any immediate urgency to convoke an ecumenical
council at the present time—Vatican II still reverberates strongly—
but by the end of the century, the situation in the Church and
the world may well demand another conciliar gathering.

2. The Synod of Bishops

One of the most significant innovations in Church governance in many centuries is the Synod of Bishops, which was established by Paul VI on September 15, 1965.[63] It had been mentioned several times earlier at Vatican II in the context of
collegiality. Article 5 of the *Decree on the Bishops' Pastoral
Office,* for example, saw the Synod as a service to the Pope and a
sign of coresponsibility: "Since it will be acting in the name of
the entire Christian episcopate, it will at the same time demonstrate that all the bishops in hierarchical communion share in the
responsibility for the universal Church." The Synod of Bishops
differs from an ecumenical council on three counts: it has a limited membership of bishops and major prelates; it has regularly
scheduled meetings every three years; and it is primarily a consultative and not a deliberative body.

The Synod of Bishops has met five times: in 1967, 1969,

---

[63] By the motu proprio *Apostolica sollicitudo, Acta apostolicae sedis,*
57 (1965), 775–80.

1971, 1974, and 1977. The purpose of the Synod is to strengthen
the unity of the episcopal college through exchange of information and discussion of critical issues facing the entire Church. Designed to assist the Pope and to act as a problem-solving assembly
engaged in the continuing process of self-renewal, it has discussed
such topics as the priesthood, justice in the world, evangelization,
and catechetics.

Many observers, including several bishops, have expressed
disappointment over the performance of the Synod. Some have
called it a "mute assembly," "a forum without power," and "a de-
bating club for bishops." These criticisms have arisen because the
Synod does not work authoritatively with the Pope in major decision-making. It is still on the fringes of genuine Roman authority.
The following suggestions may help the Synod develop its unre-
alized potential.[64]

First, the membership of the Synod should be expanded. It
should include, besides bishops and other prelates, religious and
lay representatives, both men and women.[65] A broadening of
membership—elected members with set terms—would better express the universal communion of the Church, expose the participants to a variety of views, and promote greater credibility.

Second, it should become a deliberative body. The ideal of
collegial authority, as Alexander Ganoczy notes, "will never be
truly achieved so long as the world Synod remains a purely consultative organism and not a deliberative one."[66] Such a change

[64] For the history and theology of the Synod of Bishops see A. Anton,
*Primado y colegialidad. Sus relaciones a la luz del primer Sínodo ex-
traordinario* (Madrid: Católica, 1970); Y. Congar, "Synod épiscopal,
primauté et collégialité épiscopale," in *Ministères et communion*, op. cit.,
pp. 187–227; V. Fagiolo, "Il synodus episcoporum: origine, natura, struttura, compiti," in V. Fagiolo and G. Concetti, eds., *La collegialità episcopale
per il futuro della chiesa* (Florence: Vallecchi, 1969), pp. 3–43; H. Fesquet,
Le synode et l'avenir de l'Église (Paris: Centurion, 1972); and R. Laurentin,
Le synode permanent: Naissance et avenir (Paris: Seuil, 1970).

[65] Cf. J. G. Gerhartz, "Keine Mitentscheidung von Laien auf der
Synode? Erwägungen zum Beschluss der gemeinsamen der deutschen
Bistümer," *Stimmen der Zeit*, 184 (1969), 145–59.

[66] "How Can One Evaluate Collegiality vis-à-vis Papal Primacy?" in
Papal Ministry in the Church, op. cit., 93. According to *Apostolica sollicitudo*, the Pope can give the Synod a deliberative role (*Acta apostolicae
sedis*, 57 [1965], 776). Note, however, that this would be a papal con-

would strengthen the Synod and would be a positive sign that the principle of collegiality is working.

Third, it should meet for longer periods.[67] The present period of about a month does not allow sufficient time for significant decision-making. It has been suggested that the Synod meet for six months, sufficient time for committee deliberations and general working sessions. Special financial provisions would have to be made for the lay participants.

Fourth, it should clarify its relationship to the Roman Curia, the central administration or civil service of the Church. The Curia was established formally by Sixtus V (1585–90) in 1588, and since that time it has grown steadily in power and influence. It almost has a life of its own, seemingly independent of that of the Pope or the bishops. There is truth in the adage, "Popes come and go; the Curia remains." Popes and councils have tried to reform the Curia but they have had only partial success. The high hopes of Vatican II in this regard have not been realized: "Bureaucracy has grown instead of declining. Decentralization . . . has advanced in some respects but regressed in others. . . . Nothing has been done to dismantle the structure of power and present the Church as a service to all, but especially to the poor."[68] The Curia should assist the Synod of Bishops rather than function as a parallel power-structure. Until the Vatican bureaucracy can be thoroughly reformed, the Synod of Bishops cannot perform its proper function in the Church.[69]

In discussing the implementation of the collegial ideal by

cession. An ecumenical council, on the other hand, is deliberative by nature. Yet in both instances, the Pope must give final approval.

[67] This suggestion has been made by G. Alberigo, "Pour une papauté rénovée au service de l'Église," in Renouveau écclesial et service papal à la fin du XXe siècle, op. cit., 21 and J. H. Provost, "Structuring the Church as a Communio," The Jurist, 36 (1976), 240.

[68] G. MacEoin, The Inner Elite: Dossiers of Papal Candidates (Kansas City: Sheed, Andrews and McMeel, 1978), p. xxvii.

[69] Cf. G. Zizola, "The Reformed Roman Curia," in J. A. Coriden, ed., We, the People of God, op. cit., pp. 49–77, and "Le pouvoir romain: Centralisation et bureaucratisation dans l'Église catholique," Lumière et vie, 26 (1977), 5–17; and G. Cereti and L. Sartori, "La curie au service d'une papauté rénovée," in Renouveau ecclésial et service papal à la fin du XXe siècle, op. cit., 129–41.

means of ecumenical councils and the Synod of Bishops, we have seen that the Pope's primatial role should not be conceived of as dominative authority over individuals but as a ministry that fosters the grace-filled vision of Christians to build up the Body of Christ. The function of the primacy will only be discovered, as Archbishop Ramsey observes, "by the recovery everywhere of the body's organic life with its bishops, presbyters, and people."[70] A further step in achieving that goal is a return to a more symbolic conception of the papacy.

B.   The Symbolic Approach

"The truth is we need the Pope because in this perilous age we need some one symbolically potent bishop to give expression to the Word of the Lord for our day."[71] These words of Protestant Episcopal Bishop Kilmer Myers are a sign of the growing interest among all Christians in the symbolic aspect of the papacy. There is a broad consensus today that the papacy can be most effective in worldwide Christianity if it is less juridical and more symbolic. In dealing with this crucial dimension of the contemporary papacy, I shall first make some theoretical observations about symbols and then turn to more practical matters.

1.   The Theory

If we say that the papacy is a sacred symbol, an essential element in the Christian community, then we first have to determine what we mean by symbol. Bernard Lonergan supplies us with a convenient starting point. He defines a symbol as "an image of a real or imaginary object that evokes a feeling or is evoked by a feeling."[72] Feelings, as the "affective orientation" of a

[70] *The Gospel and the Catholic Church*, 2nd ed. (London, 1956), Appendix.

[71] K. Myers, *Holy Cross Magazine* (West Park, N.Y., July 1967), pp. 2–5.

[72] *Method in Theology* (New York: Herder and Herder, 1972), p. 64. For K. Rahner, "all beings are by their nature symbolic" and "the symbol strictly speaking (symbolic reality) is the self-realization of a being in the other, which is constitutive of its essence" ("The Theology of Sym-

person, are related to objects, to their subjects, and to other feelings. The same object may evoke different feelings in different people and inspire, therefore, different symbols. Furthermore, symbols, linked as they are to affectivity, do not necessarily possess temporal permanency or logical consistency. They may undergo transformation and may also express "the existence of internal tensions, incompatibilities, conflicts, struggles, destructions."[73] Despite their fluidity, symbols are bearers of meaning and indispensable factors in social organizations.

The papacy is truly a symbol. It evokes several kinds of feelings that may even coexist in the same person: love and hate; hope and despair; security and fear; gentleness and harshness; loyalty and disinterestedness. The image of the papacy may elicit the idea of absolute power or humble service; *Unam sanctam* or *Pacem in terris*; Alexander VI or St. Pius X. Yet amid this diversity, there must be a hierarchy of symbols.

Is there an ideal symbol of the papacy? Of all the symbols that characterize the papacy today, the one that predominates, especially in ecumenical discussions, is the papacy as the symbol of pastoral unity.[74] Ideally, the Pope should express the unity of all churches through his shepherding role at the universal level. He should be the guarantor of freedom by sustaining, encouraging, and co-ordinating the various churches throughout the world. Rome, then, should be the center of guidance and concern rather than a bureaucratic monolith. As such it would function as a focal point of unity and reduce sectarianism by facilitating communication, mutual help, and pastoral love. The Pope, according to this view, would be less a lawgiver and more of an inspirational figure. Ludwig Hertling makes this point when he says that "the basic function of the Pope in the Church is not his performance of certain official duties, but simply that he be present."[75] By this

---

bol," in *Theological Investigations* [Baltimore: Helicon, 1966], 4:224 and 234).

[73] Lonergan, op. cit., p. 66.

[74] Cf. L. Scheffczyk, "Das 'Amt der Einheit': Symbol oder Wirkmacht der Einheit?" *Catholica*, 30 (1976), 227–45 and J.-J. von Allmen, "Ministère papal—ministère d'unité," in G. Alberigo et al., *Renouveau ecclésial et service papal à la fin du XXe siècle*, op. cit., 99–104.

[75] *Communio: Church and Papacy in Early Christianity*, op. cit., p. 71.

he means not that the Pope "is a lifeless rock or an abstract principle,"[76] but that he is someone whose effectiveness derives primarily not from his juridical authority but from his symbolic and sacramental role as the center of the network of churches— the focal point of the *communio*.

Other authors have pursued this theme from a sociotheological perspective. Andrew Greeley, for example, says that the religious leader is one "who understands the 'meaning system' better than others"[77] and is thus better prepared to ask probing questions and to determine priorities. Greeley believes that the papacy has to play a comforting role for the faithful and that the Pope should exhibit conviction and confidence. To be an effective sacred symbol, the Pope must appeal both to the rational and to the affective dimensions of humanity. Anthony Spencer writes in a similar vein.[78] He proposes that the Roman Catholic Church adopt Talcott Parsons' affective behavioral model of leadership, which would free the Pope from the purely administrative tasks of running the Church and allow him to perform a more inspirational function.

2. The Practice

The positive impact of symbols depends, as we have seen, on several variables: the object itself, the feeling of the subject in apprehending the object, and the cultural milieu. An important factor in the way Catholics and others perceive the papacy is the way the Pope actually exercises his office. There is some truth in the saying that style is substance and the medium is the message. The best argument for the papacy, according to Presbyterian theologian Ross Mackenzie, "would not be a theory of Petrine succession but Popes who showed in their own personal lives a love

[76] Ibid., p. 72.
[77] "Advantages and Drawbacks of a Centre of Communications in the Church—Sociological Point of View," in *Papal Ministry in the Church*, op. cit., 104.
[78] "The Future of the Episcopal and Papal Roles," *IDOC International* (May 9, 1970), pp. 63–84. Also see P. Misner, "Papal Primacy in a Pluriform Polity," *Journal of Ecumenical Studies*, 11 (1974), 239–61, esp. 254–55.

of the gospel and a desire to serve the needs of the world."[79] A papacy that avoids imperialism, authoritarianism, or paternalism has a positive symbolic impact. The respect and love that John XXIII evoked is legendary. More recently, John Paul I and John Paul II revealed a personal warmth and simplicity that was welcomed enthusiastically.

The symbolic character of the papacy also relates to the Pope as teacher. The Pope should be, as the guardian of authentic faith, sensitive to what is taught in the churches and see that it conforms to the Gospel. His charism of discernment regarding orthodox doctrine is both interpretative and evaluative. He interprets the message of Christianity and applies it to the contemporary situation. In exercising his magisterial role, it is imperative that he speak with pastoral wisdom and reach his decisions through consultation. If collegiality and coresponsibility are operative in the Church, then his direct interventions would be infrequent. Yet the Pope, as the first bishop of the episcopal college, has the right and the responsibility to intervene when the Gospel is distorted. It is he who should resolve doctrinal and disciplinary controversies. In the words of Hans Küng, the pastoral primacy can be considered "as the supreme court of appeals, mediating and settling disputes between the Churches."[80]

If the papacy adopted a more affective model of leadership there would be fewer administrative tasks for the Pope to perform. Anthony Spencer suggests that the Secretary of State would take care of the day-to-day, routine administrative business, leaving the Pope more time to act as a truly charismatic leader. The Pope would not be a figurehead, Spencer notes, because he would still have the important and difficult task of monitoring or overseeing the life of the entire Church. In doing this, he would serve as a source of strength and encouragement for the Christian community, since "it is to the affective leader that the community naturally turns for clarification of its purpose."[81]

Another element of the symbolic papacy, and perhaps its

[79] "The Reformed Tradition and the Papacy," *Journal of Ecumenical Studies*, 13 (1976), 366.

[80] *The Church* (New York: Sheed and Ward, 1967), p. 478.

[81] "The Future of the Episcopal and Papal Roles," op. cit., p. 81.

most decisive, is the episcopal or sacramental quality. The Pope is a Christian and a bishop. Hence, St. Augustine, in his characteristic neatness, says: "Peter was by nature simply a man, by grace a Christian, by still more abundant grace one of the Apostles, and at the same time the first of the Apostles."[82] The Pope, the successor of Peter and first in the College of Bishops, has a primacy that Vatican I called "truly episcopal." Like every bishop, the Pope has the tasks of sanctifying, teaching, and governing, but on the level of both the local diocese of Rome and the universal Church. "The Pope is meant to be," writes George Tavard, "for the whole Church and for his brother bishops, a symbol of what the bishop is expected to be in his diocese."[83]

The mission of a bishop is eloquently summarized in Article 16 of the *Decree on the Bishops' Pastoral Office in the Church*: "In exercising his office of Father and Pastor, a bishop should stand in the midst of his people as one who serves. Let him be a good shepherd who knows his sheep and whose sheep know him." This passage, which also applies to the Pope as a bishop, contains two important ideas: servanthood and personal contact. Both are worthy of comment.

The first theme, that of servanthood, is essential to the papacy. Enshrined in the ancient title of the Pope as "the servant of the servants of God,"[84] we find a most appropriate description of papal ministry—one that opens up immense possibilities for a symbolic understanding of the papacy. In practice, it means that the Pope in his life-style, words, and actions should communicate clearly that his ministry is to serve and not to be served. The model of the papacy, then, is not an earthly monarch but the humble Jesus of the New Testament. Today when injustice abounds in the form of racism, violence, and economic and political exploitation, the Pope should be a powerful liberating agent and inspirational force. The burning issues confronting the human family cannot be ignored by Peter's successor. Although the Pope obviously cannot solve these problems alone, he can act

---

[82] In *Joann. Evang. Tract.*, 124, 5 (PL 35:1973).
[83] "The Papacy and Christian Symbolism," *Journal of Ecumenical Studies*, 13 (1976), 352.
[84] Cf. Y. Congar, "Titres donnés au pape," in *Renouveau écclesial et service papal à la fin du XXe siècle*, op. cit., 59.

as a catalyst in raising the world's consciousness. The resolute defense of human rights should always be a prime concern of the Pope. This point was stressed and put in perspective by John Paul II in his address at Puebla, Mexico.

> Let us also keep in mind that the Church's action in earthly matters such as human advancement, development, justice, the rights of the individual, is always intended to be at the service of man, and of man as she sees him in the Christian vision of the anthropology that she adopts.[85]

The great social encyclicals of the Popes over the last century demonstrate the concern of the Church for the oppressed. They have shown, as Robert McAfee Brown asserted, that "neither the church nor the papacy exists for itself; both exist for the sake of the world, embodied in a life of servanthood."[86]

The second theme, that of personal contact, is likewise symbolically valuable. If the Pope is to act as a sacrament of Christ on earth, he must be visible. Papal visibility is achieved in a variety of ways: public and private audiences, liturgical celebrations, radio and television appearances. The most common way that people get to know the Pope is through reports about him in the media, and only secondarily through his encyclicals, addresses, and other writings. Unfortunately, papal writings are often couched in formal and stilted language and fail to reveal the personal side of the Pope. There is, however, another way in which the Pope can have direct, personal contact with his flock; that is through travel. Throughout history several Popes have left Rome and traveled widely. Papal travel has an important symbolic value.

Some Popes have traveled in the cause of peace. Leo I (440–61), for example, went to northern Italy, and near the shores of Lake Garda he persuaded Attila the Hun to spare Rome. John I (523–26) spent five months in Constantinople, and although the Emperor Justin I greeted him "as if he were Peter in person," he did not grant his requests for religious toleration.

---

[85] *Origins* (Feb. 8, 1979), Vol. 8, No. 34, 536.
[86] "Introduction" in P. J. McCord, ed., *A Pope for All Christians?* (New York: Paulist, 1976), p. 11.

In the eighth century, Leo III (795–816) went to Paderborn in Germany to ask Charlemagne for help in restoring peace to a Rome torn apart by violent factions. In the eighteenth century, Pius VI (1775–99) spent a month in Vienna trying unsuccessfully to convince Emperor Joseph II to desist from his efforts to control the Church and to change his notion that his subjects could be "Catholics without being Roman." Later the same Pope, in his eighties and partially paralyzed, was taken prisoner by Napoleon and died at Valence on his way to Paris.

Other Popes have traveled in the cause of war. John VIII (872–82) established a papal navy, which patrolled the coast of Italy against the Saracens. The well-known exploits of Julius II (1503–13), *Il Terribile*, earned him the title of "the warrior Pope." He engaged in several military campaigns in central and northern Italy in order to regain captured papal territory. His rallying cry was *Fuori i barbari!* (Out with the barbarians!)

Still other Popes traveled in the cause of Church reform. One of the most famous was Leo IX (1049–54). In order to oversee personally the implementation of reform measures, he traveled extensively throughout Italy, France, and Germany. In those countries he held over a dozen synods and issued strong decrees dealing with clerical marriage, simony, and episcopal elections. He spent only six months of his entire pontificate in Rome.

During the last hundred years, papal travel has been the exception rather than the rule. The loss of the Papal States in 1870 severely restricted papal movement. Leo XIII (1878–1903), Pius X (1903–14), and Benedict XV (1914–22) became voluntary prisoners of the Vatican and never left it after their election. Nor did they visit Castel Gandolfo, near Rome, which had served as a summer residence for many Popes since the seventeenth century. Even though the Law of Guarantees (1871) allowed the Popes to use the villa there, no Pope did so until Pius XI (1922–39) visited it in 1934. But Pius XII (1939–58) spent much time there and, in fact, died there in October 1958. Yet Pius XII traveled little and drove into the city of Rome on official business only eighteen times during the nineteen years of his pontificate.

A new emphasis on papal travel began with John XXIII (1958–63). He visited churches, hospitals, and prisons in Rome

on several occasions and in 1962 he made two trips to Loreto and
Assisi. It was Paul VI (1963–78) who traveled farther and faster
than any other Pope in history. When he went to the Holy Land
in 1964, he became the first Pope in 150 years to cross the borders
of Italy. In all, he traveled more than seventy thousand miles outside Italy; he made nine trips abroad—to the Holy Land, India,
New York and the United Nations, Portugal, Turkey, Colombia,
Switzerland, Uganda, and the Far East. There is every indication
that the present Pope, John Paul II, will continue this practice.
At this writing, he has already made major trips to Mexico, the
Dominican Republic, Poland, Ireland, and the United States.

The present and future Popes should follow the example of
those pilgrim pontiffs like Leo IX and Paul VI. They should
travel as apostles of peace and servants of the Gospel who reveal
by their very presence their deep concern for the needs of humanity. The modern world, despite the efforts of recent Popes, still
tends to think of the papacy as remote. Perhaps this is contained
in the remark of George Santayana to his friends: "I am like the
Pope; I don't return visits." A Pope on the move can show that
the papacy is not isolated from the Church and the world.
Through travel, a Pope can "stand in the midst of his people,"
develop a greater personal awareness of the problems facing the
world, and provide comfort and hope for the disadvantaged.
There is no substitute for this kind of personal and symbolic presence. The papacy never before in history has had such an opportunity to fulfill the command of Christ: "Go into the whole
world and preach the Gospel to every creature" (Mk. 16:15).

In short, we have seen how the doctrine of collegiality coun-
terbalances the long-standing monarchical idea of the papacy by
broadening the decision-making office in the Church and by emphasizing the symbolic, pastoral, and conciliar character of local
and universal Church governance. The Pope, of course, remains
the head of the Church, but functions within the College of
Bishops. This collegiality, moreover, as an answer to the objections that the papacy is imperialistic and too remote, reveals, as
we shall see in the next chapter, new possibilities and new hopes
for the ongoing ecumenical dialogue.

5 THE POPE AS ECUMENICAL PASTOR

> The reunion of a tragically divided church will not come about without some breakthrough on the understanding of the papacy.
>
> ROBERT MCAFEE BROWN[1]

A little over a century ago, the First Vatican Council called the Pope "the pastor and teacher of all Christians."[2] For some non-Roman Catholics this statement was either at best wishful thinking—a typical example of Roman grandiloquence—or, at worst, one more instance of Roman arrogance. Now as then, the Catholic teaching on the papacy is the Church's most distinguishing characteristic and, among the many issues that divide Christians, it is the one that evokes the strongest reaction. Some Orthodox Christians, for example, consider the dogmas of papal primacy and infallibility to be heresies in the formal sense. Other non-Romans, too, see these teachings as contrary to the Word of God, faith, and the Christian tradition. As a result, many consider that

---

[1] From the Introduction to P. J. McCord, ed., *A Pope for All Christians? An Inquiry into the Role of Peter in the Modern Church* (New York: Paulist, 1976), p. 12.

[2] Denzinger-Schönmetzer, 3073.

they have no other choice than to repudiate these teachings as dogmatic aberrations. Paul VI correctly assessed this attitude when he said that "the Pope, as we well know, is undoubtedly the greatest obstacle in the path of ecumenism."[3]

It is unacceptable to discuss the papacy in transition apart from the broader Christian world. The ecumenical dimension is essential. If, as George H. Tavard points out, "there will be no universal reunion without the Bishop of Rome,"[4] then it is imperative that Christians reach a common consensus on the meaning of the Petrine ministry. A better understanding of the papal office and its move toward structural reform might well make the papacy more acceptable to other churches and enable the Pope to become in fact and not just in words, "the pastor and teacher of all Christians." In this chapter on the Pope as ecumenical pastor, I shall discuss first, the present ecumenical climate, second, the major obstacles facing other Christians, and third, possible strategies of rapprochement.

I. The Ecumenical Climate

No doubt, in the last two decades the ecumenical movement has made giant strides. The relationship between Christian churches has shifted from an attitude of hostility to one of mutual concern, dialogue having replaced polemics. Especially is this evident in the ecumenical discussions of the Roman Church with the Orthodox, Anglican, and Protestant communions. Many factors have contributed to this shift. Two, I believe, are most significant. First, many Christians since Vatican II have become acutely aware of the division among Christian communities and agree with the Council that "this discord openly contradicts the will of Christ" and "provides a stumbling block to the world."[5] We have begun to realize that not only is a divided Christianity

[3] Address to the Secretariat for Promoting Christian Unity, Rome (Apr. 29, 1967) (*Documentation catholique* [May 21, 1967], col. 870).
[4] *Two Centuries of Ecumenism: The Search for Unity* (New York: New American Library, 1962), p. 65.
[5] *Decree on Ecumenism*, Art. 1.

ineffective in proclaiming the Good News but, in a much more fundamental way, that the present situation presents a challenge to all Christians to work devotedly for reunion. The awareness of the tragedy of division is in itself a healing insight from God. Christians now see that the multiplicity of competing denominations severely limits the efforts of the Church in its work for a better world.

A second factor in the development of ecumenism is the recognition of the need for some way to link the local churches to the universal Church. Thus the Lutheran-Roman Catholic Dialogue speaks of "the necessity of a specific Ministry to serve the church's unity and universal mission."[6] It calls this the "Petrine function," which it defines as "a particular form of Ministry exercised by a person, office holder, or local church with reference to the church as a whole."[7] Furthermore, the Dialogue notes that although the Petrine function has been exercised in a variety of ways by diverse office holders in the Church, the Bishop of Rome has been "the single most notable representative of this Ministry."[8] Likewise, the Venice Statement of the Anglican-Roman Catholic Dialogue affirms the need for a universal Church authority, specifically that of Rome: "It seems appropriate that in any future union a universal primacy such as has been described should be held by that see."[9] Finally, the Orthodox are not radically opposed to a universal primacy as long as it is conceived of in terms of priority or precedence and not of juridical supremacy.[10]

Many Christians who do not accept the Pope as their spiritual leader are, nevertheless, able to see a positive value in the institution of the papacy despite some of its historical abuses. They admit that the papacy has in fact functioned through its ministry of Word and Sacrament as a unifying symbol for the local churches; that it has acted as a visible and moral influence in op-

---

[6] P. C. Empie and T. A. Murphy, eds., *Papal Primacy and the Universal Church* (Minneapolis: Augsburg, 1974), No. 1, p. 10.

[7] Ibid., No. 4, p. 11.

[8] Ibid., No. 5, p. 12.

[9] No. 23 in *Origins* (Jan. 27, 1977), Vol. 6, No. 32, 507.

[10] Cf. J. Meyendorff et al., *The Primacy of Peter in the Orthodox Church* (Leighton Buzzard, Bedfordshire: The Faith Press, 1963).

position to non-Christian ideologies; and that it has been effective in proclaiming the Gospel doctrine of social justice and world peace. The papacy is judged much more benignly today, and with greater openness toward its role as an instrument of unity for the entire Christian community.

From a sociopolitical perspective every large organization needs a symbolic center to provide co-ordination, communication, and direction. Without a leadership capable of overseeing the whole, an organization can easily fall victim to stagnation, confusion of goals, and disastrous fragmentation. For as Andrew Greeley says, "Even if Christianity did not have a pope, it would have to invent one."[11] Hence, such a symbolic center is necessary if the Petrine function is to be exercised as a focal point of communication and leadership.

Why is the Bishop of Rome considered to be the most viable choice for the ministry to the universal Church? The Venice Statement gives one answer: "The only see which makes any claim to universal primacy and which has exercised and still exercises such *episcope* is the see of Rome, the city where Peter and Paul died."[12] In terms of tradition, experience, and influence, Rome can legitimately claim to be the primatial see. Moreover, it would be difficult to fashion another workable symbolic structure that would have the same strong historical roots: "Structures invested with powerful symbolic meaning cannot be created at will."[13] And even if a new primatial structure could be freshly constituted, it would still have to take into account the role of the Bishop of Rome. It would seem, therefore, that a reformed papacy offers the most realistic possibility for an institutional ministry for unifying a divided Christianity. Perhaps, as the Lutheran participants in the Dialogue with Roman Catholics expressed it: "God may show again in the future that the papacy is his gracious gift to his people."[14]

[11] "Advantages and Drawbacks of a Centre of Communications in the Church—Sociological Point of View," in H. Küng, ed., *Papal Ministry in the Church, Concilium,* Vol. 64 (New York: Herder and Herder, 1971), 101.

[12] *Origins,* op. cit., 507.
[13] *Papal Primacy and the Universal Church,* op. cit., No. 36, p. 31.
[14] Ibid., No. 28, p. 21.

II.   The Major Obstacles

To give the impression that the Orthodox or the churches of
the Reformation are on the verge of accepting the Pope as their
head would be misleading. Positive and hopeful signs of a greater
openness toward the historic papacy do abound, but hardly signs
of a massive ground swell of propapal enthusiasm. The bitter
memories and hostile attitudes of the past die slowly. Even more
significantly, for most non-Catholics, the question of the papacy,
reformed or not, does not generate any great interest. "For Lutherans, as for most Protestants," writes Lutheran theologian George
A. Lindbeck, "the Pope is of no importance. His function is negative, that is, he constitutes one of the factors which help Protestants to define what they are not."[15]

Besides antagonism and apathy, there are major problems
concerning the papacy that still divide Christians. They may be
reduced to three: divine institution, primacy of jurisdiction, and
infallibility. My intention here is not to discuss these complex issues in detail but simply to indicate what direction the present
debate is taking.

A.   Divine Institution

Catholic doctrine affirms that the papacy was established by
divine law (*ius divinum*) and is an essential and permanent structure in the Church. Thus Vatican I taught dogmatically that by
divine law Peter has perpetual successors in the primacy over the
universal Church and that the Roman Pontiff is the successor of
Peter.[16] The Council, relying on Mt. 16:17–19, Lk. 22:32, and
Jn. 21:15–17, also declared that Christ directly and immediately
conferred upon Peter the primacy of jurisdiction. Non-Catholics,
on the other hand, deny the probative value of the traditional Pe-

15 "Lutherans and the Papacy," *Journal of Ecumenical Studies,* 13
(1976), 368.
16 Denzinger-Schönmetzer, 3058.

trine texts, arguing that the papacy is a historical institution based on human law (*ius humanum*) and not a permanent feature of the Church. For example, "Lutherans have held that the papacy was established by human law, the will of men, and that its claims to divine right are nothing short of blasphemous."[17]

At the time of the Reformation, there was intense debate on the divine-right claims of the papacy. Both Catholics and Protestants agreed that divine institution meant establishment by Christ himself. But Catholics insisted that Christ personally made Peter head of the Church and that his successors in the Roman episcopate enjoy the same role. Today the debate has shifted. Many biblical scholars, both Catholic and Protestant, grant that Peter had a certain primacy among the apostles given to him by Christ, but they contend that the New Testament does not furnish explicit evidence for the continuance of that office in the Church. To admit that there is a difficulty in proving conclusively from Scripture alone that there is a succession in the Petrine function is not to say that such succession is contrary to Scripture. On the contrary, recent scholarship has shown that many of the images of Peter in the New Testament contributed to the development of the historic primatial office in the Church.[18]

Several modern Catholic ecclesiologists have attempted to reformulate the meaning of *ius divinum*.[19] One of the most promising approaches that is applicable to the papacy is that proposed by Karl Rahner[20] and Carl J. Peter.[21] It has been called a "developmental theory"[22] and its proponents have been labeled "irre-

[17] *Papal Primacy and the Universal Church,* op. cit., No. 7, p. 13.
[18] Cf. R. E. Brown, K. P. Donfried, and J. Reumann, *Peter in the New Testament* (Minneapolis: Augsburg and New York: Paulist, 1973); R. Pesch, "The Position and Significance of Peter in the Church of the New Testament," in *Papal Ministry in the Church,* op. cit., 21–35; and M. M. Bourke, "The Petrine Office in the New Testament," *Proceedings of the Catholic Theological Society of America,* 25 (1970), 1–12.
[19] A valuable article that analyzes current theories of divine establishment is A. Dulles, "*Ius Divinum* as an Ecumenical Problem," *Theological Studies,* 38 (1977), 681–708.
[20] "Reflections on the Concept of *Ius Divinum* in Catholic Thought," *Theological Investigations* (Baltimore: Helicon, 1960), 5:219–43.
[21] "Dimensions of Jus Divinum in Roman Catholic Theology," *Theological Studies,* 34 (1973), 227–60.
[22] Dulles, "*Ius Divinum* as an Ecumenical Problem," op. cit., 692–96.

versibilitists."[23] They contend that something can be of divine right without an explicit scriptural statement from Christ himself. Although a divine institution is always in conformity with Scripture and ultimately rooted in the Word of God,[24] it is possible that something can be divinely instituted even after biblical times, when a historical and free decision of the Christian community expresses the essential nature of the Church. Such a postbiblical development then becomes a permanent and irreversible reality in the Church.[25] The institution of the papacy would seem to be such an example. Historically, the Bishop of Rome at first did not function as a universal authority; it was only later that his primatial role was fully recognized. Yet since this development was directed by God and manifested a decisive and enduring element in the Church, it can be said to be divinely instituted. Thus Roman Catholics believe that "in the papacy there is a Petrine function that is not a purely human creation."[26]

To say that the papacy is divinely instituted does not mean that it is static. It is a historical reality, subject to the laws of history. It must be flexible if it is to proclaim the message of Christ effectively in a changing world. The "nature" of the papacy, its abiding quality, will be expressed in a variety of historical "forms." The two aspects are inseparable. The papacy is a permanent feature in the Church, for, as Avery Dulles points out, "it remains important in every age for the Church to possess an

[23] G. A. Lindbeck, "Papacy and *Ius Divinum*: A Lutheran View," *Papal Primacy and the Universal Church*, op. cit., pp. 193–208.

[24] In reference to the three traditional Petrine texts, Pope John Paul II said: "We are completely convinced that all modern enquiry into the 'Petrine ministry' must be based on these three hinges of the Gospel" (*Origins* [Oct. 26, 1978], Vol. 8, No. 19, 292).

[25] This does not preclude changes in the way the papacy may be exercised. The Catholic participants in the Lutheran-Catholic Dialogue noted: "While we look forward to changes in the style of papal leadership corresponding to the needs and opportunities of our times, we cannot foresee any set of circumstances that would make it desirable, even if it were possible, to abolish the papal office" (*Papal Primacy and the Universal Church*, op. cit., p. 37).

[26] C. J. Peter, "Dimension of Jus Divinum in Roman Catholic Theology," op. cit., 250.

efficacious sign of its worldwide unity and to perpetuate what has been called the 'Petrine' ministry."[27]

B. Primacy of Jurisdiction

Vatican I defined papal primacy as "full," "supreme," "ordinary," and "immediate."[28] Vatican II taught that "the Roman Pontiff has full, supreme, and universal power over the Church. And he can always exercise this power freely."[29] Orthodox and Protestant Christians do not accept this teaching on papal jurisdiction. They consider it to be without adequate scriptural foundation and an impediment to reunion. Fortunately, Vatican II also gave a more nuanced view of Church leadership. Contemporary Catholic theology, following this lead, has endeavored to make the papacy less objectionable to non-Romans. Let us examine two aspects of this development:

In the first place, most Catholic theologians agree that the definition of papal primacy in Vatican I was couched in juridical categories and was not framed in the context of a total ecclesiology. This formulation does not, of course, make it false, but it does explain some of its limitations, for Vatican I was itself historically conditioned and its terminology and concerns reflected a particular cultural milieu. Consequently, many theologians today advocate a radical change in the emphasis, expression, and formulation of papal primacy. They argue that the current style of the papacy, with its stress on juridical centralism, is not the only or even the most desirable way for the papacy to be exercised. On the contrary, they plead for a recovery of the ideal of leadership that embodies service to the Christian community rather than authority over it.

Complementing this shift from authority to service is a growing consensus among Catholics and others that the truly transitional papacy should continue the reform initiated by Vatican II

---

[27] "*Ius Divinum* as an Ecumenical Problem," op. cit., 705.
[28] Denzinger-Schönmetzer, 3064.
[29] *Lumen gentium*, Art. 22.

by de-emphasizing its monarchical authority and by embracing a collegial approach. Church authority, subordinate to Christ and the Gospel, must be seen as service: "Among pagans it is the Kings who lord it over them. . . . This must not happen with you" (Lk. 22:25–26). Concretely, the implementation of the principles of legitimate diversity, collegiality, and subsidiarity would do much to transform the papacy into an office of genuine pastoral leadership. The preceding chapter of this book dealt with that theme. Here I only note how necessary collegiality is, not merely to the inner workings of the Church, but also to its missionary vocation.

C. Infallibility

The First Vatican Council defined the doctrine of infallibility. It taught that by divine assistance the Pope is immune from error when he speaks *ex cathedra*—that is, when "by virtue of his supreme apostolic authority he defines a doctrine concerning faith or morals to be held by the universal Church."[30] Such definitions are irreformable—that is, they cannot be denied, but they can be further developed.

Non-Catholics often react negatively to this dogma. They feel not only that it is unwarranted biblically but also that it diminishes the privileged position of Christ and the Gospel, by claiming such authority for a single human being. It is irrelevant to them that over the last hundred years only one Pope has taught infallibly, namely Pius XII in defining the dogma of the Assumption in 1950. They still resent the claim, accepted as a dogma by Catholics, that the Pope *can* teach infallibly.

In the last fifteen years, many Catholic theologians have critically analyzed the doctrine of infallibility in accord with the broader vision of the Church presented by Vatican II.[31] Their

30 Denzinger-Schönmetzer, 3074.
31 An excellent recent study on infallibility is P. Chirico, *Infallibility: The Crossroads of Doctrine* (Mission, Kans.: Sheed Andrews and McMeel, 1977). Also see E. Castelli, ed., *L'infallibilité: Son aspect philosophique et théologique* (Paris: Aubier, 1970); J. T. Ford, "Infallibility: Who Won

efforts, together with the contributions made by scriptural scholars and historians, enable us to situate infallibility in its proper perspective. Moreover, the recent Lutheran-Catholic statement on "Teaching Authority and Infallibility in the Church" reveals how much common ground exists between these two major Christian denominations.[32] This statement places infallibility "in the theological categories of promise, trust, and hope rather than in the juridical categories of law, obligation, and obedience."[33] Although the two churches do not agree completely on the nature of infallibility, they do hold that it is appropriate that there be a universal Church ministry of unity, which includes "responsibility for overseeing both the Church's proclamation and, where necessary, the reformulation of doctrine in fidelity to the Scriptures."[34] Underlying much Catholic ecumenical thought are four areas of clarification and explanation concerning infallibility.

First, papal infallibility must be seen in the context of the entire Church, which Church is also infallible. An infallible definition, then, reflects the faith of the whole Church and is grounded in that faith. The faithful, moreover, receive the definition as corresponding to the meaning of the faith they possess. The assent of the faithful will never be lacking to a true infallible statement.[35] Second, an infallible teaching can only afford a partial and inadequate insight into the mystery of God. There is a continual need, therefore, to reinterpret and reformulate dogmas,

---

the Debate?" *Proceedings of the Catholic Theological Society of America,* 31 (1976), 179–92 and "Infallibility: A Review of Recent Studies," *Theological Studies,* 40 (1979), 273–305; J. Kirvan, ed., *The Infallibility Debate* (New York: Paulist, 1971); H. Küng, *Infallible? An Inquiry* (Garden City, N.Y.: Doubleday & Company, 1971); O. Rousseau et al., *L'infaillibilité de l'Église* (Gembloux: Chevetogne, 1963); G. Thils, *L'infaillibilité pontificale* (Gembloux: J. Duculot, 1969); and B. Tierney, *Origins of Papal Infallibility* (Leiden: E. J. Brill, 1972).

[32] This study, part of the continuing Lutheran-Roman Catholic Dialogue, appears in *Theological Studies,* 40 (1979), 113–66.

[33] Ibid., "Roman Catholic Reflections," No. 5, 139.

[34] Ibid., "Common Statement," No. 41, 132.

[35] Cf. Y. Congar, "La réception comme réalité ecclésiologique," *Revue des sciences philosophiques et théologiques,* 56 (1972), 364–403, and A. Grillmeier, "Konzil und Rezeption," *Theologie und philosophie,* 45 (1970), 321–52.

in order to discern their meaning more accurately.[36] Third, every infallible definition is historically conditioned, as *Mysterium ecclesiae* noted, by the expressive power of the language used; by the limited context of faith and knowledge in a particular situation; by the limited intention of dealing with specific concerns; and by the changeable thought patterns of a given epoch.[37] Fourth, "the ultimate trust of Christians is in Christ and the gospel, not in the doctrine of infallibility, whether of Scripture, the Church, or the pope."[38] These four observations help theologians to ground their discussions more soundly, as well as to develop a more acceptable ecumenical base.

III.   Some Possible Strategies

Before discussing the specific ways the papacy could function in worldwide Christianity, I must consider for a moment its basic purpose. Today, many argue that the papacy should embody the ideals of service and unity—should, indeed, be the organ of unity by inspiring, promoting, and preserving a graced bonding of Christian churches. The Pope, as "the servant of the unity of the Church and its universal primate,"[39] should co-ordinate the various local churches and foster their fidelity to Christ. Roman Catholic tradition has insisted on the unitive function of the Petrine ministry. For example, Vatican I stated that Peter was placed at the head of the other apostles in order to be a visible and permanent foundation that would preserve all believers in "the unity of

[36] Cf. P. Chirico, "Dynamics of Change in the Church's Self-understanding," *Theological Studies*, 39 (1978), 55–75.

[37] *Mysterium ecclesiae* was issued on June 24, 1973, by the Sacred Congregation for the Doctrine of the Faith. English translation: *Declaration in Defense of the Catholic Doctrine on the Church Against Certain Errors of the Present Day* (Washington, D.C.: United States Catholic Conference, 1973).

[38] "Teaching Authority and Infallibility in the Church," op. cit., "Common Statement," No. 51, 136.

[39] M. Sheperd, "How Can We Arrive at a Theological and Practical, Mutual Recognition of Ministries? An Anglican Reply," in H. Küng and W. Kasper, eds., *The Plurality of Ministries, Concilium,* Vol. 74 (New York: Herder and Herder, 1972), 95–96.

both faith and of communion."[40] The Lutheran-Catholic Dialogue explains that the primatial ministry "serves to promote or preserve the oneness of the church by symbolizing unity, by facilitating communication, mutual assistance or correction, and collaboration in the church's mission."[41] The Venice Statement of the Anglican-Roman Catholic Dialogue develops this same idea:

> Primacy fulfills its purpose by helping the churches to listen to one another, to grow in love and unity and to strive together towards the fullness of Christian life and witness; it respects and promotes Christian freedom and spontaneity; it does not seek uniformity when diversity is legitimate, or centralize administration to the detriment of local churches.[42]

Similarly, Orthodox Christians view primacy as an expression of the Church's unity and faith. In particular, they see it as an expression of "solicitude for all the churches" insofar as their authentic faith is concerned. Thus Alexander Schmemann, a Russian Orthodox theologian, writes that the purpose of the primacy is "to express and preserve the unanimity of all churches to keep them from isolating themselves into ecclesiastical provincialism, loosing the Catholic ties, separating themselves from the unity of life."[43]

Keeping in mind these ideas about the purpose of the primacy, we ask: Can the Pope function in the future as "the pastor and teacher of all Christians?" Can there be a union of Christians in which the Pope would act as a spiritual authority, recognizing

---

[40] Denzinger-Schönmetzer, 3051.

[41] *Papal Primacy and the Universal Church,* op. cit., No. 4, p. 12.

[42] No. 21 in *Origins* (Jan. 27, 1977), Vol. 6, No. 32, 507.

[43] "The Idea of Primacy in Orthodox Ecclesiology," in *The Primacy of Peter in the Orthodox Church,* op. cit., p. 49. Schmemann also quotes with approval the following passage from P. Batiffol, *Cathedra Petri. Unam Sanctam,* 4 (Paris: Cerf, 1938), p. 28: "The 'papacy' of the first centuries is the authority exercised by the Church of Rome among other Churches, authority which consists in caring after their conformity with the authentic tradition of faith . . . and which is claimed by no other Church but the Church of Rome." M. A. Fahey gives a survey of recent ecumenical activity among the Orthodox in "Orthodox Ecumenism and Theology: 1970–78," *Theological Studies,* 39 (1978), 446–85.

the legitimate traditions and regional autonomy of the different churches? It is possible, yes; but any prediction of success, especially in the foreseeable future, would clearly be premature. My concern here is to explore what steps the papacy can take to create the condition for the possibility of eventual reunion. Barring something like a nuclear disaster—which, ironically, might impel the surviving Christians to unite—the process will be a long one. It is unthinkable that the Catholic Church will repudiate the doctrinal definitions of Vatican I and the Marian dogmas. Nor is it probable that the Orthodox and the Protestants will suddenly embrace these teachings and accept the Pope as their primate. What, then, should be done?[44]

Here are some suggested ways for the Roman Church to act. Implicit in them, of course, is the reciprocal duty of other Christian churches to make corresponding moves toward this ecumenical goal. These suggestions are illustrative, not exhaustive; but they do require, since they touch critical areas, a serious hearing and evaluation. Beginning with an already existing international structure, the World Council of Churches, we shall examine complementary processes, such as summit meetings and magisterial co-operation, and even the feasibility of some institutional structure, limited perhaps but unified in the Spirit.

A.   The World Council of Churches

In the near future, the papacy should reconsider the advisability of becoming a member of the World Council of Churches, the largest and most influential non-Catholic organization working for Christian unity. With a fellowship of nearly three hundred churches, most of them national groups, its members represent all the major Christian denominations (including the Orthodox and the Old Catholics), with the exception

---

[44] See A. Dulles, *The Resilient Church* (Garden City, N.Y.: Doubleday & Company, 1977), esp. Chap. 9, "Ecumenical Strategies for a Pluralistic Age," pp. 173–90, and J. W. Baker, "The Petrine Office: Some Ecumenical Projections," in *Papal Primacy and the Universal Church*, op. cit., pp. 213–24.

of the Southern Baptists, some Lutheran groups, several Pentecostal churches, and, most conspicuously, the Roman Catholics. It exercises no legislative power over member churches. According to its recently revised Constitution, its purpose is "to call churches to the goal of visible unity in one faith and in one eucharistic fellowship expressed in worship and in common life in Christ, and to advance toward that unity in order that the world may believe."[45] The World Council seeks to raise ecumenical, missionary, and social consciousness and to be a forum for sharing theological insights.

Despite its lack of official membership in the WCC, the Catholic Church maintains a close relationship with it.[46] The Joint Working Group is the principal organ for co-ordinating exchanges between Rome and the World Council. Catholics also participate as members with full voting rights in the Faith and Order Commission, which has produced some significant doctrinal statements.[47] In 1968, the WCC and the Pontifical Commission for Justice and Peace established the Committee on Society, Development, and Peace (Sodepax). Finally, there are Catholic observer-consultants at all the major WCC meetings.

Rome, however, has moved cautiously toward full membership in the WCC for several reasons. The first issue is theological —a concern that Catholic participation might undermine the doctrinal uniqueness of Rome and create the impression of religious indifferentism. Yet in the 1950 Toronto statement of the World Council, there is a partial answer to this objection. It made clear that membership does not presuppose any one ecclesiology and does not imply "that each Church must regard the other member

---

[45] In D. M. Paton, ed., *Breaking Barriers: Nairobi 1975* (Grand Rapids: Eerdmans, 1976), pp. 317–18.

[46] Cf. "Patterns of Relationships Between the Roman Catholic Church and the World Council of Churches," in *Catholic Mind*, 70 (1972), 22–54; "Collaboration Between the Catholic Church and the World Council of Churches," in Secretariat for Promoting Christian Unity, *Information Service* (1975), No. 27, pp. 25–30; and M. Walsh, "Between the Assemblies," *The Month*, N.S. 8 (1975), 308–11.

[47] Cf. *One Baptism, One Eucharist and Mutually Recognized Ministry: Three Agreed Statements*, FO paper No. 73 (Geneva: World Council of Churches, 1975).

Churches as Churches in the true and full sense of the word."[48]
The second issue is practical. Both Catholics and Protestants fear
that the WCC might be unbalanced by the membership of one
Church whose size is greater than the combined membership of
the entire Council. Most Christians feel, as Robert McAfee
Brown remarks, that "Catholic membership would engulf the
council, upset all balances, and make many smaller churches ap-
prehensive that they were simply going to be 'absorbed' by
Rome."[49] The details of representation and voting rights would
have to be carefully worked out. But as the experience of the
United Nations reveals, the task is troublesome. The one Church-
one vote principle disregards the significance of population size;
yet to use population size alone would render smaller churches irrelevant in decision-making.[50]

On the more positive side, Catholic membership in the
WCC might significantly change the ecumenical movement and
usher in a vital era of development. It would give considerable
impetus to the work of ecumenism on the international level,
would open up several exciting possibilities for a closer collaboration among the local churches, and would bring the Pope into
frequent contact with other Christian leaders. The role of the
Pope as an official of the WCC would, naturally, be different
from his position as head of the Catholic Church. This dual function would necessitate beforehand a clear determination of
specific authority and responsibilities.

[48] G. K. A. Bell, ed., *Documents of Christian Unity,* Fourth Series
(New York: Oxford University Press, 1958), p. 220.
[49] *The Ecumenical Revolution: An Interpretation of the Catholic-
Protestant Dialogue* (Garden City, N.Y.: Doubleday & Company/Image
Book, 1969), p. 44.
[50] Another reason that may dissuade Rome from seeking full membership in the WCC at this time is the continuing debate over the aid the
World Council gives to certain political groups in southern Africa. It recently gave eighty-five thousand dollars to the Patriotic Front in Rhodesia.
Many of the member-churches strongly object to supporting groups who
use violence to achieve political goals. The Salvation Army, for example,
has withdrawn from active membership, and other churches in Europe and
the United States have threatened to withhold contributions.

B. Summit Meetings

In the absence of a single spokesman for all Christians, the Pope should initiate regular—annual or semiannual—meetings with the spiritual leaders of other communions, not just papal audiences but meetings of some duration with preparation, agenda, and scheduled working sessions. They could be held at Rome or at some neutral location. At first, these meetings would afford an opportunity for world religious leaders to get to know each other and to share their common concerns. In time, specific issues would inevitably be discussed and, eventually, statements would be issued, statements prophetic and symbolic rather than juridical or binding, which would show that even separated Christians can come together in charity to provide mutual encouragement and direction. The witness character of such meetings would be impressive, for, though not formal ecumenical councils, they would be substantial steps in that direction. Consider how important ecumenically were the meetings of Pope Paul VI with the Patriarch of Constantinople, the Archbishop of Canterbury, and the Coptic Patriarch. Is there any reason why they should be so infrequent or exclusive?

Anglican theologian J. Robert Wright made a suggestion that might well lead, as a practical matter, to some kind of interaction at the summit. His recommendation was simple and unobjectionable—namely, that the Vatican offer to put on its mailing list all Anglican bishops who request it. Why restrict this to Anglicans? Should not all non-Roman Church leaders—bishops, patriarchs, church presidents, and others—receive, if they wish, all the regular, nonconfidential material that the Holy See sends to its own bishops? Certainly, some of the information received from these mailings would furnish important background material for later summit meetings. Wright feels that such a communication of information would be a practical way for leaders "to test the value of papal primacy and form their own estimates of the desirability of having a single personal focus of leadership for the church's unity and mission."[51]

C.   Magisterial Co-operation

> To promote a more ecumenical dimension in our Church's teaching function, we recommend that Catholic leaders invite Lutheran church authorities to participate in the formulation of Catholic doctrine, in a consultative capacity, seeking to follow and even go beyond the precedent set by the participation of non-Catholic observers at Vatican Council II.[52]

This suggestion, made by the Catholic participants in the Lutheran-Catholic Dialogue, should be extended to other churches. The Pope might even change the traditional practice of the curial administration and invite representatives from the major Christian denominations to participate in the meetings of the Roman congregations. At present, there are no official, permanent, non-Catholic members of the Roman Curia. Although occasionally observer-consultants from other churches do participate in some special meetings, they do not take part in the plenary sessions. I would suggest that there be permanent, nonvoting members from other Christian communities attached to the Curia, who would have a voice but not a vote, would attend all meetings, and would be expected to take the usual committee assignments. They would also report back regularly to their own churches.

This proposal might evoke the criticism that it goes too far—one more step in the deterioration of Catholic identity. The plan, however, should be executed gradually, subject to evaluation and revision; the number of non-Romans would be limited with only a consultative vote. Others might complain that the proposal does not go far enough, that non-Catholic members should also have

---

[51] "Anglicans and the Papacy," *Journal of Ecumenical Studies,* 13 (1976), 402–3.
[52] "Teaching Authority and Infallibility in the Church," op. cit., "Roman Catholic Reflections," No. 58, 157.

full voting rights. This is a difficult question both theologically and politically. At present, it would seem wiser to grant the non-Catholic members only consultative status.

The advantages of magisterial co-operation are manifold. It would provide a stable and active liaison between Rome and other Christian communities; it would bring non-Catholics into the heart of the Church's central administration to the mutual benefit of all; and, finally, it would give positive support to ecumenism at the highest level in the various churches. But most of all, it would be a significant development in the exercise of the teaching authority of the universal Church. By encouraging other Christians to participate in the preparation of important doctrinal and social statements, the Church would help project a strong and persuasive witness to the world. With the goodwill of the participants and the assured guidance of the Holy Spirit, magisterial co-operation could do much to advance the cause of Christian unity.

D. Institutional Unity

Much more difficult to achieve than membership in the World Council of Churches or participation in ecclesial summit meetings or co-operation in magisterial functions is the formation of a political institution comprising all the Christian churches. A neutral and naïve observer might surmise that the task is a relatively easy one, since most Christians would agree with Vatican II that "the true Church established by Jesus Christ the Lord is, indeed, one and unique."[53] This observer would also note that the various Christian institutions even now form a larger spiritual institution, a multi-institutional one; for the Roman, Orthodox, Anglican, Lutheran, and other churches—admittedly independent and doctrinally diverse—do actually share a common unity in Christ.

The big question is how these many different institutions can form one comprehensive institution, a political one reflecting their

[53] *Decree on Ecumenism*, Art. 1.

underlying spiritual bond. Must they be converted into one or other of the existing churches or into some newly formed Church? I shall bypass any discussion of the conversion alternative at this time, for it seems to demand a currently unacceptable, and perhaps even ultimately an unwise sacrifice of ecclesial identities. Instead, I shall now touch upon what may be the only feasible alternative, the multi-institutional model. This, as the name indicates, reflects the principle of unity amid variety. The ecumenical goal should be to resolve divisiveness without jeopardizing diversity, for, as John Macquarrie notes: "Diversity is just as essential as unity to the well-being of the Christian church."[54] According to Avery Dulles, "the greatest value of the ecumenical movement, as we have known it thus far, is that . . . it introduced into the religious sphere the benefits of heterogeneous community."[55]

If the many Christian churches do manage to achieve political unity through a multi-institutional body, they would still have the problem of determining the symbol and center of this unity. Karl Rahner says that in a united Church, the individual member-churches would continue to possess a relative juridical autonomy, but "we may reasonably assume that they would admit a certain function for the Petrine ministry."[56] Two subsequent ecumenical conferences have made similar recommendations. In 1974, the Lutheran-Catholic Dialogue conceived of a future reconciliation which, while preserving "the self-government of Lutheran churches within a communion,"[57] would also recognize some form of papal ministry. Ten years later, in 1976, the Venice Statement of the Anglican-Roman Catholic Dialogue agreed that if Church unity is to be realized, it must be under the authority of the Pope, since "Rome is the only see which makes any claim to universal primacy . . . it seems that in any future union, a universal primacy should be held by that see."[58]

[54] *Christian Unity and Christian Diversity* (Philadelphia: Westminster, 1975), Preface.
[55] *The Resilient Church*, op. cit., p. 182.
[56] *The Shape of the Church to Come* (New York: Seabury, 1974), p. 105.
[57] *Papal Primacy and the Universal Church*, op. cit., p. 23.
[58] No. 23 in *Origins* (Jan. 27, 1977), Vol. 6, No. 32, 507.

Despite these tentative moves toward union, difficulties remain. One of the greatest obstacles to a multi-institutional Church with a papal ministry or universal primacy is the state-analogue fallacy, whereby both Church and state are viewed externally as the same kind of institution, one ultimately involving a strong government, a legal order, and power politics. Since some of history's most memorable Popes have clearly been temporal rulers, the nagging fear still persists: Is not every institution necessarily structured in terms of power, and will not this multi-institutional Church prove to be an authoritarian Roman trap?

Of primary importance in all ecumenical discussions, especially those focused on the role of the Pope, is a sound understanding of what is meant by institution, lest negotiations be permanently stalled. To clarify and even reformulate the notion of institution is necessary if it is to be used successfully in bringing Christian churches together. This book is not the place to make that attempt, although I have tried to do it elsewhere.[59] What is needed here is simply to note the ecumenical implications of the notion of institution as it involves the role of the Pope.

This limited appreciation of institution is required, since the very idea of a multi-institutional institution is too often overlooked—a missing of the forest because of the trees. A moment's consideration reveals that this institutional complex is the basic concern of ecumenism, for the Christian churches are institutions. Any larger unity that they form will also be institutional and a multi-institutional one if the member-churches retain any autonomy. But because we are so accustomed to speak of the "institutional Church" as referring only to the external, legal, or juridical aspects of the Church that is sacrament and mystery, we fail

---

[59] "The Church as Institution: A Reformulated Model," *Journal of Ecumenical Studies* 16 (1979), 425–47. In this article I analyzed the contributions of the legal philosophers known as the "French Institutionalists" (M. Hauriou, G. Renard, and J. Delos) and applied their theory of institution to the Church. Also see G. Hasenhüttl, "Church and Institution," in G. Baum and A. Greeley, eds., *The Church as Institution, Concilium,* Vol. 91 (New York: Herder and Herder, 1974), 11–21, and M. Kehl, *Kirche als Institution: Zur theologischen Begründung des institutionellen Charakters der Kirche in der neueren deutschsprachigen katholischen Ekklesiologie* (Frankfurt: Knecht, 1976).

to appreciate the incarnational aspect of institution, which is necessary if the whole Christian community is to make a unified response to the Christ event.

Without attempting an elaborate analysis of the notion of institution, I shall just present some basic insights to expand the awareness of this prosaic and theologically undervalued aspect of the Body of Christ. Perhaps the most enlightening facet is seen in Georges Renard's memorable description of an institution as "the communion of men in an idea."[60] Applying this to the Church, we see that the *congregatio fidelium* is just that, the communion of believers in the Christ event. The Church has other dimensions, but this one gives the Body its oneness and its cohesiveness. This *idée directrice*, to use Maurice Hauriou's words,[61] is the heart of my definition of an institution: a stable communion of men in an idea for the shaping and sharing of values through a pattern of practices, or, formulated differently, a social pattern of co-operation for human good constituted by meaning. Through the common idea, the will of the founder, here Christ, prevails over the wills of the adherents, so there is unity and continuity. Since Christ wants one flock and one shepherd, his idea should be participated in by all who call him Lord. Institution is the necessary human instrumentality if Christ's will is to be done.

Although this communion in an idea does require some principle of organization, Renard points out that the more intimate the participation in the directive idea, the less actual governing is needed. On the other hand, "the less intimate an institution becomes, the more rules you will see appearing."[62] Applying this observation to a united Christian Church, we see how minimal will be the "institutional" aspects—the structures, prescriptions, and sanctions. The first reason for this limited legalism is the intensely intimate participation by believers in the Christ event; the second is that since the member-churches are semi-autonomous, they

---

[60] *La théorie de l'institution* (Paris: Recueil Sirey, 1930), p. xvi.

[61] According to Hauriou: "The most important element of every corporate institution is the idea of the work to be realized in a social group" ("La théorie de l'institution et de la fondation," *Cahiers de la nouvelle journée*, 4 [1925], 12).

[62] *La théorie de l'institution*, op. cit., p. 290.

would necessarily be responsible for most of the rule-making for their own denominations. These two considerations are extremely important in ecumenical discussions, for they clearly insure that the Pope in this universal Church—this multi-institutional institution—will be more a symbol than a ruler, more charismatic than juridical, a principle of unity whose strength resides in the convictions of others, rather than on his own political power.

Since I have discussed the question of a multi-institutional Church in general, my next task is to examine it more concretely in order to see how legitimate diversity and papal ministry can be harmonized in practice. The issue, then, concerns the coexistence of a variety of ecclesial typologies within the one Church of Christ.[63] Ecumenists have made various proposals, the most promising of which are the uniate and federal models, the one, however, requiring conversion to Roman Catholicism, the other clearly admitting confessional diversity.

1. The Uniate Model

This model is patterned after the present relationship that exists between the Roman Catholic Church and the "uniate" Eastern Catholic churches. Rome recognizes and respects the diversity and the unique historical tradition of these churches; it does not demand strict uniformity but allows for differences in liturgical, canonical, and devotional expression. Vatican II's *Decree on Eastern Catholic Churches,* for example, reaffirmed the rights and privileges of the Eastern churches and spoke with affection of their venerable apostolic heritage. The decree, however, also made it unequivocally clear that all the Catholic churches of the East

[63] Cardinal Willebrands, president of the Secretariat for Promoting Christian Unity, explains the idea of ecclesial typologies as follows: "When there is a long, coherent tradition, commanding men's love and loyalty, creating and sustaining a harmonious and organic whole of complementary elements, each of which supports and strengthens the other, you have the reality of a *typos*" (*Documents on Anglican-Roman Catholic Relations* [Washington, D.C.: USCC, 1972], p. 39). For a valuable discussion of this concept see A. Dulles, *The Resilient Church,* op. cit., pp. 185–89 and E. Lanne, "Pluralism and Unity," *One in Christ,* 4 (1970), 430–51.

share the same faith, the same sacraments, and the same government as the universal Church and are "equally entrusted to the pastoral guidance of the Roman Pontiff, the divinely appointed successor of St. Peter in supreme governance over the universal Church."[64] In a word, the Eastern Catholic churches have accepted the claims of the Pope and have placed themselves under his obedience.

The uniate model would allow non-Catholic churches to unite with Rome and still preserve much of their own tradition, canon law, and forms of worship. They could be united with the Roman Church without being absorbed into it, since they could be accorded some status of self-government and treated as sister churches. The present Orthodox, Anglican, Lutheran, and other communions would be considered as rites. Yet all of them would accept the primatial authority of the Pope.

Official Roman Catholic reaction to the uniate model, as described here, would, I feel, be positive. The Holy See would see it as a desirable way to unite a divided Christianity, since there is a historical precedent for it that respects papal prerogatives. This model corresponds closely to the traditional Roman view of reunion, which encouraged the "return" of the "separated brethren" through a kind of *quid pro quo* arrangement. Rome would allow the other churches to keep much of their cherished tradition, if they in turn accept certain Catholic doctrinal teachings, especially those concerning papal primacy.

Non-Catholic reaction to the proposed uniate model has been largely negative.[65] The Orthodox, for example, do not accept the primacy of papal jurisdiction, at least as formulated in Vatican I and Vatican II. They also feel strongly about uniatism in general and, in fact, consider the present status of the "uniate"

---

[64] Art. 3.

[65] John Macquarrie, however, writes: "I believe that the best existing model for Christian unity is that which we find in the relation between the Roman Catholic Church and the so-called 'Uniat' churches of the East" (*Christian Unity and Christian Diversity*, op. cit., p. 43). Dulles remarks: "While I do not substantially disagree with Macquarrie's proposal, I would wonder whether uniatism, as the term is generally understood, is the best model" (*The Resilient Church*, op. cit., p. 187–88). Also see J. T. Ford, " 'An Ecumenical Church'—Problems and Possibilities," *Ecumenical Trends* (Nov. 1978), 145–48.

churches as a serious impediment to ecumenical dialogue with the East. Furthermore, they object to the tendency of Rome to reduce the differences between the East and the West to matters of rites, discipline, and way of life. In response, Alexander Schmemann writes that the Orthodox "affirm that the liturgical and canonical traditions of the East cannot be isolated from doctrinal principles which it implies and which constitute the real issue between Roman Catholicism and Eastern Orthodoxy."[66]

Protestants, too, generally reject the uniate model, since it would put them under the authority of the Pope and, hence, pose a threat to their religious identity. For them, uniatism has too many unanswered questions: the nature and exercise of papal primacy and infallibility; the exact canonical status that would be granted to Protestant churches; and the content of the "profession of faith" that would be required for membership. But in the final analysis, the principal objection seems to be a juridical one—the jurisdictional authority of the Pope. Lutheran theologian Joseph A. Burgess illustrates this attitude:

> A uniate model, even under another name and updated, is not acceptable. A uniate Church, even if it is permitted many traditions and styles of its own, finally is subject to Roman jurisdiction. Although the term "sister church" might be used, in those borderline cases where primacy and infallibility inevitably are brought in, one sister becomes the "big sister" or the "mother."[67]

2. The Federal Model

According to this model, individual churches would join together institutionally on the basis of their common Christian faith; each Church would have broad juridical autonomy and

[66] "A Response," in W. M. Abbott, ed., *The Documents of Vatican II* (New York: America Press, 1966), p. 386.

[67] "Lutherans and the Papacy: A Review of Some Basic Issues," in P. J. McCord, ed., *A Pope for All Christians?*, op. cit., pp. 38–39. This same objection is made by M. Sheperd, "How Can We Arrive at a Theological and Practical, Mutual Recognition of Ministries?," op. cit., 96; J. Robert Wright, "Anglicans and the Papacy," op. cit., 397; and G. A. Lindbeck, "Lutherans and the Papacy," op. cit., 375–77.

keep its own traditions; and each Church would recognize the Pope as embodying the Petrine ministry and accept him as its spiritual leader without necessarily accepting all the claims connected with his office. In this multi-institutional communion, Rome would be a symbol and center of unity, but would encourage the legitimate diversity of all the churches.

The following portrait of the Pope, drawn from many sources, describes his role in the federal Church of the future.[68] The principal task of the Pope would be to unite the individual churches with the universal Church. Without possessing doctrinal or juridical authority of himself, he would function as a spokesman for the entire Church, to which he would be accountable; for the papal office would be viewed as established by human law with a primacy of honor and leadership. The Pope would have a fixed term of office and be subject to removal for cause. Vis-à-vis the leaders of other churches, he would be *primus inter pares* (the first among equals), hence the chief shepherd, pastor, and guide of the entire Christian world.[69] In practice, he would function as moderator and arbitrator. In ecumenical councils, he would be presiding official, taking the initiative on occasion, but always dependent on the consensus of the assembly. His power would be suasive and symbolic rather than authoritarian.

How can we assess the federal model? Negatively, a federal Church might be a utopian fantasy that makes the Pope a mere figurehead and at best establishes an artificial unity, a kind of

---

[68] Besides the studies already referred to, the following also discuss this question: K. McDonnell, "Papal Primacy: Development, Civilization, and Changing Styles," in *Papal Primacy and the Universal Church*, op. cit., 172–93; S. Harkianakis et al., "Can a Petrine Office Be Meaningful in the Church?," in H. Küng, ed., *Papal Ministry in the Church*, op. cit., 115–46; and P. Misner, "Papal Primacy in a Pluriform Polity," *Journal of Ecumenical Studies*, 11 (1974), 239–61.

[69] In this context, some authors speak of the possibility of a plural papal leadership. G. A. Lindbeck, for example, wonders whether a kind of *troika* would be feasible ("Primacy and *Ius Divinum*: A Lutheran View," in *Papal Primacy and the Universal Church*, op. cit., p. 200), and P. Misner suggests that perhaps the Pope, the ecumenical patriarch, and a representative of the World Council of Churches could form a *troika* ("Papal Primacy in a Pluriform Polity," op. cit., 259–60).

peaceful coexistence, another bureaucracy contributing very little to inner Christian unity. Even so, its formation might well encounter great resistance. Positively, however, a loose federation of Christian churches with the Pope as symbolic center might provide Christianity with a greater sense of religious identity. It would safeguard the distinctive character and freedom of the member-churches but at the same time unite them on the basis of shared commitment. It would also give worldwide Christianity a greater moral authority and enable the message of Christ to be more effectively proclaimed. Moreover, the federal model, whatever opposition it may face, seems to be the most feasible means of realizing the union of all churches in Christ.

The Roman Catholic Church, certainly, would be in a unique position in the proposed federation, for the Pope would be the head of his own Catholic Church as well as of the federal Church. Catholics, of course, would have to recognize his ultimate jurisdictional and doctrinal authority, but other member-churches would not, even though they would grant him some limited power. The Pope's twofold role, however, raises some difficulties. First, the Church's present central administration should be thoroughly restructured to provide broad and equitable ecumenical representation. Second, the ecumenical Petrine office should be harmonized with the Pope's obligations to his own Catholic faithful. Third, procedures for the election of the Pope should be clearly worked out ahead of time, especially those concerning the eligibility of the electors. However desirable it might seem to have an ecumenical election, such a course would raise the problem that non-Catholics would be choosing the magisterial authority binding fully only Catholics.

Even if the political and procedural aspects are satisfactorily arranged, for many, the chief impediment to Christian reunion remains the dogmas of the Roman Catholic Church. Several ecumenists have seen a way out of this impasse by suggesting that Rome should not set down as an absolute condition for union acceptance of any dogma issued since the Orthodox and Protestant churches have been separated from Rome. In particular, they point to the dogmas of papal primacy and infallibility and the Marian dogmas of the Immaculate Conception and the Assumption.[70] This proposal would not mean that the other churches would deny these teachings, but that they would be allowed to interpret them according to the spirit of the Gospel. Some have further suggested that all future dogmatic pronouncements be made only by a genuine ecumenical council—that is, one including all Christian churches.

It is impossible to predict how union will be eventually achieved—either through a uniate or federal model or through some other, still undetermined, manner. There is, nevertheless, clearly a need for some kind of institutional unity that would preserve the plurality of Christian traditions. Both of the models that I have discussed have their advantages and disadvantages. Nor can we overlook the fact that at the present there does not seem to be an intense desire among Christians—either at the leadership or at the grass-roots level—to establish a worldwide Church organization. Interest, however, in this possibility might be generated if Rome and the other centers of Christian leadership began actively working on concrete proposals. Rome should take the initiative, for it has a crucial role in resolving such issues as: the doctrinal requirements for incorporation; the nature and limits of the Pope's ecumenical authority; the extent of autonomy for member-churches; and the question of ministry and sacramental sharing.

From a Roman Catholic perspective, the reform of the papacy will be a major factor in the movement toward reunion. Karl-Heinz Ohlig wisely observes that "if models for a future institution of unity are to be effective ecumenically, they cannot be developed on the basis of a monarchical governing office."[71] This means that the papacy in the future has to become much more charismatic, prophetic, and collegial. Yet even if these goals are realized in the near future, it is unlikely that Christians would

[70] See A. Dulles, "Dogma as an Ecumenical Problem," *Theological Studies*, 29 (1968), 397–416, and "A Proposal to Lift Anathemas," in *Origins* (Dec. 26, 1974), Vol. 4, No. 27, 417–21. It is also discussed in the Lutheran-Catholic Dialogue, "Teaching Authority and Infallibility," op. cit., Nos. 42–50, 152–55.

[71] *Why We Need the Pope. The Necessity and Limitations of Papal Primacy* (St. Meinrad, Ind.: Abbey Press, 1975), p. 142.

immediately unite. A much more realistic scenario is that reunion will occur only after a long series of mutual testing and adjustment. Thus J. Robert Wright correctly observes that all Christians have to face "the probability that the eventual visible reunion of all the separated churches can take place only gradually and in a somewhat random way in various regions of the world, 'at different paces in different places.' "[72]

Ecumenism will continue to be a priority for the papacy in transition. Individual Popes can do much to encourage mutual sharing and co-operation. The reunion of a divided Christianity will not come easily. When unity does occur, it will not be simply because of the untiring work and prayers of Popes, Christian leaders, and dedicated believers, but primarily because of the gift of the Holy Spirit: "And hope does not disappoint, because the charity of God is poured forth in our hearts by the Holy Spirit who has been given to us" (Rm. 5:5).

[72] "Anglicans and the Papacy," op. cit., 402.

6 THE POPE AS ELECTED LEADER

> When the selection of the highest
> priest is being taken care of, let him to
> be preferred above all whom the clerics
> and the people have agreed to ask for.
>
> POPE LEO I[1]

No man is born a Pope; he becomes one when he is so designated by others. Peter was personally selected by Christ to hold a prominent position in the apostolic college, but there is nothing in Scripture—no dominical statement, no procedural norm—that deals with the appointment of his successors. The election of the Pope, then, is in the sphere of ecclesiastical and not divine law. Each Pope has the right to establish the norms that will be used in the naming of his successor. Popes have regularly exercised this prerogative and in this century alone there have been eight significant papal decrees dealing with election. The latest legislation, used in the elections of John Paul I and John Paul II, is the apostolic constitution *Romano pontifici eligendo,* issued by Paul VI on October 1, 1975.[2] In this chapter, I shall first discuss the

---

[1] Letter to the Bishop of Thessalonica (*PL* 54:673).
[2] *Acta apostolicae sedis,* 67 (1975), 609–45.

historical evolution of papal elections and then treat some perti-
nent theological issues.

I. Election by Clergy and People

For about a thousand years, the Pope was elected by the clergy
and people of Rome. Although there is only fragmentary evidence
about the lives of the very early Popes, it is generally agreed that
the Bishops of Rome were selected in the same way as bishops in
other parts of the Christian world.[3] From the end of the first century, there are two indications of this process. The Didache, a
document of Syrian origin, stated: "Elect for yourselves bishops
and deacons, men who are an honor to the Lord, of gentle dispo-
sition, not attached to money, honest, and well-tried."[4] Clement
of Rome, in the last decade of the first century, wrote a strong letter to the Corinthian Church, rebuking it for deposing some of
their officials: "We deem it an injustice to eject from the sacred
ministry the persons who were appointed by them [the Apostles]
or later, with the consent of the whole Church, by other men of
high repute."[5] These documents do not mention the Bishop of
Rome but it is likely that he too was elected by the community.

Eusebius of Caesarea (d. c. 339) described the election of
Pope Fabian (236–50) and its extraordinary circumstances. A
dove landed on Fabian's head and "the whole body exclaimed,

[3] In writing this chapter I have found the following studies most
useful: T. Ortolan, "Élection des papes," *Dictionnaire de théologie catholique*, IV, 2281–319; G. Thils, *Choisir les évêques? Élire le pape?* (Paris:
Lethielleux, 1970); E. Roland, "Élection des évêques," *Dictionnaire de
théologie catholique*, IV, 2256–81; P. Granfield, *Ecclesial Cybernetics: A
Study of Democracy in the Church* (New York: Macmillan, 1973); R. Eno,
"Shared Responsibility in the Early Church," *Chicago Studies*, 9 (1970),
129–41; L. Swidler and A. Swidler, eds., *Bishops and People* (Philadelphia:
Westminster, 1970); J. E. Lynch, "Co-responsibility in the First Five Centuries: Presbyterial Colleges and the Election of Bishops," *The Jurist*, 31
(1971), 14–53; and F. L. Ganshof, "Note sur l'élection des évêques dans
l'empire romain au IVe et pendant la première moitié de Ve siècle," *Revue
internationale des droits de l'antiquité*, 4 (1950), 467–98.
[4] Didache, 15. *Die Apostolischen Väter*, F. X. Funk and K. Bihlmeyer (Tübingen: J. C. B. Mohr, 1956), I: 8.
[5] First Epistle of Clement, 44 (Funk and Bihlmeyer, I: 59).

with all eagerness and with one voice, as if moved by the one spirit of God, that he is worthy; and without delay they took him and placed him upon the episcopal throne."[6] This legendary procedure, however, did not set a precedent. The next Pope, Cornelius (251–53), was elected in the more traditional manner, which Cyprian described in a letter to Antonianus: "Cornelius was made bishop by the judgment of God and of His Christ, by the testimony of almost all the clergy, by the vote of the people who were then present, by the assembly of venerable bishops and good men."[7]

In his letters, Cyprian frequently referred to the election of bishops and clearly indicated that it involved all of the community: the clergy, the laity, and the neighboring bishops.[8] He described the three principal phases of the process: the *testimonium* —a public manifestation by the community of the candidate's qualifications; the *suffragium*—an act (either by voting or some other indication of preference) by which the community indicated whom they wished to be bishop; and the *judicium*—a final approval of the entire electing body (including the bishops) of the candidate chosen. This process, according to Cyprian, was followed in Africa, Rome, Spain, and throughout almost all of the provinces.

In the fourth and fifth centuries, popular elections continued, but the neighboring bishops assumed a greater role. Two Popes in particular stressed the role of the community. Celestine I (422–32), in a letter to the bishops of Gaul, wrote: "Let no bishop be given to a community against its will; the consent and desire of the clergy, people, and nobility is required."[9] Leo I (440–61) agreed: "No consideration allows making bishops of those who have not been chosen by the clerics, sought for by the people, and consecrated by the provincial bishops with the consent of the metropolitan."[10] Leo also left us with the classical

[6] *Historia ecclesiastica*, 6, 29 (PG 20:587, 590).

[7] *Ep.* 55, 8 (*Corpus scriptorum ecclesiasticorum latinorum*, ed. G. Hartel [Vienna: Apud C. Geroldi Filium, 1871] 3:629–30).

[8] Cf. P. Granfield, "Episcopal Elections in Cyprian: Clerical and Lay Participation," *Theological Studies*, 37 (1976), 41–52.

[9] *Ep.* 4, 5 (PL 50:434).

[10] *Ep.* 167 (PL 54:1203).

reason for such participation: "He [the bishop] who is in charge of all, should be chosen by all."[11]

In the sixth and seventh centuries, the clergy and the bishops took a more prominent part in electing the Bishop of Rome, and influential lay members of the community (civil and military officials) exercised a greater role than the ordinary citizen. A council held at Rome in 769 decreed that only clerics could vote in a papal election and that the role of the laity should be reduced to greeting the newly elected Pope as "Lord of all."[12] This decree, however, did not gain immediate acceptance; lay participation still played some part in the procedure. As late as 1049, we find Leo IX (1049–54) refusing to assume the papal office until he had received public approval.[13] Ten years later, the cardinals were made the exclusive papal electors.

Two principal factors dictated the need for a radical reform in the procedure for electing a Pope: the abuses that frequently accompanied papal elections, and the progressive interference by civil rulers. These reforms occurred sporadically from the fourth to the eleventh centuries.

First, many abuses undermined the traditional practice. For instance, after the Edict of Milan (313), papal elections were too often the scene of riotous demonstrations and bloodshed. Pagan historian Ammianus Marcellinus described the disputed election of Pope Damasus and the antipope Ursinus in 366: "In a single day 137 corpses were found, and . . . it was only with difficulty that the long-continued frenzy of the people was afterward quieted."[14] Antipopes and rival factions, a problem even before Constantine, kept increasing after his death. Ortolan calls the following six centuries "a scandal for the faithful and a joy for the pagans."[15] In the tenth century, the so-called Iron Age of the pa-

---

[11] *Ep.* 10 (PL 54:634).

[12] *Monumenta germaniae historica, Concilia,* ii, No. 14, p. 86.

[13] Cf. H. Tritz, "Die Hagiographischen Quellen zur Geschichte Papst Leos IX," *Studi Gregoriani,* 4 (1952), 191–364.

[14] Translation from Loeb Classical Series, trans. J. C. Rolfe (Cambridge: Harvard University Press, 1964), III, Bk. 27, 4, 14.

[15] Ortolan, op. cit., 2289. The pagan prefect, Praetextatus, looked with envy on the wealth of the Roman episcopacy in the fourth century. He said: "Make me the bishop of the city of Rome, and I will immediately

pacy, the office fell perhaps to its lowest level. Papal elections were often manipulated through gross political intrigue. An expert in Machiavellian politics was the infamous Marozia, whom Christopher Dawson can literally call "the Senatrix, mistress, mother, and murderess of Popes."[16] During that same century, there were at least thirty Popes or antipopes. So bad was the reputation of the papacy that the French bishops at the Council of Saint-Basle de Verzy in 991 could make the following bitter comments about the Popes: "Is it to such monsters, swollen with their ignominy and devoid of all knowledge human or divine, that the innumerable priests of God throughout the world who are distinguished by their knowledge and virtues should have to be submitted?"[17]

Second, emperors, kings, and influential political figures openly interfered in pontifical elections. They controlled and confirmed elections, imposed and deposed Popes, and settled conflicts between rival claimants. From the fourth century to the eleventh, Christian emperors, Ostrogoth and Carolingian kings, and Italian feudal rulers all vied with one another in trying to dominate the papacy.

In time, an imperial *placet* or formal approbation by the emperor was required before a papal election was legitimate. When the capital was in Constantinople, papal representatives had to go there, receive approval from the emperor, and return to Rome before the newly elected Pope could be installed or exercise any jurisdiction. As a result, from the middle of the sixth century to nearly the end of the seventh, long delays were common, usually only three or four months, but in two instances (after the death of Honorius I in 638 and of Agatho in 681), the delay lasted nineteen months. The period of the Italian feudal rulers (900–64), as we saw above, was dominated by powerful families who were unscrupulous in their dealings with the papacy. This practice continued in the next century with Otto and his succes-

---

become a Christian" (Jerome, *Liber contra Joannem Hierosolymitanum, ad Pammachum* [PL 23:361]).

[16] *The Making of Europe: An Introduction to the History of European Unity* (New York: New American Library, 1956), p. 230.

[17] Ibid., pp. 234–35.

sors. Otto I made Leo VIII (963–65) a Pope, and his pontificate was a stormy one. In 963, he is said to have issued a bull giving Otto I and his successors the right in perpetuity to name the Pope and also archbishops and bishops.[18] Although this bull is now considered to be a forgery of the investiture period, the Ottos acted in accord with its provisions. Depositions and impositions of Popes were frequent. Clearly, then, by the beginning of the eleventh century, the time for a radical reform of the papal election procedure was long overdue.

II. Election by the Cardinals

The office of cardinal developed slowly in the Roman Church.[19] Originally, the title referred to those bishops, priests, and deacons who were attached to a church other than the one for which they were ordained. By the end of the eighth century, during the pontificate of Stephen III (768–72), the cardinals were a group who took care of the liturgical services in the major Roman basilicas. Their powers grew, and eventually they were given administrative functions. By the beginning of the eleventh century, they had become the main consultants and advisers to the Pope. Finally, in 1059, Nicholas II (1059–61) made them papal electors.

Nicholas II, a native of Burgundy, had a short but important pontificate. In 1059, he issued the decree *In nomine Domini*, the first decisive contribution of the Gregorian reform.[20] It was drafted by Nicholas with the help of Hildebrand and Peter Damian. The aim of the decree was to enable the Church to regain

[18] The text of the bull can be found in *Monumenta germaniae historica, Constitutiones,* I, Appendix X, No. 448, 665 ff.

[19] Cf. S. Kuttner, "*Cardinalis:* The History of a Canonical Concept," *Traditio,* 3 (1945), 129–214; G. Alberigo, *Cardinalato e collegialità. Studi sull'ecclesiologia tra l'XI e il XIV secolo* (Florence: Vallecchi, 1969), and M. Andrieu, "L'origine du titre de cardinal dans l'Église romaine," in *Miscellanea Giovanni Mercati* (Città del Vaticano: Biblioteca Apostolica Vaticana, 1946), V: 113–44.

[20] Cf. H. Krause, "Das Papstwahldekret von 1059 und seine Rolle im Investiturseit," *Studi Gregoriani,* 7 (1960).

control of the papacy by ensuring free and peaceful elections. It sought to avoid the disruptions that frequently accompanied popular elections and also to eliminate imperial influence. Success was only partial. The cardinal bishops gained the predominant role in the election of the Pope; the participation of the clergy and the laity was reduced to a formality. Peter Damian explained the respective functions: "The cardinal bishops make the principal judgment; second, the clergy give assent; third, the people give applause."[21] The decree did not grant the emperor the right of confirmation but simply suggested that he be informed of the election. Rome considered this a concession given to Henry IV, not something that would automatically pass on to his successors.

The decree of 1059 did not immediately solve all the problems connected with papal elections. During the rest of the century, there were many antipopes supported by Henry IV and Henry V. In general, however, the decree was observed. The most notable breach of the rule giving cardinals the exclusive vote occurred at the election of Martin V at the Council of Constance in 1417. He was elected by twenty-two cardinals but also by thirty prelates—six from each of the five major nations at the Council: Italy, France, Spain, Germany, and England.

Later Popes refined the legislation of Nicholas II. Alexander III (1159–81), responding to interferences from the Hohenstaufen, in particular Frederick Barbarossa's support of several antipopes, issued the constitution *Licet de evitanda* at the Third Lateran Council in 1179.[22] It contained two important provisions: the inclusion of all cardinals (bishops, priests, and deacons) in the election of the Pope and the requirement of a two-thirds majority of the electors. There was no mention of any imperial confirmation nor any reference to the lower clergy or the laity. The cardinals were now the exclusive electors of the Pope.

The two-thirds-majority rule was designed to avoid the possibility of any candidate's being elected by a single faction within the electoral college. In the past, an election by a simple majority

21 PL 144:243.
22 Text in G. Alberigo et al., eds., *Conciliorum oecumenicorum decreta* (Freiburg: Herder, 1962), p. 187.

vote had often resulted in schism. Some of the cardinals, refusing to accept the choice, would seek an antipope. The two-thirds-majority rule, however, was a move toward consensus and compromise, which helped guarantee that the candidate finally elected would be acceptable to the group as a whole. It did not eliminate the possibility of disputed elections, but made them less likely.[23]

The procedures of 1179 also provided for speedier elections and greatly reduced the length of time the Holy See was vacant. Most elections were completed in a few days or weeks after the death of the Pope. There were, however, two famous exceptions in the thirteenth century that revealed the need for further legislation. The first occurred after the death of Celestine IV (1241), who reigned for only seventeen days. Owing primarily to the machinations of Frederick II, who imprisoned some of the cardinals and sent others away, the papacy was vacant over eighteen months, until Innocent IV (1243–54) was finally elected. The second unusual incident took place in 1268 at the death of Clement IV (1265–68). The cardinals, meeting in Viterbo, were unable to decide on a candidate. Months passed and the authorities of Viterbo, acting on the advice of St. Bonaventure, locked the cardinals in the archbishop's palace, put them on bread and water, and even tore down the roof of the building. At last, after a vacancy of two years and nine months—the longest election in papal history—the cardinals elected Gregory X (1271–76).

Gregory X, in order to avoid the repetition of such long vacancies, promulgated a law regulating the conclave in the bull *Ubi periculum* at the Second Council of Lyons in 1274. It decreed that ten days after the death of a Pope, the cardinals were to assemble in the papal palace and there, in a room locked in on all sides, were to conduct the election. The provisions were stringent.

> But if, God forbid, within three days from the time they enter the aforesaid room, the cardinals have not provided the Church with a pastor, they must for the period of

[23] Pius XII changed this rule slightly to two-thirds majority plus one. Cf. Apostolic constitution *Vacantis apostolicae sedis, Acta apostolicae sedis,* 28 (1946), 87.

five days immediately following, on each day, be content at their noon and evening meals with only one dish. If at the end of that time they have not provided a pastor, then they shall be served only bread, wine, and water till they have done so. During the time of the election, the cardinals may receive nothing from the papal treasury, nor from any other revenue accruing to the Church from whatsoever source during the time of the vacancy.[24]

The Fifth Lateran Council (1512–17) also dealt with papal elections. The bull *Si summus rerum opifex* of Julius II (1503–13), issued at the fifth session of the Council, decreed that the cardinals have the sole responsibility for the election and that even if an ecumenical council is in session at the time of a Pope's death, it should be immediately suspended.[25] Subsequent Popes have repeated that provision. Julius II also declared that any simoniacal papal election is invalid, and the candidate elected an apostate. Pius X abrogated this stipulation in 1904. Likewise, Paul VI, in 1975, condemned "the detestable crime of simony" but "removed the nullity of simoniacal elections . . . in order that the validity of the election of the Roman Pontiff may not be challenged for this reason."[26]

III. The Present Legislation

The apostolic constitution *Romano pontifici eligendo* of Paul VI now contains the law on papal elections. But there is also a body of unwritten customs and rituals, some of which are still used.

---

[24] Latin text in *Conciliorum oecumenicorum decreta*, op. cit., p. 291. The English translation here is taken from H. J. Schroeder, *Disciplinary Decrees of the General Councils* (St. Louis: B. Herder, 1937), p. 332. This decree on the conclave was suspended by Adrian V in 1276, and a year later it was revoked. It was finally restored in 1294 by Celestine V.

[25] *Conciliorum oecumenicorum decreta*, op. cit., 576–79. In another decree, Lateran V condemned an abuse that had grown up during the years —the looting of the cardinals' homes when the Holy See was vacant and the electors were in conclave ("Contra invadentes domos cardinalium," ibid., 625–26).

[26] *Romano pontifice eligendo*, op. cit., No. 79, 641. English translation from *Origins* (Nov. 27, 1975), Vol. 5, No. 23, 366.

Who is eligible for election to the papacy? In theory, any baptized, male Catholic who is capable of accepting the election and of exercising authority may be elected. There is no provision in the law governing the candidate's age, nationality, or status in the Church. In practice, however, most of the Popes in the last several hundred years have been Italian cardinals over fifty years of age. With the exception of John Paul II, the last non-Italian Pope was the Dutchman Adrian VI (1522–23); the last non-cardinal to be elected was Urban VI (1378–89), who was Archbishop of Bari; and the last Pope who was a member of a religious congregation was the Camaldolese monk Gregory XVI (1831–46).

Who elects the Pope? Since 1179, the College of Cardinals has acted exclusively as papal electors. No eligible cardinal can be excluded from the election, even if he is under the penalty of excommunication, suspension, or interdict. These censures are temporarily suspended during the election. But a cardinal who has resigned or who has been canonically deposed cannot participate. Today canonists agree that the right of the cardinals to elect the Pope is based only on ecclesiastical law.

In recent years, some modifications have been made relative to the cardinal electors. The Code of Canon Law (Canon 232, 1) declared that cardinals must be at least priests—the last nonpriest cardinal was Giacomo Antonelli (d. 1876), Secretary of State under Piux IX. In 1962, John XXIII ordered that all cardinals in the future would also be bishops;[27] Paul VI, in 1970, barred all cardinals over eighty years of age from participating in papal elections.[28] Both John and Paul greatly enlarged and internationalized the College of Cardinals, whose number had been fixed at seventy by Sixtus V in 1586. At the death of Pius XII there were 57 cardinals; at the death of John XXIII there were 87; and at the death of Paul VI there were 129. Today there are more than 50 nations represented in the college, with about one third from the Third World. At the conclaves of 1978, for the first time in history, a majority of the 111 electors were non-Europeans.

[27] *Cum gravissimas, Acta apostolicae sedis,* 54 (1962), 256–58.
[28] *Ingravescentem aetatem,* ibid., 62 (1970), 810–12.

The maximum number of cardinal electors was set at 120 by Paul VI.[29]

The present legislation forbids, under pain of excommunication, any elector to accept "under whatsoever pretext, from whatsoever civil authority, the task of proposing the *veto* or *exclusiva*."[30] This is a reference to a practice that existed since the sixteenth century whereby several of the powerful Catholic nations of Europe—Austria, France, and Spain—attempted to use the *veto* to exclude a particular candidate they did not favor. The last instance of this usage was in the conclave following the death of Leo XIII in 1903. The Austrian Emperor, through Cardinal Puzyna, vetoed the candidacy of Cardinal Rampolla del Tindaro. Pius X was elected at that conclave and, early in his pontificate, he condemned this practice.[31]

What is the conclave? The conclave is both the assembly of the cardinal electors and the place where it meets. Paul VI gave the following description:

> By conclave is understood those clearly defined places, having as it were the character of a sacred retreat, where, after the invocation of the Holy Spirit, the cardinal electors choose the Supreme Pontiff, and where they and the other officials and assistants, together with any conclavists there may be, remain day and night until the election has taken place, without having any dealings with extraneous persons or things.[32]

The conclave must begin at least fifteen days after the Pope's death but not more than twenty. During this period before the conclave, the cardinals meet formally to discuss the law governing the election, the state of the Church, and the kind of Pope who is needed. They do not propose names at this time but try to arrive at a consensus on the qualifications required in the next Pope. The long preconclave period is designed to shorten the time of the actual conclave. Electioneering and the formation of any

29 *Romano pontifici eligendo*, op. cit., No. 33, 622.
30 Ibid., No. 81, 641; *Origins*, 366.
31 *Commissum nobis* (Jan. 20, 1904).
32 *Romano pontifici eligendo*, op. cit., No. 42, 624; *Origins*, 361.

pacts, agreements, or arrangements between the cardinals is strictly forbidden. Unlike elections in the secular world, there are no declared candidates, no official parties, and no public campaigning. Some informal lobbying does occur, perhaps based on Paul VI's statement that "We do not, however, have the intention of forbidding the exchange of views concerning the election during the period in which the See is vacant."[33]

The cardinal electors live in small, specially built rooms in the Vatican and cannot leave until a Pope is elected. The quarters are simple and there is no communication with the outside through letters, newspapers, telephone, television, or radio. Some find the confinement trying, especially in a sweltering Roman summer. Cardinal Siri of Genoa, for example, claimed in a moment of poetic exaggeration that "in a certain sense it is like a living hell." Of recent years, however, the conclaves have not been excessively long. In this century, conclaves have averaged three days.

Secrecy governs every aspect of the conclave. The cardinals and other officials take a solemn oath promising, under pain of excommunication, not to reveal anything that takes place in the conclave. The number of possible excommunications that threaten the cardinals at every turn has led Peter Hebblethwaite to refer to the conclave as "a dangerous occasion of sin." All the votes and private notes of the cardinals are burned. At the end of the conclave, a document is prepared that gives the results of each balloting session. It is kept in a sealed envelope in the Vatican archives and cannot be opened without the explicit permission of the Pope. No recording, reproducing, or transmitting device is allowed within the precincts of the conclave. To see that this prohibition is observed, officials make regular searches of the area.

How is the election conducted? The present norms describe in detail the three traditional types of election, which are also to be followed if a Pope resigns. The first, election by acclamation

[33] Ibid., No. 82, 642; *Origins*, 366. This provision was generously interpreted by the cardinals during the two conclaves of 1978. For a fascinating account of these conclaves see P. Hebblethwaite, *The Year of Three Popes* (Cleveland: W. Collins, 1979) and A. Greeley, *The Making of the Popes 1978* (Mission, Kan.: Andrews & McMeel, 1979).

or inspiration, occurs "when the cardinal electors, as it were through the inspiration of the Holy Spirit, freely and spontaneously, unanimously and aloud, proclaim one individual as Supreme Pontiff."[34] There has to be complete unanimity, and each cardinal has to indicate his assent either orally or by writing.

Election by delegation, the second type, must be agreed upon by every one of the cardinals. They then elect an uneven number of delegates—from nine to fifteen—and specify the procedure the delegates must follow. This would involve, for example, deciding whether the delegation should simply propose a name to the rest of the cardinals or directly carry out the election.

Election by scrutiny, the third type, is the usual method and consists of written ballots. The candidate who receives two thirds plus one is considered elected. Four ballots are held each day: two in the morning and two in the afternoon. If after three days— that is, after twelve ballots—no one has been elected, then balloting is suspended for a time, with a maximum of one day for prayer and discussion. Then seven more ballots can be taken and, after another pause, seven more. Then, if still no election has taken place, the electors must choose one of the following options: (a) to continue voting in order to arrive at the necessary two-thirds-plus-one majority; (b) to agree unanimously to elect by delegation, or by the absolute majority of votes plus one, or by voting for one of the two candidates who gained the greatest number of votes in the preceding ballot.

To the faithful waiting in St. Peter's Square, black smoke coming from the chimney in the Sistine Chapel is a sign that the balloting must continue; white smoke, that a Pope has been elected and that they will soon hear the words: *Annuntio vobis gaudium magnum. Habemus Papam!* The Pope gives his blessing *urbi et orbi* and receives the applause of the multitude—the last vestige of popular participation in papal elections.

At the end of the conclave, the newly elected Pope is asked: "Do you accept your canonical election as Supreme Pontiff?" If he accepts, he is then asked: "By what name do you wish to be called?" The tradition that the Pope take a new name is an interesting aspect of papal history, a long-standing practice but not

[34] Ibid., No. 36, 632; *Origins*, 363.

an ancient one. For centuries, Popes kept their own names, but this precedent was broken in the sixth century when a man named Mercury was elected Pope. He decided that it would be more fitting to have a Christian name than the name of a pagan god so he took the name John II (533–35). The next Pope to change his name was Octavian, who took the name John XII (955–64). By the eleventh century, this practice became quite common. In 1009, for example, a candidate who was known as Peter Pig's Mouth (to distinguish him from his father, Peter the Shoemaker) was elected and understandably took a new name, Sergius IV (1009–12). When Pietro Barbo was elected, he wished to take the name Formosus II. The cardinals, however, objected, since the name (which means handsome) might be taken to be an unseemly reference to his good looks. He then selected the name Mark, but since this was the rallying cry of the Venetian troops, it too was rejected. He settled on the name Paul II (1464–71). The most popular papal names have been John, Pius, Benedict, Clement, Leo, Gregory, and Innocent. There has never been a Peter II. John Paul I was the first Pope ever to choose a double name and the first Pope since Lando (913–14) to have an original name.

In conclusion, papal elections are unpredictable events, as the 1978 conclaves proved dramatically. Despite countless forecasts and lengthy assessments of front-running *papabili*, the results showed once again the wisdom of the Roman proverb "He who enters the conclave a Pope, leaves it a cardinal." The activity of the Holy Spirit, that silent member of the conclave, continues to surprise us. Paul VI warned the electors not to decide on the basis of friendship or aversion and not to be influenced by pressure groups, suggestions from the media, or the desire for popularity. The criterion he gives is pragmatic but deeply spiritual:

> But having before their eyes solely the glory of God and the good of the Church and after imploring God's help, they shall give their vote to the person whom they judge to be more suited than the others to govern the universal Church fruitfully and usefully.[35]

35 Ibid., No. 84, 642; *Origins*, 366.

IV.   Some Theological Questions

The method for electing Popes has undergone several major
refinements over the centuries but only one truly radical development: the shift in the eleventh century, from election by the people to election by the cardinals. The procedure, however, raises
many theological questions, which I shall now treat. A future
Pope may confront some of them.

A.   The Naming of a Successor

Can a Pope name his successor? There is a historical precedent. Felix IV (526–30), in order to prevent a schism after his
death, appointed the archdeacon Boniface as his successor and
conferred upon him the pallium. On the death of Felix, Boniface
became Pope and, after some initial difficulty, was accepted by
the Roman synod. The question remains: Was Boniface Pope because he was appointed by Felix or because he was approved by
the synod? A year later, Boniface (530–32) appointed his own
successor but rescinded this arrangement before his death.

Some theologians would deny that the Pope can legitimately
name his successor.[36] Others maintain that it is per se possible,
since Peter in all likelihood named his successor, and there is no
explicit prohibition in divine law against it.[37] Ortolan makes a
distinction between designating a successor and recommending a

---

[36] Cardinal Cajetan argued that the direct election of a successor
by a reigning Pope would be invalid (Scripta theologica, Vol. 1, De
comparatione auctoritatis papae et concilii cum apologia eiusdem tractatus,
ed. V. Pollet (Rome: Angelicum, 1936), Cap. 17, No. 736. Also see
C. Journet, The Church of the Word Incarnate (London: Sheed & Ward,
1955), I: 479–80, and I. Salaverri, De ecclesia Christi in Sacrae theologiae
summa, 2nd ed. (Madrid: Biblioteca de autores cristianos, 1952), p. 635.

[37] Canonists J. A. Abbo and J. D. Hannan note: "Moreover, it is
also clear that the authority of the Roman Pontiff is full and supreme and
that there is no positive prohibition of this exercise of it found in any
provision of the divine law" (The Sacred Canons [St. Louis: B. Herder,
1952], I: 286).

possible candidate. He says: "Up to the end of the fifth century, the usage existed at least of asking the Pope, in view of a vacancy of the Holy See, what candidate he would recommend to the electors."[38]

The present law of the Church backed by centuries of tradition prohibits this method of selection. Pius IV (1559–65) ruled in 1561 that the Roman Pontiff could never choose his own successor or appoint someone with the right of succession, even if each and every cardinal agreed.[39] Today the theological question is unresolved. Although it is possible to conceive of a grave situation in the future that might prompt a Pope to name his successor, the traditional election would still be the wiser course.

B. The Beginning of Papal Authority

Traditionally, a newly elected Pope who was not a bishop or a priest was ordained to these offices as soon as possible. This practice was common during the first ten centuries when bishops were rarely chosen to be Popes: The overwhelming majority of candidates were priests, deacons, and, occasionally, laymen, such as Benedict VIII (1012–24) and John XIX (1024–32). The first bishop from another diocese to become a Pope was Marinus I (882–84), the Bishop of Caere in Etruria. Moreover, while Rome awaited imperial confirmation of the election, there were frequent delays, as long as several months, before episcopal ordination. Indeed, Severinus (640) and Leo II (682–83) waited a year and a half before becoming bishops.

Canon 219 of the Code of Canon Law seems to imply that even before becoming a bishop, the one elected Pope has full papal power, for it states: "The Roman Pontiff, legitimately elected, obtains by divine right full power of supreme jurisdiction as soon as he has accepted the election." This canon seems to reflect the medieval distinction between the power of order and

[38] Ortolan, op. cit., 2282.
[39] Raynaldus, *Annales ecclesiastici: 1198–1566* (Lucques: L. Venturini, 1756), 15:121.

the power of jurisdiction. Accordingly, the crucial element in papal primacy is the power of jurisdiction, which the Pope receives at his election, and not the power of order, received at episcopal consecration. Hence, Walter Ullmann asserts that "it was never a requirement for the exercise of papal powers that the pope had to be consecrated."[40] Likewise Eric Mascall writes: "Whereas the episcopate is a sacramental function in the Church, the papacy is a juridical and administrative one."[41]

Historical precedent, especially from the Middle Ages, tends to justify a literal interpretation of Canon 219. But Vatican II sought to return to the much earlier idea that order and jurisdiction are not two separate powers but fundamentally one.[42] The Pope, then, is not merely the administrative head of the Church; he is at the same time the Bishop of Rome and leader of the episcopal college. The episcopal character is a necessary element in the office of the papacy. The sacramental nature of the papal office was further stressed in *Romano pontifici eligendo*, which qualified Canon 219. "The intention is clear," remarks Yves Congar, "the Pope is essentially the Bishop of Rome."[43] The decree described the beginning of papal authority as follows:

> After the acceptance, the person elected, if he has already received episcopal ordination, is immediately bishop

[40] "Leo I and the Theme of Papal Primacy," *The Journal of Theological Studies*, N.S. 11 (1960), 28, n. 1. This preoccupation with papal jurisdiction is also found in Augustinus Triumphus (d. 1328), who said that "papa est nomen jurisdictionis." See M. Wilks, "Papa est nomen jurisdictionis," *The Journal of Theological Studies*, N.S. 8 (1957), 71–91 and 258–71.

[41] *The Recovery of Unity* (London: Longmans, Green, 1958), p. 208. It should be noted, however, that even in the Middle Ages the Church recognized the close connection between papal authority and episcopal ordination. Stephen (752), for example, who died three days after his election and before he was made a bishop, is not included in many of the medieval lists of Popes. Also Innocent III (1198–1216) and Boniface VIII (1294–1303) reconfirmed all the papal acts made before they were ordained bishops.

[42] See *Lumen gentium*, Art. 21: "But episcopal consecration, together with the office of sanctifying, also confers the offices of teaching and of governing."

[43] "Bulletin d'ecclésiologie: Conciles et papauté," *Revue des sciences philosophiques et théologiques*, 60 (1976), 297.

of the Church of Rome, true Pope, and head of the college of bishops; and by that very fact he acquires and can exercise full and supreme power over the universal Church. Should the person elected not yet have the episcopal character, he shall be ordained bishop immediately.[44]

If the person elected does not yet have the episcopal character, homage and obedience are given to him and the announcement made to the people only after he has been ordained bishop.[45]

The problem is how to relate Canon 219, which states that one who is elected Pope (even if he is not a bishop) has by "divine right full power of supreme jurisdiction," with the view, succinctly expressed by W. Bertrams, that "the office of the supreme pastor of the Church is constituted . . . through episcopal consecration and mission."[46] In other words, the question is what authority does a Pope who is a layman, deacon, or priest have before he becomes a bishop? Admittedly, today this situation would be unheard of, but the theological problem does remain.

I shall make three observations about the beginning of full papal authority. First, every newly elected Pope who is not a bishop is morally and canonically bound to accept episcopal ordination, since his papal authority is essentially linked to the episcopal character. The Pope cannot be the Bishop of Rome and in communion with the members of the episcopal college unless he himself is a bishop. Second, an elected Pope not yet a bishop is, to quote J. Hortal Sanchez, "truly designated by God and worthy of all veneration, but he does not yet possess the pontifical *cathedra*."[47] He is not yet a universal teacher but rather an adminis-

---

[44] *Romano pontifici eligendo*, op. cit., No. 88, 644; *Origins*, 367.
[45] Ibid., No. 89, 644; *Origins*, 367.
[46] "De missione divina et de consecratione episcopali tamquam constitutiva officii supremi ecclesiae pastoris," *Periodica de re morali canonica liturgica*, 65 (1976), 187.
[47] *De initio potestatis primatialis Romani Pontificis: Investigatio historico-iuridica a tempore S. Gregorii Magni usque ad tempus Clementis V* (Rome: Gregoriana, 1968), p. 89. The latest draft of the *Lex fundamentalis ecclesiae* of the proposed new Code of Canon Law states in Canon 30: "The Roman Pontiff, duly elected, acquires full and supreme power in the Church by divine right when he accepts the election and is ordained a bishop"

trator of the Holy See. In more canonical terms, Bertrams argues that before an elected Pope becomes a bishop, he has *ius ad rem* concerning the primatial power over the entire Church, which becomes *ius in re,* actual and complete, only after his ordination. Third, if a newly elected Pope adamantly refuses to be ordained a bishop, he could possibly be removed from office. Here deposition would be grounded on an intrinsic aspect—the failure to achieve fully constituted papal authority.

In brief, we see here an instance of the development of ecclesiological doctrine. Vatican II and *Romano pontifici eligendo* have in effect reinterpreted Canon 219 by emphasizing the unity of the powers of order and jurisdiction. Hence, the true beginning of full papal authority requires both designation and ordination. Since usually episcopal ordination precedes designation by the College of Cardinals, election suffices. Canon 219 thus accurately describes what happens in the usual situation. Vatican II, however, forces us to a theological reformulation of what actually constitutes papal power—the essential unity of order and jurisdiction.

C. The Electoral College

In the early 1970s, there were several reports from Rome that Paul VI planned to broaden the electoral college to include the patriarchs and some representatives from the Synod of Bishops. The Pope himself even alluded to this question.[48] The final document on election procedures, *Romano pontifici eligendo,* made no such provision. Theologians have argued both for and against changing the membership of the electoral college.

Theologians in favor of continuing the practice of having only the cardinals elect the Pope present the following reasons. First, the election of the Bishop of Rome has always been the exclusive prerogative of the Church of Rome, and not even the patriarchs of the East before the schism interfered with this process.

(*Communicationes,* 1977, 114–16). Also see J. M. R. Tillard, "The Jurisdiction of the Bishop of Rome," *Theological Studies,* 40 (1979), 3–22.

[48] At a consistory on May 5, 1973 (*Acta apostolicae sedis,* 65 [1973], 163).

Second, there is an intimate relationship between the College of Cardinals and the Roman Church. The collège is the senate of the Pope, and its members serve as the Pope's closest advisers through their work in the Curia. The cardinals are chosen both for their ability to assist the Pope in the governance of the universal Church and for their qualities as future electors. In a sense, they are part of the clergy of Rome, their international character making them especially valuable as electors. Third, it is ecclesiologically unsound to make some bishops electors, because it would conflict with the doctrine of collegiality and the theology of the local Church. Hervé-Marie Legrand, for example, feels that the proposal to expand the electorate rests on a universalist ecclesiology that is opposed to the collegial ideal.[49] The autonomy of the local Church of Rome should be preserved and not sacrificed to a distorted notion of collegiality. Thus, Roberto Tucci suggests that a change in the traditional practice would create the impression that the Pope "was a kind of delegate of the universal Church or at least elected as universal Bishop and not the Bishop of a particular Church."[50] Fourth, it would be ecumenically damaging if patriarchs of the Eastern Catholic churches were made electors. This would adversely affect Rome's relationship with the Orthodox churches, who would feel that a long and sacred tradition had been repudiated.

Theologians who advocate a change in the membership of the electorate give two principal arguments. First, the theology of shared responsibility demands it. The sacramental dignity and equality of the People of God allow them to share in the life and decision-making of the Church—including the selection of its pastors, bishops, and Pope. For centuries the Church encouraged the popular election of bishops. The principle of Leo I is still valid today: "He who is in charge of all, should be chosen by all."[51] Second, the College of Cardinals is not truly representative of the

[49] "Ministère romain et ministère universel du pape. Le problème de son élection," in G. Alberigo et al., *Renouveau ecclésial et service papal à la fin du XXe siècle, Concilium* (French ed.), No. 108 (Paris: Beauchesne, 1975), 43–54.

[50] "The Election of the Roman Pontiff: A Juridical and Pastoral Document," *L'osservatore romano* (English ed.) (Dec. 11, 1975), p. 9.

[51] *Ep.* 10 (PL 54:634).

universal Church. Its members are appointed and not elected.
The Pope, therefore, can influence the type of successor to be
chosen. This procedure may provide stability and continuity, but
it also encourages inbreeding. Most of the cardinals who voted in
the elections of John Paul I and John Paul II had been named
by Paul VI. Furthermore, the College of Cardinals does not represent the various constituencies within the Church. The Catholic
laity have no voice in papal elections; the wisdom and experience
of women are not represented; the bishops, priests, and religious
are likewise excluded. "As far as the election of the Pope is concerned," writes Hans Küng, "it is a matter of special importance
that this should be handed over by the College of Cardinals—
which is in no way representative and is in any case an anachro-
nism—to the council of the bishops and the lay council."[52]

Both schools of thought raise valid issues, but it seems to me
that those who suggest a broader membership of the electoral college are on surer ground. True, the autonomy of the local church
is precious, but Rome is unlike any other local church. To elect a
Pope is not only to elect the Bishop of Rome but also to choose
someone who will be the supreme pastor of the universal Church.
However close the cardinals may be to Rome, they are not
Romans, and the Bishop of Rome, as is presently the case, is not
necessarily from Rome. The See of Rome is unique, so what is
needed is an electoral procedure that would give some voice to the
international membership of the Church at all levels.

Paul VI wisely recommended that "the electoral body should
be named beforehand and should not be too numerous, so that it
may be convened easily and without delay."[53] A small but truly
representative group would be ideal. At the present, when bishops are still not elected by the faithful, it may be utopian to

[52] *Truthfulness: The Future of the Church* (New York: Sheed &
Ward, 1968), pp. 172–73. Cardinal Suenens suggests the following change
in the electoral college in accord with the doctrine of collegiality. He writes:
"This would require, for instance, that the electoral body should be, in the
first place, the whole body of bishops, and then, as a second step, a nar-
rower college of bishops; or should application be made directly to the
Synod of Bishops?" (J. de Broucker, *The Suenens Dossier: The Case for
Collegiality* (Notre Dame, Ind.: Fides, 1970), p. 28.

[53] *Romano pontifici eligendo*, op. cit., Proem., 610.

think that in the near future papal elections will be conducted by representatives from the lay, clerical, and episcopal ranks. A first phase, however, could be initiated by making the presidents of the national episcopal conferences electors or by granting a vote to some members of the Synod of Bishops. Episcopal conferences might also be encouraged to submit to the Holy See and the Synod of Bishops the names of possible candidates. Likewise, there might be input from lay and clerical organizations concerning the future needs of the Church and priorities for the papal ministry. In time, this might lead to plans that would include both lay and clerical participation in papal elections.

D. The Reform of the Conclave

Is there still a need to play out the medieval drama of locked doors, sealed windows, multiple oaths, threats of excommunication, occasional searches, and smoke signals? The secrecy of the recent conclaves was by no means absolute, since detailed accounts of the balloting appeared in several newspapers and magazines all over the world. The Church should not have to shroud its decision-making and to veil its human side by an exaggerated secrecy. The electors should be allowed to discuss possible candidates by name even before the election. Furthermore, many of the cardinals do not know each other well. Consistories are rarely held and, with the development of the Synod of Bishops, this is not likely to change. The electors, whoever they may be, might meet regularly to consider the future direction of the papacy and to discuss possible successors.

Serious thought should also be given to the place where the conclave is held. In the past, papal elections have been held at St. John Lateran, the Quirinale Palace, and at several papal residences outside of Rome, as well as in the Vatican. The present cramped quarters in the Vatican are ill suited for a large assembly of live-in electors. If the conclave is supposed to have about it the character of a retreat, then it might profitably be moved to another place in Rome—a monastery, college, or religious house—that has more suitable accommodations and can provide a more spiritual atmosphere. The problem of location would, of course, be irrelevant if the present conclave system were abolished. Yet there is a definite value for the electors to be together during the course of the election and to share a moving religious experience.

E.   The Papacy and Rome

Must the successor of Peter always be the Bishop of Rome, or could the primacy be attached to another see? These questions have more than an academic interest when one considers the uncertainty of Italy's future with Eurocommunism and even the possibility of nuclear war. Is it possible that a future Pope could be the Bishop of Dublin, Toronto, or Tokyo?

This question was debated at Vatican I. The First Schema of the Constitution on the Church stated that the Roman Pontiff is the successor of St. Peter by divine law.[54] The final conciliar text, *Pastor aeternus,* however, did not go that far. It declared that the Roman Pontiff is St. Peter's successor, but left open the question of the basis of that union and its permanence.[55] Bishop Dupanloup, for example, said that "it is not certain at this time that the true successor of Peter will always have, by divine law, his see at Rome."[56] The Bishop of Granada, on the other hand, suggested that the relationship between Rome and the primacy be defined as of divine law, but he was told: "The Most Reverend Father has spoken learnedly and piously, but not every pious opinion can be put into a dogmatic constitution."[57]

Theologians have debated this question for centuries.[58] Some

[54] Mansi, 51:552.
[55] Denzinger-Schönmetzer, 3058.
[56] Mansi, 51:969.
[57] Ibid., 52:720.
[58] For a more recent discussion of this issue see C. Journet, *The Church of the Word Incarnate,* op. cit., 427–38; G. van Noort, *Christ's Church* (Vol. 1 of *Dogmatic Theology*) (Westminster, Md.: Newman, 1961), 273–77; I. Salaverri, *De ecclesia Christi in Sacrae theologiae summa,* op. cit., pp. 633–35; G. Thils, *Choisir les évêques? Élire le pape?,* op. cit., 85–89; and R. La Valle, "Engagement du pape en tant qu'évêque de Rome," in G. Alberigo et al., *Renouveau ecclésial et service papal à la fin du XXe siècle,* op. cit., 75–86.

(de Soto and Bañez) argued that the primacy is joined to the Roman See only by ecclesiastical law and hence, for a good reason, can be separated. Others (Cajetan, Cano, Bellarmine, Billot, and Journet) maintained that the connection is based on divine law and thus inseparable. Charles Journet, for example, contends that the jurisdiction of the Bishop of Rome is fused with his jurisdiction over the universal Church, because St. Peter "was expressly led . . . by the divine will to unite the papacy to the See of Rome for all future time."[59] Bellarmine and Billot took this one step farther and held that the link between Rome and the papacy is indestructible and that Rome, which will exist to the end of time, will always have some clergy and faithful. A more moderate view is held by Perrone and Journet, who argue that if Rome were totally obliterated and the Pope forced to live elsewhere, he would continue to be the *de jure* though not the *de facto* Bishop of Rome.

Tradition and theological opinion seem to favor some kind of divinely willed foundation linking the primacy to Rome. The matter, however, is not definitively settled, and discussion continues. Avery Dulles, for example, notes that it is theoretically possible "that the bishop of another city might hold the primacy," but adds that Catholics, because of tradition, "would be reluctant to see the primacy transferred elsewhere."[60] At present, since there is no imminent threat to Rome, the question remains a purely theological one. Whatever may happen in the future, the papal office will be localized somewhere and the Pope will still retain his episcopal status and his linkage with St. Peter, whose see was Rome.

F. The Papal Term of Office

Traditionally, Popes have been elected for life. The longest pontificate was that of Pius IX (1846–78), who served for thirty-one years and seven months. The shortest was that of Stephen (752), who was Pope for only three days. In the nineteenth cen-

---

[59] Journet, op. cit., 430.
[60] *The Resilient Church* (Garden City, N.Y.: Doubleday & Company, 1977), p. 120.

tury, six Popes ruled for an average of seventeen years. So far in this century, excluding the thirty-four-day "September papacy" of John Paul I, the average has been twelve years.

The proposal to limit the time of papal service suggests either a fixed term of office or retirement at a fixed age. Both formulations exclude lifetime tenure. There are no explicit scriptural or dogmatic statements, so let us examine some of the arguments for and against this proposal.[61]

The principal argument against a term of office for the Pope is tradition: Popes have always ruled for life and should continue to do so. Cardinal Suenens, who spoke out forcefully at Vatican II in favor of an age limit for bishops, stopped short of applying it to the Pope because: "It is clear from the nature of the case that this need for an age limit does not apply to the Supreme Pontiff; the universal good of the Church demands that he remain in office for life."[62] Although the Belgian cardinal did not explain why "the universal good of the Church" would exempt the Pope from any limitation on his term of office, several reasons may be suggested. Perhaps a term of office or an age limit for the Pope might weaken the idea of the Pope as the enduring, visible symbol of Church unity. Frequent changes in the highest leadership position in the Church might disturb the Christian community, subtly introduce the feeling of discontinuity, and seriously restrict the Pope in his long-term pastoral planning. A further disadvantage is that a fixed date might set the stage for a political campaign before the Pope's term had expired, the last few years of which might be a kind of marking time, a suspension of leadership that the Church could ill afford. Or if the Pope could be re-

[61] Much of the literature deals with the episcopal rather than the papal question. Cf. A. Auer, G. Biemer et al., "Limited Term of Office for Residential Bishops," in L. Swidler and A. Swidler, eds., *Bishops and People*, op. cit., 22–37 and J. Neumann, "Election and Limitation of Term of Office in Canon Law," ibid., 54–70.

[62] In H. Küng, Y. Congar, and D. O'Hanlon, eds., *Council Speeches of Vatican II* (Glen Rock, N.J.: Paulist Deus Book, 1964), p. 119. H. Küng, however, insists that "there must be an age-limit for the Pope too. . . . A Pope with a recognized time-limit, and therefore a more exact distinction between office and individual, would make the character of the Petrine office as an office of service much clearer" (Editorial in *Papal Ministry in the Church, Concilium*, Vol. 64 [New York: Herder and Herder, 1971], 10).

elected, the period might be for him a time of subtle campaigning and compromising even more harmful to the Church.

The above considerations have to be taken seriously, for one does not tamper lightly with a system that has survived for nearly two millennia. Nevertheless, if we reject a monarchical view of the papacy—no monarch has a term of office—and accept a more pastoral and collegial concept of Church leadership rooted in loving service, then an age limit or fixed term for the Pope has definite advantages.

The principal reason for suggesting a fixed retirement date for the Pope is that the burden of carrying out the universal ministry of the Church requires extraordinary strength and energy. As history tragically recounts, even the Popes are subject to the various ills, physical, mental, and moral, that the rest of mankind is heir to. An established retirement age might substantially reduce the probability of untoward developments as the Pope ages. Although the Pope would be theoretically free to disregard this terminal norm if it were merely a statutory and not a constitutional prescription, it would still have strong suasive power and would give a failing Pope a graceful way out of the papacy. The critical and complex problems facing the Church need a leader who can deal with them vigorously, adapt to changing times, and put effective reforms into practice. Do not the same reasons supporting the retirement of bishops at seventy-five years of age apply equally to the Pope?[63] An age limit would benefit both the believing community and the Pope himself who, through a long and difficult pontificate, might easily become complacent, intransigent, or simply exhausted.

A set term of office for the Pope would also have several advantages. Such a practice would facilitate the regular circulation of fresh ideas, energy, and talent within the papacy; introduce a greater sense of urgency in the direction of the Church; and prevent an ineffective Pope from causing spiritual harm to the Church.

The Church of the future, then, should thoughtfully con-

[63] On the retirement of bishops see *Decree on the Bishops' Pastoral Office in the Church*, Art. 21 and *Ecclesiae sanctae*, I: 11 (*Acta apostolicae sedis*, 58 [1966], 763).

sider three alternatives: first, retain the present practice of life-time tenure; second, establish an age limit of seventy years of age for the Pope (five years less than that required of bishops because of the greater demands of the office); and third, set a term of ten years with the possibility of one extension of five years.[64] Any change in the tradition will, of course, demand a careful assessment of advantages and disadvantages, with the ultimate criterion always being the greater good of the Church.

To conclude, the process of papal elections has been an uneven one, evolving gradually and painfully. Its first discernible shape was the voice of the clergy and people of the city of Rome; its most recent, that of the balloting of the elite College of Cardinals. Procedures have improved over the centuries, but more needs to be done—perhaps even a limited return to the spirit of the past, with a greater participation by a more representative electorate. But however justly and prudently carried out, an election is, after all, only the beginning of a papal reign, so we must next consider the ways in which that reign reaches its inevitable termination.

[64] J. Blank suggests a seven-year term with the possibility of one re-election ("Gefangener seiner einegen Tradition," in G. Denzler, ed., *Papsttum heute und morgen* [Regensburg: F. Pustet, 1975], p. 38), and G. Hasenhüttl, a five-year term with one re-election (ibid., "Nicht mit-herrschen, sondern mitdienen," p. 71). Richard P. McBrien suggests a tenure of ten years, renewable (*The Remaking of the Church* [New York: Harper & Row, 1973], p. 93).

7 THE LOSS OF THE PAPACY

> No mortal shall presume to rebuke
> his [the Pope's] faults, for he who is to
> judge all is to be judged by no one, un-
> less he is found straying from the faith.
>
> GRATIAN[1]

Papal authority can be lost in several ways, the most obvious of which is death. Although most of the Popes have died from natural causes, many have died as martyrs. Allegedly, the first twenty Popes were martyred, but in some instances the evidence is scanty and even dubious. The latest act of antipapal violence was the assassination attempt by a knife-wielding Bolivian painter against Paul VI during his visit to Manila in November 1970.

Death, even though violent, effectively terminates a papal reign without presenting any theoretical problems. Not so the two main nonlethal modes of termination, the voluntary and the forced—resignation and deposition. A third mode, retirement at a set age or after a set term, is possible but is arguably reducible to

---

[1] *Decretum Gratiani, Dist.* 40, c. 6 (*Corpus iuris canonici*, I, ed. E. Friedberg [Leipzig: B. Tauchnitz, 1879], col. 146). I would like to acknowledge here that the first part of this chapter, on papal resignation, is substantially the same as my article "Papal Resignation," *The Jurist*, 38 (1978), 118–31.

one of the other two—that is, the Pope voluntarily retires in accordance with an established canonical norm, or the Church is empowered to enforce the constitutional norm whether he agrees or not. All we need examine here are the two main modes: resignation and deposition.

I. Papal Resignation

The last few years of the pontificate of Paul VI sparked widespread speculation about the desirability and the probability of papal resignation. Although that concern ended with the death of the Pope in August 1978, the question of resignation may well surface in the future. Let us take a new look at an old issue, a tranquil look at what was once, as the thirteenth century became the fourteenth, a crisis in practical ecclesiology. This conflict was not over abstract dialectics but over political survivalship; it was sectarian, it was venal, it was vindictive—but it was also theologically enlightening. It helped decide a theoretical issue, only to leave for succeeding generations the thorny problem of concrete application.

Resignation simply means the voluntary giving up for a just cause of an ecclesiastical office—here the supreme office of the papacy—and is similar to deposition, since the effect is essentially the same, the loss of office. Yet, since one is active, the other passive; the one voluntary, the other coercive; the theological implications are vastly different. In this section, I shall consider three basic aspects of papal resignation: the possible precedents, the medieval conflicts, and the canonical norms.

A. The Possible Precedents

Ten men—not all of them familiar names, even to those discussing resignation—have been proposed at one time or another as examples of papal resignation. They are Clement I, Pontian, Cyriacus, Marcellinus, Martin I, Benedict V, Benedict IX, Gregory VI, Celestine V, and Gregory XII. Medieval theologians frequently mentioned Clement, Cyriacus, and Marcellinus; contemporary writers also mention Celestine, Gregory XII, and, occasionally, Pontian, Martin, Benedict V, Benedict IX, and Gregory VI. To determine the reliability of using them as precedents, I shall examine each separately and, with the exception of Celestine, chronologically. I discuss Celestine last, for his situation is both the strongest one for resignation and the one that occasioned the greatest of the medieval debates, which I shall deal with in the following section.

1. CLEMENT I (88–97). There is no unanimity in the patristic evidence concerning Clement's career. Irenaeus (*Adv. haer.* 3, 3, 3) and Eusebius (*Hist. eccl.* 3, 15, 34) placed Clement as the third successor of St. Peter after Linus and Cletus. Tertullian (*De praescrip.* 32), however, wrote that Clement was consecrated by Peter and, hence, his immediate successor. In an attempt to reconcile these inconsistent statements, Epiphanius (*Panarion* 27, 6), while agreeing with Tertullian, claimed that Clement gave up the pontificate to Linus for the sake of peace and became Pope again after the death of Cletus. Assuming that Epiphanius is correct, which is problematic, there is an added complication—the theory that the papacy at that time was not monarchical but collegial, with possibly a revolving presidency.[2] In short, the Clementine precedent for papal resignation is unclear and uncertain.

2. PONTIAN (230–35). At the end of his fifth year in the papacy and during the persecution of Maximinus Thrax, Pontian was exiled to the mines of Sardinia. It appears that, thus separated from Rome and with little hope of returning, he resigned his papal office and was succeeded by Anterus.[3] The

---

[2] Cf. M. Bévenot, "Clement of Rome in Irenaeus's Succession List," *Journal of Theological Studies*, 17 (1966), 98–107 and D. F. Wright, "Clement of Rome and the Roman Succession in Irenaeus," ibid., 18 (1967), 144–54.

[3] See reference in the Liberian Catalogue of the fourth century in *Liber pontificalis*, ed. L. Duchesne (Paris: E. Thorin, 1886), 1:5.

scanty biographical information we have about Pontian gives us no details about his alleged resignation.[4]

3. CYRIACUS. This is a clear case of a nonexistent Pope, a fictional character created in the Middle Ages and widely accepted then as real. The legend was that in the third century Cyriacus was the Pope between the reigns of Pontian and Anterus. Supposedly, he received a heavenly command to resign his papacy and to accept martyrdom with St. Ursula's eleven thousand virgins—which number itself is a pious exaggeration.[5] According to von Döllinger, "delusion, visionary fantasy, and baseless credulity worked together to create a Pope who is as unreal and as purely illusory as Pope Joan."[6]

4. MARCELLINUS (296–304). This Pope is said to have sacrificed to the pagan gods and, having been found guilty by the bishops, accepted their judgment and removed himself from the papacy. The historical validity of this story is questionable. Augustine (Contra litteram Petil. 2, 92, 202) rejected it as a Donatist fabrication. Contemporary scholars, likewise, discount the authenticity of Marcellinus' abdication.[7]

5. MARTIN I (649–55). In the midst of a bitter controversy with the Emperor Constans II over monothelitism (the heretical doctrine that Christ possessed only a single will), Martin was deported in 653 to Constantinople. Tried at the imperial court, he was found guilty of treason and exiled to Cherson in the

---

[4] Cf. F. X. Seppelt and G. Schwaiger, Geschichte der Päpste (Munich: Kösel, 1964), p. 17.

[5] John of Paris cited Cyriacus as an example of papal resignation. He noted, however, that he was not in the catalogue of the Popes, because the cardinals "credebant ipsum non propter devotionem sed propter oblectamenta virginum dimisisse papatum" (De potestate regia et papali, Chap. 24. The text is found in J. Leclercq, Jean de Paris et l'ecclésiologie du XIIIe siècle [Paris: J. Vrin, 1942], p. 253).

[6] J. J. I. von Döllinger, Die Papst-Fabeln des Mittelalters (Stuttgart: J. G. Cotta, 1890), p. 53. Although Cyriacus is mentioned in some early editions of the Roman Breviary, he is not found in the accepted list of Popes. Cf. A. Mercati, "The New List of Popes," Mediaeval Studies, 9 (1947), 71–80.

[7] Cf. von Döllinger, op. cit., pp. 57–61; E. H. Röttges, "Marcellinus-Marcellus. Zur Papstgeschichte der Diokletianischen Verfolgungszeit," Zeitschrift für katholische Theologie, 78 (1956), 385–420; and A. Amore, "Il preteso 'lapsus' di Papa Marcellino," Antonianum, 32 (1957), 411–26.

Crimea, where he died in 655. However, the Roman clergy in 654, a year before Martin's death, fearing that the emperor would install a monothelite Pope, elected Eugene I. Although there is no evidence that Martin formally resigned the papacy, there is an indication that he knew that a successor had been elected and that he apparently approved the choice; for, in a letter to a friend in Constantinople, he prayed for the continued orthodoxy of the Romans and "especially for the pastor who is now placed over them."[8]

6. BENEDICT V (964). The events surrounding Benedict's resignation, after a reign of only one month, are complex and disputed. In 955, John XII was elected Pope but was later deposed by a Roman synod that in turn elected Leo VIII. After John died, the Romans elected Benedict V, who had participated in the election of Leo but now repudiated him. This action so infuriated Emperor Otto I that, with Leo, whom he considered to be the true Pope, he convened a synod at the Lateran to deal with the matter. If the chronicler Liutprand, Bishop of Cremona, can be believed, Benedict agreed with the charge that he had usurped the papacy, and on June 23, 964, he accepted deposition.[9]

7. BENEDICT IX (1032–48) and 8. Gregory VI (1045–46). These two Popes can be taken together, since their careers are intertwined. Benedict IX, who had obtained the office by simony, resigned the papacy on the condition that John Gratian (Gregory VI) would grant him a comfortable pension. After Benedict's departure, Gregory was deposed at the Council of Sutri (1046) on the grounds of simony. Later Benedict was also deposed. Thus in neither case do we have an instance of pure resignation, because of the simoniacal involvement and the depositions.[10]

[8] Regesta pontificum romanorum ab condita ecclesia ad annum post Christum natum 1198, ed. P. Jaffé (Leipzig: Veit, 1885), I, No. 2081, 235.

[9] Liudprandi historia Ottonis in Monumenta germaniae historica (Scriptores), Ser. 4, Tom. 3, 346.

[10] Cf. C. J. Hefele and H. Leclercq, Histoire des conciles (Paris: Letouzey et Ané, 1911), IV, 2:981–91; G. Borino, "L'elezione e la deposizione di Gregorio VI," Archivo della Società Romana di Storia Patria, 39 (1916), 142–252 and 295–410; and E. Amman and A. Dumas, L'Église

9. GREGORY XII (1406–15). During the Great Western
Schism, there were three claimants to the papacy: from Rome,
Avignon, and Pisa. At the Council of Constance, the Avignon
and Pisan Popes were deposed and Gregory XII, of the Roman
line, resigned.[11] However, the chaotic atmosphere of the Church
at that time,[12] the uncertainty over the legitimacy of any of the
contenders,[13] and the unusual character of the Council[14] make it
impossible to find in Gregory's resignation a sound precedent.

10. CELESTINE V (1294). Peter of Morrone, at the age
of about eighty, was elected Pope on July 5, 1294. He was the
founder of a small Benedictine group of hermits and had a widespread reputation for holiness and asceticism. One of his electors,
Cardinal James Colonna, said of him: "The fame of his sanctity
was so great that it moved the cardinals to make him Pope."[15] Yet
he was ill suited for the administrative complexities and the political intrigues of the papal court.[16] Subservient to Charles II of
Naples, exploited by the unscrupulous, and deeply unhappy at
having left his solitary life, he was soon overwhelmed by the
office and decided to resign. He gave for his reasons: humility,
the desire to lead a more perfect life, and physical and mental in-
capacity to govern the Church.[17] On December 13, 1294, after a

au pouvoir des laïques [Vol. 7 of Histoire de l'Église by A. Fliche and
V. Martin] (Paris: Bloud & Gay, 1943), 89–97.

[11] Cf. H. Zimmermann, Papstabsetzungen des Mittelalters (Graz:
H. Böhlaus, 1968), pp. 273–95.

[12] Cf. L. Salembier, The Great Schism of the West (London: Kegan
Paul, Trench, Trübner, 1907) and W. Ullmann, The Origins of the Great
Schism (London: Burns, Oates, and Washbourne, 1948).

[13] Cf. K. A. Fink, "Die Wahl Martinus V," in Das Konzil von
Konstanz, ed. A. Franzen and W. Müller (Freiburg: Herder, 1964), pp.
138–51.

[14] Cf. A. Franzen, "Das Konzil der Eihheit," ibid., pp. 69–112.

[15] Analecta bollandiana, XVI: 476.

[16] The Liber pontificalis called Celestine "a man of God but not
expert in secular matters" (op. cit., 2:468). Clement V (1305–14), in his
bull canonizing Celestine V, said he was a Pontiff "inexperienced in the
government of the universal Church" (Regestum Clementis papae V—Anni
8 & 9—LX–LXI [Rome: Ex typographia Vaticana, 1888], No. 9688, p. 294).

[17] The statement of Celestine at his abdication is found in Annales
ecclesiastici, ed. C. Baronius and A. Theiner (Barri-Ducis: L. Guérin, 1871),
p. 145.

reign of only five months, he resigned. T. S. R. Boase describes the final dramatic exit: "On 13 December Celestine read his own abdication in full consistory, stripping the robes of his great office from him, a pathetic scene, in which the Pope showed to better advantage than in any of the more grandiose moments of his pontificate."[18] On December 24, 1294, Cardinal Benedict Gaetani was elected Pope as Boniface VIII.[19] He was a canon lawyer and a veteran of papal service. One of the problems he faced, as we shall see presently, concerned the legitimacy of his own election.

Of the ten cases of resignation I have discussed, only Celestine V offers a solid example.[20] His resignation initiated an intense, at times acrimonious, theological debate. The strong, abrasive character of Boniface VIII and the personal ambitions and political motivations of others further complicated the issue.

B.   The Medieval Conflicts

1.   The Adversaries

The chief opponents of papal resignation and, hence, of the validity of Boniface's election were the two Colonna cardinals, James and his nephew Peter. Although both had voted for Boniface in 1294, three years later they were openly opposed to him. The reasons were clear. Boniface demanded that the treasure

---

[18] *Boniface VIII* (London: Constable, 1933), p. 50.

[19] Boniface explained the resignation of Celestine in his *Littera coronationis* (Jan. 24, 1295). The text is given in *Les registres de Boniface VIII*, G. Digard et al., eds. (Paris: E. de Boccard, 1939), No. 1, cols. 1–4.

[20] Celestine V is immortalized in literature. Petrarch and Boccaccio were laudatory of Celestine's actions. It is generally thought, however, that Dante in *The Divine Comedy* placed him in hell:

> When some among them I had recognized,
> I looked, and I beheld the shade of him
> Who made through cowardice the great refusal.

> *The Divine Comedy*, trans. Henry
> Wadsworth Longfellow (Boston: James
> R. Osgood, 1871), Canto III, 58–60, p. 11.

(taken by a relative of the Colonnas, Stephen Colonna) be returned, that Stephen surrender, and that Boniface himself be
given three large Colonna palaces. The Colonnas quickly took
the offensive, and in 1297 issued three manifestos against Boniface, denouncing him as a usurper, heretic, simoniac, and illegitimate Pope and calling for a general council to settle the matter.[21]
Philip the Fair of France[22] and the Spiritual Franciscans,[23] both
stanch supporters of Celestine, were sympathetic to the arguments
made by the Colonnas against the validity of papal resignation,
specifically Celestine's resignation.

Articulate defenders of papal resignation, nevertheless, were
not lacking. Chief among them were the Franciscan Peter John
Olivi,[24] Godfrey of Fontaines,[25] Peter of Auvergne,[26] the Augus-
tinian Giles of Rome,[27] and the Dominican John of Paris.[28] They

[21] The three Colonna manifestos are published in H. Denifle, "Die
Denkschriften der Colonna gegen Bonifaz VIII und der Cardinale gegen
die Colonna," in Archiv für Litteratur-und Kirchengeschichte, 56 (1889),
493–525. The letter of the cardinals was very polemical, dismissing the
Colonnas as "not so much schismatics as madmen" (ibid., 529). For the
few theologians from the University of Paris who agreed with the Colonnas
against the legitimacy of the papacy of Boniface VIII see Chartularium
universitatis parisiensis, ed. H. Denifle and A. Chatelain (Paris: Delalain,
1891), II, No. 604, p. 77.

[22] On this issue see G. Digard, Philippe le Bel et le saint-siège,
1285–1304 (Paris: Libraire du Recueil Sirey, 1936).

[23] Cf. D. Douie, The Nature and Effect of the Heresy of the Fraticelli
(Manchester: Manchester University Press, 1932).

[24] He wrote De renuntiatione papae in 1295. Text edited by P. L.
Oliger in Archivum franciscanum historicum, 11 (1918), 366–73.

[25] He discussed this matter in Quaestio IV of his Quodlibetum XII,
written in 1295. Text in J. Hoffmanns, ed., Les Quodlibets XI–XIV de
Godefroid de Fontaines in Les philosophes Belges (Louvain: Éditions de
l'Institut Supérieur de Philosophie, 1932), V: 96–100.

[26] In Quaestio XV of his Quodlibetum I, written in 1296. The text
is still in manuscript form, but a summary of it is given by J. Leclercq, "La
renonciation de Célestin V et l'opinion théologique en France du vivant
de Boniface VIII," Revue d'histoire de l'Église de France, 25 (1939),
183–92.

[27] Giles wrote De renuntiatione papae in 1297. Text in J. T.
Rocaberti, ed., Bibliotheca maxima pontificia (Rome: I. F. Buagni, 1698),
II, 1:1–64.

[28] John of Paris discussed resignation in Chap. 23–25 of his De
potestate regia et papali, op. cit., pp. 251–60. He summarized, with some
significant differences, the lengthy text of Giles and also borrowed from
Godfrey of Fontaines.

were all educated at the University of Paris and all, in spite of their personal feelings about Celestine and Boniface,[29] unanimously asserted the legitimacy of papal resignation. Moreover, they accepted the principle of Gratian that the Pope is beyond all human judgment, ecclesiastical or civil, except when judged to be heretical,[30] since heresy is the equivalent to death and a heretical Pope has actually separated himself from the Church.

This unanimity had limits, for there was a significant difference between Giles of Rome and John of Paris on how precisely papal authority could be lost. Giles of Rome explained that a living Pope could cease being a Pope in two ways: either he falls into clear heresy and is deposed by a council, or he renounces his office voluntarily, with or without the consent of the cardinals who elected him. Giles vigorously rejected the possibility of a forced deposition for a nonheretical Pope.[31] To allow this, he felt, would be to deny the *plenitudo potestatis* inherent in the papal office.

John of Paris, on the other hand, held that "the Pope can renounce his office and even unwillingly be deposed."[32] To prove the deposition of a *"papa noluntarius,"* he cited the *Glossa ordinaria,*[33] which said that a Pope could be deposed not only for heresy but also for any notorious crime or vice. John concluded that if a Pope was found guilty of a serious crime and did not reform after being admonished, then his contumacy was equivalent to heresy and was grounds for deposition. Moreover,

[29] For example, Olivi was a major figure among the Spiritual Franciscans and a stanch supporter of Celestine V (cf. Douie, op. cit., 81–119); Giles of Rome was a defender of papal monarchy and of Boniface VIII; and Peter of Auvergne and John of Paris both signed a document calling for a general council against Boniface VIII (cf. *Chartularium universitatis parisiensis,* op. cit., II: 634).

[30] In addition to the text of Gratian quoted in n. 1, there is also another important text from the *Decretum* concerning the Pope: *"Neque ab Augusto neque ab omni clero neque a regibus neque a populo iudex iudicatur"* (C. 9, q. 3, c. 13, *Decretum Gratiani,* op. cit., col. 610).

[31] Cf. *De renuntiatione papae,* op. cit., 20, 21, 56. Giles also stressed the voluntary character of resignation and equated it with self-deposition.

[32] *De potestate regia et papali,* op. cit., 252.

[33] *Glossa ordinaria decreti,* Dist. 40, c. 6. The position of John of Paris is discussed by Brian Tierney in *Foundations of the Conciliar Theory* (Cambridge: Cambridge University Press, 1955), pp. 157–78.

he did not think it necessary for a council to depose the Pope; the College of Cardinals could undertake that task, since the plenitude of papal authority is diffused throughout the Church and the cardinals represent the Church.[34]

2. The Arguments

Each of the principal spokesmen in this controversy discussed, more or less, the same arguments—about a dozen of them—which, however, can be reduced to four main ones. In treating them individually, I shall give the position of the opponents of the right of papal resignation and then the response of the proponents of that right.[35]

The first argument is that the Pope has no human superior to receive his resignation, for no human agent can remove what he cannot confer. But papal authority, the highest created power, is conferred by God alone and hence can be taken away by God alone. Two axioms described the exempt and unique status of the Pope: (a) *Prima sedes a nemine iudicatur*. The Pope may be the judge of all, but he can be judged—and removed from office—only by God. (b) *Nemo est iudex in causa sua*. The Pope is no judge in his own case, and hence he cannot baptize, absolve, or ordain himself, nor can he remove himself from his supreme office by resignation.

The proponents of resignation answered by distinguishing between papal power in itself and in a particular person. Thus, while papal power is given by God, it is not given immediately but through human mediation: the consent of the electors and the acceptance of the elected. For a sufficient reason the elected (the Pope) may withdraw his consent. This is what happens in resignation. A Pope may freely give up what he has freely accepted.

[34] John of Paris held that the cardinals were *"loco totius cleri"* (215); *"in loco totius cleri et totius populi"* (254), and *"vice totius ecclesiae"* (257).

[35] In writing this section, I have found most helpful the article by W. Ullmann, "Medieval Views on Papal Abdication," *Irish Ecclesiastical Record*, 71 (1949), 125–33.

The objection that there is no superior capable of receiving a Pope's resignation was answered directly by Olivi. He argued that since the cardinals act "in the place of a superior" (*vices superioris*) in electing a Pope and urging him to accept the election, they would act in the same manner in accepting his resignation. He even said that the validity of the resignation depends on its acceptance by the cardinals.[36] Giles of Rome[37] and John of Paris,[38] however, took a different view. They held, citing the dubious precedent of Cyriacus, that even if the people, clergy, and cardinals do not agree, a Pope may still resign.

The second argument against resignation is that the Pope and the universal Church are joined by a spiritual bond of marriage, just as are a bishop and his diocese. A spiritual marriage is stronger than a carnal marriage between husband and wife. Thus, if not even God will dissolve a properly ratified and consummated carnal marriage, then he clearly will not allow the dissolution of the spiritual contract between the Pope and the Church. Therefore, resignation is impossible.

The response focused on the weakness of the marriage analogy. Giles of Rome[39] and John of Paris,[40] for example, argued that a spiritual bond may be greater than a carnal one, not because it is more durable but because it is more worthy. Furthermore, a bishop can be transferred by the Pope to another diocese and for a sufficient reason a bishop can be removed from his diocese.[41] A consummated sacramental marriage, however, cannot be dissolved. Peter of Auvergne pointed out that while there is a prohibition in Scripture against the dissolution of a carnal marriage (Mk. 10:7 and Mt. 19:9), there is no similar prohibition against terminating the union between the Pope and the Church.[42] The theologians in favor of papal resignation main-

[36] *De renuntiatione papae*, op. cit., 364.
[37] *De renuntiatione papae*, op. cit., 9, 62.
[38] *De potestate regia et papali*, op. cit., 253.
[39] *De renuntiatione papae*, op. cit., 29, 30.
[40] *De potestate regia et papali*, op. cit., 256. Also Godfrey of Fontaines, op. cit., 96.
[41] Bishops also had the right to renounce their sees. Cf. Alexander III in *Decretales*, I, xiii, 1.
[42] Cf. J. Leclercq, "La renonciation de Célestin V," op. cit., 188.

tained that if the Pope can allow bishops to resign for the good of
the Church, then, for like reasons, he can resign himself. What is
permitted to inferiors is permitted to superiors.

The third argument against resignation is that the power of
papal jurisdiction, which is universal and supreme, confers an indelible character on the person possessing it. To suggest that a
Pope can resign would imply that he would lose this indelible
character. Since that would be impossible, resignation is not allowed.

This argument, called by Olivi the *"principalissima ratio"* of
many of his opponents, is rejected by him as "false and falla-
cious."[43] Olivi and others contended that there is a radical
difference between the power of order and the power of jurisdiction. By the former, the Pope can absolve sins, celebrate Mass,
and confer orders. By the latter, he is teacher, ruler, and judge of
all Christians. The Pope and the ordinary bishop possess the same
spiritual power; they differ in their administrative and jurisdictional authority. The power of jurisdiction has no sacramental
quality, nor does it confer an indelible character. Since the power
of jurisdiction is not a permanent element, it is not an impediment to papal abdication. A resigned Pope loses his jurisdictional power but not his spiritual power.

The fourth and final argument is that nothing is more necessary in the Church than a stable authority that preserves the faith
intact. If a Pope could freely resign, then great harm would come
to the Church because of scandal and schism.

The defenders of papal resignation acknowledged that frivo-
lous and frequent resignations would be detrimental to the
Church. They all agreed that resignation should be an exceptional step, permitted only under the most serious circumstances.
They proposed the following reasons as legitimate: (1) public
awareness of a crime; (2) avoidance of scandal; (3) canonical ir-
regularity; (4) bodily defect; (5) old age and infirmity; (6) defect
of knowledge and discretion; (7) insanity, weakness of spirit, or a
similar impediment; (8) total ineptitude and uselessness; (9) mal-
ice of the people that the Pope cannot correct and can no longer

43 *De renuntiatione papae,* op. cit., 358.

tolerate; (10) desire to enter religious life; (11) fear for his own salvation; and (12) the order, status, and public good of the universal Church.[44]

In conclusion, the debate among medieval theologians over papal resignation was intense but brief. In 1298, Boniface VIII, admittedly an interested party, issued an authoritative statement in the *Liber sextus* that the Roman Pontiff could resign.[45] Although the discussion continued, that precise issue after the death of Boniface in 1303 eventually came to have only academic interest.[46] By that time, the common teaching of the theologians was that even though papal resignation would be a rare occurrence, it was possible for a Pope to resign legitimately and meritoriously for the good of the Church. Some, however, reasoned that the arguments for papal resignation also logically justified papal deposition, since the *justa causa* could be the same in both instances.[47] This development set the stage for the major theological question in the fourteenth and fifteenth centuries: the superiority of a general council over a Pope.

C.   The Canonical Norms

The *Codex iuris canonici* of 1917 deals with the question of the resignation of ecclesiastical offices in Canons 184–91. The specific issue of the resignation of the Pope is treated in Canon 221: "If the Roman Pontiff resigns, the validity of his resignation does not depend on its acceptance by the cardinals or anyone

[44] These reasons are taken from the writings of the five defenders of papal resignation, from Innocent III, *De renuntiatione*, C. 10, I, 9, and from the *Glossa ordinaria decreti*, c. 12, C. VII, q. 1.

[45] *Liber sextus*, I, vii, 1.

[46] No significant material on papal resignation is present in the writings of the canonists after the death of Boniface. See Alexander de Sancto Elpidio, *De ecclesiastica potestate* (c. 1324) in J. T. Rocaberti, *Bibliotheca maxima pontificia*, op. cit., II: 7, 36–37; and Augustinus Triumphus, *Summa de potestate ecclesiastica* (1325), Rome, 1584.

[47] Thus M. J. Wilks writes: "To acknowledge that the pope can resign is halfway towards admitting that he can be deposed" (*The Problem of Sovereignty in the Later Middle Ages* [Cambridge: Cambridge University Press, 1963], p. 497).

else." The majority of the commentators on the Code do little more than repeat the rule.[48] It is clearly not a controverted point in the recent canonical tradition. Some observations, however, can be made.

First, the canon assumes that a Pope can resign. This is taken for granted as an accepted principle with no hint of the historical crisis that the resolution of this issue engendered.

Second, the point of affirmation of the canon is not so much the right of the Pope to resign as it is his exclusive possession of this right. He needs the consent, permission, or acceptance of no one. Furthermore, the Code, in preserving this supremacy, nowhere suggests that a Pope could be deposed—not even for heresy, although this omission would not abrogate relevant common-law principles.

Third, papal resignation should be a free and unconstrained act. Thus, a resignation coerced by an external force that cannot be resisted would be invalid. But what of a resignation made through grave fear or fraud? According to Canon 103, §2, acts performed under the influence of grave and unjustly induced fear are valid, unless the law provides otherwise. Such a provision is

---

[48] I have consulted the following authors: J. A. Abbo and J. D. Hannan, *The Sacred Canons* (St. Louis: B. Herder, 1952), I: 287–88; C. Augustine (Bachofen), *A Commentary on the New Code* (St. Louis: B. Herder, 1918), II: 208–16; M. Bargilliat, *Praelectiones iuris canonici* (Paris: Baston, Berche, and Pagis, 1923), I: 240–41; U. Beste, *Introductio in codicem* (Collegeville, Minn.: St. John's Abbey Press, 1938), p. 231; A. Blat, *Commentarium textus codicis iuris canonici* (Rome: F. Ferrari, 1921), II: 200–2; T. Lincoln Bouscaren and A. C. Ellis, *Canon Law: A Text and Commentary* (Milwaukee: Bruce, 1946), p. 154; G. Chelodi and E. Bertagnolli, *Ius de personis iuxta codicem iuris canonici* (Trent: Libr. Edit. Tridentum, 1927), pp. 248–50; 264–65; G. Cocchi, *Commentarium in codicem iuris canonici ad usum scholarium* (Turin: Marietti, 1940), III: 25–27; M. Coronata, *Institutiones iuris canonici* (Rome: Marietti, 1950), I: 372–74; F. Della Rocca, *Manual of Canon Law* (Milwaukee: Bruce, 1958), p. 186; B. Ojetti, *Synopsis rerum moralium et iuris pontifici* (Rome: S. C. de Propaganda Fide, 1912), III: s.v. "resignatio," cols. 3422–27; P. Maroto, *Institutiones iuris canonici* (Madrid: Editorial del Corazón de Maria, 1919), II: 183–84; A. Vermeersch and I. Creusen, *Epitome iuris canonici* (Mechlin-Rome: H. Dessain, 1949), I: 292; F. X. Wernz and P. Vidal, *Ius canonicum* (Rome: Gregoriana, 1928), II: 434–42; S. Woywood, *A Practical Commentary on the Code of Canon Law* (New York: J. F. Wagner, 1943), I: 86.

made in Canon 185: "A resignation made through grave fear unjustly induced, or through fraud, or substantial error, or simony is null and void."

Fourth, a Pope who wishes to resign must communicate his intention in some manner to the Church.[49] In other words, an occult or purely private act of resignation is insufficient; some kind of public declaration or action must be present before the papal office can be said to be vacant.

Fifth, a papal resignation made without a legitimate reason is valid but not licit.[50] Thus, if a Pope resigns for an unworthy motive, he may be morally reprehensible and may later even regret his decision, but his resignation is still valid.[51] The law, however, does not prohibit the possibility, unlikely though it may be, of the re-election of a Pope who has resigned.

Before concluding this section on resignation, I would like to reaffirm that resignation is a drastic and unsettling move. Obviously, since Pope John Paul II, elected in his late fifties, is clearly healthy, effective, and popular, there is no question of resignation. Nevertheless, there is no guarantee that the present Pope or one or other of his successors will never find himself so circumstanced that resignation would not be prudent and praiseworthy. Indeed, whenever a Pope becomes unable to function adequately as the leader of the Christian community and whenever his continuance in office becomes seriously harmful to the Church, he would seem to be morally obliged to resign.

The idea of resignation, however, has at least one major drawback. It might well, when once used even for a just reason, set a dangerous precedent that would encourage special-interest groups to pressure the Pope to resign for a variety of reasons not necessarily conducive to the good of the universal Church. Such political pressure could severely curtail the effectiveness of a beleaguered Pope and increase the divisiveness and polarization within the Church itself.

[49] Cf. Maroto, op. cit., 183; Wernz-Vidal, op. cit., 436; and Coronata, op. cit., 373.

[50] Cf. Cocchi, op. cit., 27; Chelodi-Bertagnolli, op. cit., 267; and Wernz-Vidal, op. cit., 436.

[51] Cf. Coronata, op. cit., 373.

As things now stand, resignation is a theological and a canonical alternative for a reigning Pope. It will undoubtedly be rarely used—even if strong reasons press for such a decision. The Pope can resign, but he does not have to resign. The question that then presents itself—a much harder question—is: Can the Pope even be forced to resign, can he be deposed? In the next section I try to see whether or not there is this more drastic remedy proportioned to serious and pressing need.

II.   Papal Deposition

If by deposition we mean simply the forcible removal of a Pope from office, then history supplies us with numerous examples, not only from the Middle Ages but even from the early centuries. In fact, during the first 15 centuries of Christianity, there were a host of contested elections, nearly 40 antipopes, and intense interference with many reigning Pontiffs. For example, the Council of Constance, prior to the election of Martin V in 1417, deposed John XXIII of the Pisan line (whose number thus passed on to our own Pope John 5½ centuries later) and Benedict XIII of Avignon. Similarly, the unofficial rump Council of Basel in 1439 deposed Eugene IV (1431–47) and elected the last antipope, Felix V, who eventually resigned.

Instances could be multiplied, but a thousand forcible depositions do not necessarily make a single valid deposition. So we must ask two basic questions: Can any papal deposition be valid? If so, under what conditions? The fundamental issue is whether or not the principle of absolute papal immunity from all human judgment can be preserved, if depositions are deemed legal. The canonical and theological answers to these perplexing questions are historically intertwined. Yet the answers are important not because future depositions are envisaged, but because they focus sharply on the allocation of jurisdictional power between the Pope and the rest of the Church.[52]

[52] In preparing this section of deposition, the following works have been most useful: H. Küng, *Structures of the Church* (New York: Thomas

A. The Canonical Question

The canonical debate originated with the *Decretum* of Gratian (c. 1140). A number of times, Gratian asserted without qualification that a Pope could be judged by no one, not even a general council; that, in fact, the Pope is beyond all human judgment, civil or ecclesiastical. Yet he did grant a single exception, namely, that for heresy, and heresy alone, the Pope could be judged: "[The Pope] is to be judged by no one, unless he is found straying from the faith."[53] It should be noted here that the concept of heresy is more precise now than it was in the Middle Ages.[54] Today heresy is the public and pertinacious denial or doubt of a specific truth formally proposed by the Church as divine faith. In the Middle Ages, however, heresy was much broader—an attitude to a number of things: a proud and deliberate contempt of Church discipline; antagonism to the teaching authority of the Church; and any threat to the vital life of faith in the Christian community, not just the denial of an article of faith.

Among the commentators on the *Decretum*, the decretists, Rufinus (d. before 1192) held that schism as well as heresy is

---

Nelson & Sons, 1964), pp. 249–68; B. Tierney, *Foundations of the Conciliar Theory*, op. cit.; W. Ullmann, *The Growth of Papal Government in the Middle Ages*, 3rd ed. (London: Methuen, 1970); H. Zimmermann, *Papstabsetzungen des Mitelalters* (Graz: H. Böhlaus, 1968).

[53] *Dist.* 40, c. 6. Brian Tierney remarks that upon this one text "was built a formidable edifice of canonistic speculation" (*Foundations of the Conciliar Theory*, op. cit., p. 57).

[54] Two articles by Albert Lang are especially useful: "Die Gliederung und Reichweite des Glaubens nach Thomas von Aquin und die Thomisten. Ein Beitrag zur Klärung der scholastischen Begriffe: fides, haeresis und conclusio theologica," *Divus Thomas*, 20 (1942), 207–36, 335–46, 21 (1943), 79–97, and "Die Bedeutungswandel der Begriffe 'Fides' und 'Haeresis' und die dogmatische Wertung der Konzilsentscheidungen von Vienne und Trient," *Münchener theologische Zeitschrift*, 4 (1953), 133–46. Also see J. Russell, "Interpretations on the Origins of Medieval Heresy," *Mediaeval Studies*, 25 (1963), and K. Rahner, *On Heresy* (New York: Herder and Herder, 1964).

cause for deposition, since schism always results in heresy.[55] This idea was taken one step forward by Huguccio (d. 1210), who wrote a lengthy gloss on the Gratian text.[56] He concluded that not only heresy but also other notorious crimes such as fornication, robbery, and simony were quivalent to heresy. Such crimes gravely injure the Church and are grounds for deposition. Huguccio, however, faced the perennial problem of how even a heretical Pope could be tried when no court was competent to decide the legal fact of his heresy. To avoid this difficulty, he argued for a kind of automatic excommunication based on the presumption of guilt. When a Pope falls into heresy he is less (minor) than any Catholic, is no longer Pope, and, in fact, has convicted himself. Huguccio carefully qualified his position. He insisted that a Pope could only be deposed if he publicly affirmed a known heresy and resolutely adhered to it even after several admonitions. Occult heresy or suspicion of heresy was not enough. The Pope's heretical teaching had to be public and in accord with an acknowledged heresy.

Other canonists also treated the question of papal deposition. Joannes Teutonicus (d. 1246) said that a Pope could be deposed even for secret heresy and did not distinguish between old and new heresies. John of Paris (d. 1306) agreed with Huguccio that heresy and other notorious crimes were cause for papal deposition and also added incompetence. He maintained that both resignation and forced deposition were possible, since the Pope receives his jurisdictional power from the whole Church, and for a serious reason it could be taken away by the College of Cardinals, who act in the name of the Church. Giles of Rome (d. 1316) took a different view and held that a Pope could be deposed only for heresy.

Later canonists, like William of Ockham (d. 1349) and Marsilius of Padua (d. 1342), proposed an extreme form of conciliarism that made the general council superior to the Pope. At the end of the fourteenth century, the debate over papal deposi-

---

[55] Die Summa Decretorum des Magister Rufinus, ed. H. Singer (Paderborn: F. Schöningh, 1902), Dist. 40, c. 6, p. 96.

[56] The entire gloss is reprinted in Tierney, Foundations of the Conciliar Theory, op. cit., pp. 248–50.

tion intensified primarily because of the practical issues brought about by the Great Western Schism. By 1409, there were three claimants to the papal throne. Moderate conciliarists—Franciscus Zabarella (d. 1417), Pierre d'Ailly (d. 1420), and Jean Gerson (d. 1425)—felt that the "royal way of the council" was the only solution to end the terrible schism that was destroying the unity of the Church. They strongly believed that a general council was superior to the Pope in matters of faith and that in extreme situations it could, for the good of the entire Church, exercise its right of deposition. The Council of Constance adopted these views and acted accordingly.

The present Code of Canon Law makes no explicit statement concerning the possibility of papal deposition for heresy or for any other reason. Its purpose was to defend papal primacy and not to limit it. Hence, Canon 1556 states: "The First See can be judged by no one" (*Prima sedes a nemine iudicatur*).[57] Commentators on the Code, however, do discuss the problem of the loss of papal jurisdiction. They generally agree that by notorious or manifest heresy or schism a Pope is *ipso facto* deprived of his juridical power. This would also be true of a Pope who was clearly insane and could be proven to be so.[58] Mental illness is seen as the legal equivalent to death. Only the human acts of a Pope are valid, and an insane Pope is incapable of exercising his ministry. The commentators on the Code do not as a rule mention incompetence or gross moral behavior as grounds for removal.

B.   The Theological Question

During the Middle Ages and also at the time of the Reformation, theologians debated how the Church should deal with a

---

[57] This ancient canonical maxim originated as a forgery at the time of Pope Symmachus (498–514) and was later included in the *Decretum of Gratian*.

[58] Three Popes are frequently cited as having shown signs of severe mental problems: Boniface VIII (1294–1303), Urban VI (1378–89), and Paul IV (1555–59). See H. Küng, *Structures of the Church*, op. cit., pp. 258–59, n. 21.

heretical Pope.[59] In those turbulent times, the charge of heresy was frequently leveled against several Popes. The Colonna cardinals, for example, called Boniface VIII (1294–1303) a heretic, the Dominican Johann von Falkenberg accused Gregory XII (1406–15) of heresy, and Savonarola said of Alexander VI (1492–1503): "I declare in the first place and I affirm it most certainly that this man is not a Christian; he no longer believes that God exists and this scales the height of all infidelity and impiety."[60] The most controversial instance of papal heterodoxy concerned Honorius I (625–38). More than forty years after his death, the Third Council of Constantinople (680–81) condemned monothelitism and named Honorius among its adherents on the basis of a letter he wrote to Sergius I, the patriarch of Constantinople. This condemnation was repeated at Nicaea II (787) and Constantinople IV (869–70).[61] Obviously there was no question of deposition here, because the accusation of heresy was made posthumously, the real question being that of papal infallibility. The multiplicity of the interpretations of this case illustrate the difficulty that contemporaries might have in definitively proving a heresy charge.

Medieval theologians generally took for granted that a Pope could be heretical.[62] Even ardent papalists argued in that manner.

---

[59] For an analysis of the papalist response see J. A. Mirus, *The Dominican Order and the Defense of the Papacy in the Renaissance* (Princeton, N.J.: Princeton University Press, 1973) and "On the Deposition of the Pope for Heresy," *Archivum historiae pontificiae*, 13 (1975), 231–48. Also see R. Manselli, "Le cas du pape hérétique vu à travers les courants spirituels du XIVe siècle," in E. Castelli, ed., *L'infallibilité: Son aspect philosophique et théologique* (Paris: Aubier, 1970), pp. 113–30.

[60] *Le lettere di Girolamo Savonarola*, ed. R. Ridolfi (Florence: L. S. Olschki, 1933), p. 206.

[61] Cf. J. Chapman, "The Condemnation of Pope Honorius," *Dublin Review*, 139 (1906), 129–54 and 140 (1907), 42–72; R. Bäumer, "Honorius I," *Lexikon für Theologie und Kirche*, 2nd ed. (1961), 5:474–75; and P. Galthier, "La première lettre du pape Honorius," *Gregorianum*, 29 (1948), 42–61.

[62] Albert Pighius (d. 1542), however, was one of the first Catholic theologians to hold that a Pope cannot fall into heresy. Robert Bellarmine referred to Pighius and said that his opinion was probable but not the certain or common opinion at that time. Cf. *Opera omnia, De controversiis christianae fidei*, I, *De Romano pontifice*, Liber II, cap. 30 (Naples: J. Giuliano,

Thus John of Torquemada (d. 1468) wrote: "Were the Pope to command anything against Holy Scripture, or the articles of faith, or the truth of the sacraments, or the commands of the natural or divine law, he ought not to be obeyed, but in such commands he is to be disregarded."[63] The precise problem the theologians faced was the relationship between the traditional teaching of papal primacy, which included immunity from judgment, and the possibility of a heretical Pope. In a word, how can a heretical Pope be deposed? Two solutions were suggested.

The first solution proposed divine or *ipso facto* deposition. This view was held by Petrus de Palude (d. 1342), John of Torquemada, Robert Bellarmine (d. 1621), and others. They argued as follows. A heretical Pope separates himself from the Church and is thereby cut off from it; he no longer remains a member of the Church, because he has denied the faith. Without faith he cannot be a Christian and because of his public and adamant disbelief he should be shunned. Such a Pope, however, is not deposed by the Church, which has no authority over him, but by divine law: "Whoever does not believe is already judged for not believing in the name of God's only Son" (Jn. 3:18). Heresy, then, is a kind of spiritual suicide. A Pope who teaches a clearly heretical doctrine in the public forum and refuses to accept the admonitions of his brethren has, by those facts, already lost his papal authority. A general council simply declares what has taken place.

A second solution suggested ecclesial deposition. Such an opinion was proposed in varying degrees by Cardinal Cajetan (d. 1524), Melchior Cano (d. 1560), Francisco Suarez (d. 1617), and John of St. Thomas (d. 1644). It sought to find a middle road between conciliarism and *ipso facto* deposition. According to this opinion, a heretical Pope is not automatically deprived of his authority but ceases to be Pope only after the Church establishes his

---

1856), 418. At Vatican I, Bishop Gasser rejected the view of Pighius (Mansi, 52:1218). Also see H. McSorley, "Some Forgotten Truths About the Petrine Ministry," *Journal of Ecumenical Studies*, 11 (1974), 208–37.

[63] *Summa de ecclesia* (Venice: M. Tramezium, 1561). Lib. II, c. 49, p. 163B. Trans. from J. H. Newman, *A Letter Addressed to His Grace the Duke of Norfolk on Occasion of Mr. Gladstone's Recent Expostulation* (New York: The Catholic Publication Society, 1875), p. 68.

guilt. Thus Suarez noted: "If the Pope becomes an incorrigible
heretic after the declaratory sentence of this crime has been made
against him, he ceases to be Pope."[64] This does not mean that the
council is above the Pope, because the council's judgment is declaratory and not deliberative; the judgment does not cause deposition but merely confirms it. Yet a formal sentence from the
Church is necessary to preserve order and to remove publicly a
source of scandal. Suarez rejected the view that the College of
Cardinals alone can depose a Pope and argued, rather, that it is
the principal duty of the bishops, "the ordinary shepherds and
pillars of the Church."[65] If provincial or regional councils are unable to agree on this matter, then a general council should be
called. Should the Pope try to prevent this, "one is under no obligation to obey him, since he abuses his power against justice and
the common good."[66]

The ecclesiological balance of the second solution makes it
most attractive. It avoids extreme conciliarism and protects papal
primacy in a reasonable manner. Moreover, it would seem to
apply not only to a heretical Pope but also to one who is schismatic or insane. But what of a Pope whose actions do not fall into
the above categories but who is totally inept or grossly immoral
and who causes grave scandal and injury to the Church? Some, as
we saw earlier, would equate such crimes with heresy, which
would be adequate grounds for removal from office. Others, however, would stop short of applying the conciliar solution to any
situation except that of heresy, schism, and, perhaps, insanity.
How, then, would the Church deal with a wicked Pope? Medieval theologians suggested several remedies for correcting such
abuses. They apply primarily to wicked Popes and only partially
to incompetent ones. John of Torquemada suggested the following course of action: humble admonition; fraternal correction
drawn from Scripture and the lives of the saints; devout prayer;
personal resistance by the cardinals; refusal to accept illegal
benefices or promotions; and the convoking of a council by the

[64] *Opera omnia* (Paris: L. Vivès, 1858), Vol. 12, Tract. I, Disp. X,
De summo pontifice, Sect. VI, 317.
[65] Ibid., 318.
[66] Ibid.

cardinals for the purpose of admonition, not deposition. If all else fails, one must follow the example of God and patiently tolerate the unfortunate situation.[67]

Cardinal Cajetan made a similar but more forceful proposal. He admonished the princes and prelates not to be indifferent to papal abuse but to take positive action.

> Let them oppose the abuse of power which destroys, by suitable remedies as not obeying, not being servile in the face of evil actions, not keeping silence, by arguing and by urging leaders to follow the example of Paul and his precept found at the end of the Epistle to the Colossians [4:17]: "Tell Archippus, 'See that you fulfill the ministry you have received in the Lord.'" [Do this] and there will be little or no abuse of power.[68]

Cajetan, who lived under the pontificate of Alexander VI (1492–1503), had some experience with wicked Popes. He realized that human remedies are not always successful, arguing that prayer is the principal remedy that Christ has given the Church for the removal of "a believing but incorrigible Pope." Thus: "Let us turn to Christ, and the Pope, were he frantic, furious, tyrannical, a destroyer, dilapidator, and corrupter of the Church, will be overcome."[69]

Today communication systems, both ecclesial and secular, make it unlikely that a scandalous or harmfully inadequate Pope would long remain unnoticed. In all probability, appropriate action would be taken by the College of Cardinals, the Synod of Bishops, or the national episcopal conferences. Moreover, the outcry of negative public opinion might force such a Pope to resign, not that he would have to do so. If, on the other hand, the Pope should prove to be heretical, schismatic, or insane, then perhaps "the way of the council" would be used again. It does not

---

[67] *Summa de ecclesia*, op. cit., Lib. II, c. 106, pp. 246A–248B.

[68] *Scripta theologica*, Vol. I, *De comparatione auctoritatis papae et concilii cum apologia eiusdem tractatus*, ed. V. Pollet (Rome: Angelicum, 1936), Cap. 27, No. 412, pp. 179–80. Trans. from H. McSorley, op. cit., 216.

[69] Ibid., No. 420, p. 184.

follow, however, that there is an urgent need now to draw up legal norms for papal deposition. "To demand that law should foresee and make provision for every abnormal situation," as Bishop Butler observes, "is to relapse into legalism."[70]

Papal resignation and deposition are unusual and unsettling events in the Christian community. A fixed term of office or a fixed age limit for the Pope would presumably reduce the possibility of such drastic actions. Nevertheless, in the absence of such norms, it seems preferable for the conclusion of a papal reign to be left to the wisdom of Divine Providence rather than to the uncertainties of partisan politics and the inevitable controversies over whether the Pope should be pressured to resign or be forcibly deposed. In short, the peace and unity of the Church may, in the meantime, be best served by reliance on that final deposition that is death.

[70] C. Butler, *The Theology of Vatican II* (London: Darton, Longman & Todd, 1967), p. 106.

8 THE POPE OF THE FUTURE

> It matters little whether the new
> Pope be Bergamasque or not. Combined
> prayers should ensure that he be a wise
> and gentle man, and that he be a holy
> man and one who spreads holiness.
>
> POPE JOHN XXIII[1]

The papacy, despite its divine origins and its two-thousand-year history, still remains subject to change. Since the Church is in the world, it reflects its secular matrix even to the point sometimes of aping its methods. Yet again and again, it takes stock of itself and returns to its own unique heritage. We began this book by noting seven key transitions in papal history, from the Church's political toleration in 313 through its long and often disastrous flirtation with temporal power, occasioning numerous reforms and resulting at times in divided leadership and more permanently in divided membership. We saw, in the last hundred years, a re-emphasis on spiritual power, first its centralization, then its collegial partici-

[1] From a letter to the Bishop of Bergamo written by Angelo Cardinal Roncalli on the eve of the conclave of 1958 at which he was elected Pope John XXIII. Cited in M. Trevor, *Pope John* (Garden City, N.Y.: Doubleday & Company/Image Books, 1968), p. 244.

pation. After these major transitions, we find ourselves in the modern era, an era of theological pluralism and technological jeopardy, the papacy becoming less monarchical and more collegial, its focus less juridical and more pastoral and ecumenical. These new directions for the papacy give hope of a revitalized Christianity.

An intangible but hardly abstract sense of tradition enveloping the office and its holders may be the most significant obstacle to progress. To strike out in new directions is an awesome responsibility for a Pope, for the mantle of papal tradition rests heavily upon his shoulders. No Pope reaches the Vatican without a rich knowledge of Church history and a deep kinship with his predecessors. The impressive installations of John Paul I and John Paul II, with the choir in the background singing *Tu es Petrus,* symbolize perfectly the historical continuity of the office and the immense moral burden a Pope must bear.

Papal tradition, however, need not retard decision-making. The example of many Popes in the past who have faced new challenges or solved old problems by radically creative actions shows that tradition can be a springboard, not just a barrier. The force of circumstances necessitating prompt and proper decisions is always coupled with the light of the Holy Spirit, so that the papal "householder brings out from his storeroom things both new and old" (Mt. 13:52).

In this, the final chapter, I shall look to the future of the papacy. My criteria must be grounded in the past and shaped and inspired by the present, but, of course, not totally determined by it, for as Dean Inge warned: "The man who marries the spirit of the times soon finds himself a widower." So my criteria will be based on the inherent pastoral nature of the Petrine ministry. Theologians are ever suggesting ways of reforming the papacy.[2] This habit intensified after Vatican II and especially in the last

----

[2] For example, the *De consideratione* of St. Bernard of Clairvaux to Eugene III in the middle of the twelfth century; the *Libellus ad Leonem X* of P. Giustiniani and P. Quirini in 1513; and the *Consilium de emendenda ecclesia* commissioned by Paul III in 1537.

years of the pontificate of Paul VI.[3] The following observations, as part of this tradition, are made hopefully and humbly, since it is impossible to plot precisely the course of the papacy in transition. Now that we are at the beginning of a new pontifical era, with a Pope who could lead the Church into the third millennium, our yearning for papal updating and restructuring has increased. The personalities, institutions, and events of the future will continue to surprise us, but we can try to sketch the immediately apparent items on the papal agenda and the requisite qualifications for future Popes.

I. The Tasks Ahead

As the Pope learns to function less as a monarch and more as a colleague and pastor, he may find his office proportionately more difficult and complex. Yet, if his new role is fulfilled, as it can be with the help of the Spirit and the prayers and co-operation of the faithful, there will also be a welcome revitalization of the Christian Church. The issues the Pope faces are many and controversial, not all of them are susceptible of immediate solution, but they are required items on the papal agenda. Let us note briefly some of the major concerns of the papacy in the last years of the twentieth century. Of the ten issues discussed, the first six are specifically Roman Catholic problems, while the next four affect also the wider human community.

[3] In addition to the studies already cited throughout this book, the following appeared from 1974 to the death of Paul VI in 1978: *Servitium,* 8 (1974), 729–866; *Journal of Ecumenical Studies,* 11 (1974), 257–314 and 13 (1976), 345–404; G. Denzler, ed., *Das Papsttum in der Diskussion* (Regensburg: F. Pustet, 1974); H. Stirnimann and L. Vischer, eds., *Papsttum und Petrusamt* (Frankfurt: O. Lembeck, 1975); A. Brandenburg and H. J. Urban, eds., *Petrus und Papst* (Münster: Aschendorff, 1977). Since Pope Paul's death several popular items have also appeared: the statement of a group of ten international theologians, *Time* (Aug. 21, 1978), p. 71; "An Agenda for the Papacy" by R. P. McBrien, C. Davis, and L. Swidler in *Commonweal* (Sept. 1, 1978), pp. 560–64; and the January/ February 1979 issue of *New Catholic World* is devoted to the pastoral agenda of Pope John Paul II.

A. Vatican II

The Second Vatican Council (1962–65) marked the end of the Counter-Reformation and introduced a new consciousness of the Church and its mission. Reaction to it has differed. Peter Hebblethwaite, for example, called it "the most momentous event in the history of the Roman Catholic Church in this century,"[4] and Cardinal Siri of Genoa said it was "the greatest mistake in recent ecclesiastical history."[5] Both views have their contemporary adherents. That the reforms of Vatican II have met some resistance should not be surprising. Nearly every general council of the Church has been followed by a serious crisis. Vatican I had its Old Catholics and later the Modernists, and Vatican II has its Traditionalists and Radicals.

The full promise of Vatican II has not yet been realized. It has not reached what John Paul II calls "a maturity of movement and of life." In his first address as Pope, he said that the primary duty of his pontificate would be to promote "with prudent but encouraging action the most exact execution of the norms and directions of the Council."[6] This commitment is most welcome, because Rome itself has often failed to apply some of the major theological and pastoral principles of the Council. If the Holy See consistently carries out the ideas of Vatican II and encourages the faithful to accept them, then the Council will become what it was intended to be: an instrument of genuine reform and reunion. The Church, guided by decisive papal leadership, should continue to apply the teachings of Vatican II to the life of the universal and local Church by fostering the renewal of the liturgy, the laity, the priesthood, and the religious life. Such reform efforts may well significantly help in resolving the present vocation crisis. Fidelity to the directives of Vatican II is first in the papal agenda. The name taken by the last two Popes, John Paul, signifies this

4 *The Runaway Church* (New York: Seabury, 1975), p. 10.
5 Ibid., p. 12.
6 *Origins* (Oct. 26, 1978), Vol. 8, No. 19, 291.

continuity with the spirit of the Council, which was begun by John XXIII and completed by Paul VI.

B. Collegiality

One of the central themes of this book has been collegiality. Earlier, in Chapter 4, I expressed the hope that the papacy would become more collegial, that power and decision-making would be more widely diffused, and that there would be an increase in the sharing of responsibility between the Pope and the College of Bishops. The Pope needs the collective wisdom of the episcopate to help him resolve the pressing questions facing the Church. Concretely, this means an aggressive move to decentralize papal authority; to increase the function of the Synod of Bishops in the governance of the Church; and to give greater autonomy to episcopal conferences and diocesan councils. This kind of co-operation should extend to all levels of the Church; subsidiarity and legitimate diversity should be positively promoted. The Pope will not cease to be the head of the Church and the final arbiter in disputes, but he will emphasize his role as a fellow bishop who rules within rather than over the Church. Rigid centralization and anything that smacks of imperialism should have no place in the renewed papacy. The ideal for Church decision-making is clearly expressed by the Canon Law Society of America:

> The making of general policy decisions at the level of the universal Church should be reserved to the Pope and the Synod. The function of the Curia is to assist in the execution of these decisions. In the course of such execution, the Curia may issue administrative directives concerned with interdiocesan or supranational questions. The Curia should have no administrative authority in purely local matters.[7]

[7] In J. A. Coriden, ed., We, The People of God . . . : A Study of Constitutional Government for the Church (Huntington, Ind.: Our Sunday Visitor, 1968), p. 15.

C. Vatican Bureaucracy

The complexity and intransigence of the Church's central administration are legendary. Future Popes should work to improve the cumbersome Vatican bureaucracy by reorganizing the congregations, secretariats, commissions, tribunals, and other offices with an eye to greater efficiency and pastoral sensitivity. The internationalization process, begun by recent Popes, should continue, especially in respect to middle-management positions and diplomatic posts where Italians still predominate. Younger personnel, whose theological views represent the broad spectrum of legitimate contemporary thought, should be employed. Likewise, the number of women, lay and religious, should be greatly increased in the curial offices. Of the 3,000 employees of the Vatican, only 250 are women, admittedly an improvement over ten years ago, when there were only a dozen. But even today no women hold important executive or decision-making positions in the curial congregations. Lack of priestly ordination should not disqualify women from key administrative offices. Finally, Christians from other denominations should be invited to participate as consultants in the work of the Curia. In a word, the Curia should reflect the reformed papacy: pastoral, service-oriented, and responsive to the signs of the times.

D. Lay Participation

Vatican II recognized functional differences among members of the Church but also taught that the baptized share a fundamental sacramental dignity and equality. This theological truth, rooted in Scripture, has only begun to be implemented in the practical life of the Church. Much more, therefore, needs to be done, and the papacy in transition should foster greater lay participation in decision-making. An immediate priority is to devise a new procedure for the selection of bishops that would allow for an active lay voice. Many Catholics would agree with the observation of Hans Küng:

> For as long as I can contribute advice and work, but am excluded from decision-making, I remain, no matter how many fine things are said about my status, a second-class member of this community: I am more an object that is utilized than a subject who is actively responsible.[8]

E. Theological Issues

The Pope is the principal teacher in the Christian community with the responsibility of preserving the unity of faith and communion. Today this task is awesome, because nearly every aspect of the traditional teaching on faith and morals is the subject of intense theological debate. The issues include: Christology; Mariology; ecclesiology; the sacraments; sexual morality; birth control; abortion; divorce and remarriage; priestly celibacy; ordination of women; communal absolution; and intercommunion. Richard P. McBrien, for example, suggests that the new Pope symbolize his "unambiguous and progressive" leadership by revoking the teaching *Humanae vitae* against contraception; by abolishing mandatory celibacy for priests; and by beginning efforts that would eventually lead to the ordination of women to the priesthood and the episcopacy, the first step of which would be the admission of women to the diaconate.[9] Although John Paul II does not at this stage in his pontificate appear to accept these recommendations, the issues have not died. The result of much of the contemporary discussion on these and other questions has been a mixture of valuable insights and unsettling ambiguity. Should debate on these issues continue?

Some would urge the Pope to issue stern warnings to theologians who approach heterodoxy; to excommunicate those who are

---

[8] "Participation of the Laity in Church Leadership and in Church Elections," *Journal of Ecumenical Studies*, 6 (1969), 512.

[9] *Commonweal*, op. cit., p. 561.

clearly straying from the faith, and to allow only uniform texts
approved by the Holy See to be used in seminaries. Others, insist-
ing on the necessity of historical consciousness and development
of doctrine, contend that theological pluralism is essential to the
growth of tradition and that if the process of reinterpretation is allowed to continue, then a consensus will emerge that will deepen
our grasp of the faith. An international group of well-known theologians, speaking before the election of John Paul I, made a
relevant observation about the Pope as teacher:

> Free from anxiety, he should be able to give positive
> guidance rather than prohibition in all the decisive ques-
> tions affecting life and death, good and evil, including
> those matters where human sexuality is involved. He
> should not be a doctrinaire defender of ancient bastions,
> but rather—with all due respect for continuity in the
> Church's life and teaching—he should be a pastoral
> pioneer of a renewed preaching and teaching in the
> Church.[10]

One of the most critical of all theological issues is the role of
the magisterium or, to put it differently, the relationship between
the theologians and the magisterium. Most would agree with
John Paul II that "the objective importance of the magisterium
should always be kept in mind and safeguarded."[11] But what this
means in practice is still controverted. The old dichotomy between the *ecclesia docens* (the teaching Church) and the *ecclesia
discens* (the learning Church), with the theologians relegated to
the second group, must be rethought, for the charism of teaching
is found in both theologians and bishops. The Pope should encourage responsible theological debate by giving positive support,
guidance, and, at times, correction. The Pope has the undeniable
right and duty to teach and to preserve doctrinal integrity, but he
should use corrective measures only rarely and always with due
process.

10 *Time*, op. cit., p. 71.
11 *Origins* (Oct. 26, 1978), Vol. 8, No. 19, 293.

F. Canon Law

The present Code of Canon Law, with its 2414 canons, was promulgated in 1917 and went into effect a year later. Early in his pontificate, John XXIII announced his intention to modernize the Code and, on March 28, 1963, he established the Pontifical Commission for the Revision of the Code. Drafts of the new Code have been circulated, but the reaction has been largely negative. To quote the Canon Law Society of America: "The revision of law proposed to date is not acceptable in substance."[12] The Commission has been criticized for the secrecy that surrounds the revision process; for the failure to incorporate the ecclesiological principles of Vatican II; and for the lack of broad consultation. In respect to the latter, the CLSA notes: "Those who will be directly affected by various elements of the law—the Christian faithful, men or women, clergy, religious or lay—are not being consulted."[13] To remedy these deficiencies, the present Pope should restructure the Commission, clarify its mandate, and improve its procedures. Since universal Church law is so vital an element in the life of the Christian community, its revision should reflect the true nature of the Church and the needs of its members.

G. Spiritual Leadership

In an age of widespread unbelief, the papacy should help rekindle the spiritual aspirations of humanity. It is commonplace today to hear that Western civilization has forsaken the spiritual and embraced the material. Alexander Solzhenitsyn, for example, in his commencement address at Harvard University on June 8, 1978, criticized the West for its spiritual exhaustion, loss of cour-

[12] "A Statement Concerning the Revision of the Code of Canon Law," *The Jurist*, 38 (1978), 209.
[13] Ibid., 213.

age, moral mediocrity, and rationalistic humanism. "The human soul," he said, "longs for things higher, warmer, and purer than those offered by today's mass living habits."[14] In similar terms, John Paul I said in his inaugural address: "The danger for modern man is that he would reduce the earth to a desert, the person to an automaton, brotherly love to a planned collectivization, often introducing death where God wishes life."[15]

The papacy, whose greatest asset may well be its moral and inspirational authority, has to confront this situation. As part of its duty of evangelization, the papacy should work tirelessly to move the minds and hearts of people by exhortation and example. It should continue compassionately to heal the wounds that society inflicts on its members and to offer love, hope, and truth—all of which are necessary to build a renewed sense of spiritual worth. One way to accomplish this would be for the Pope to travel extensively as an apostle of Gospel spirituality. Papal travel should not be merely a public-relations device, but an opportunity for the Pope to demonstrate visibly his solidarity with all humanity.

H. Social Justice

Of the four billion people in the world, two thirds of them live below the level of subsistence. If the Church is to follow the Gospel mandate of love, then it should be the spokesman for this voiceless majority. Disadvantaged and oppressed peoples everywhere should be able to look to the Pope as their advocate. The Pope should work to sensitize the moral consciences of the affluent nations in order to encourage them to develop a global economic and political system that is built on justice and not on the exploitation of others. Widespread hunger, illiteracy, and the loss of basic human rights are world problems. Civil society has the primary duty to provide a life of dignity and peace, but when it fails to do so, the Church should use its moral authority to remind it of its responsibilities. The papacy should show the poor

14 *Time* (June 19, 1978), p. 33.
15 *Origins* (Sept. 7, 1978), Vol. 8, No. 12, 179.

of the world that it cares about them and is at their service. The words and actions of John Paul II during his trip to Mexico in 1979 illustrate how this can be done effectively. Finally, in its own quest for justice, the Church should not be blind to its own failings. It should honestly assess its own laws, policies, and programs to see that there is no trace of discrimination or exploitation, but rather a manifestation of love and justice of all in Christ.

I. Ecumenism

As the leader of the largest and most influential Christian body in the world, the Pope can exercise tremendous moral persuasion and encouragement in the cause of ecumenism. The words of John Paul I should be acceptable to any successor of Peter: "We intend to dedicate our prayerful attention to everything that would favor union. We will do so without diluting doctrine but, at the same time, without hesitation."[16] Moreover, a papal style that exhibits a genuine evangelical spirit and shuns authoritarianism in every form can do much in bringing Christians together. Besides considering Catholic membership in the World Council of Churches and the establishment of regular summit meetings with other Christian leaders, the Pope should also foster magisterial co-operation, institutional unity, pulpit and altar fellowship, and collaboration in works of social justice among Christians, as well as strengthen the ties that exist between the Jews, the Moslems, and other religious peoples.

J. Communism

According to Karl Marx, "the abolition of religion as the illusory happiness of the people is required for their real happiness." Atheism is the official position of the governments of Eastern Europe, and yet there are some sixty million Roman Catholics liv-

16 Ibid., p. 180.

ing in Russia and the Communist-bloc nations. An estimated 95 per cent of the populations of Poland and Lithuania are Catholic; 65 per cent in Hungary; and 60 per cent in Czechoslovakia. In the last twenty years, beginning with John XXIII, the Vatican has altered its policy toward the Marxist regimes of Eastern Europe, moving from confrontation to détente, from denunciation to dialogue. Paul VI was the chief architect of *Ostpolitik*, and Archbishop Casaroli, head of the Council for the Public Affairs of the Church, its leading negotiator and roving diplomat. Casaroli has since been made Secretary of State by John Paul II. Pope Paul, who met with several high-ranking Communist leaders, was able to win some concessions from a few nations: the right of the Church to nominate bishops, to teach religion, to celebrate Church festivals in public, and to accept a limited number of seminarians. Vatican efforts, however, have been criticized by both exiles from Eastern Europe and by some Catholics in the West who are strongly anticommunist. They argue that the concessions granted to the Church were minimal in view of the continuing religious persecution in those countries, and they urge the Vatican to take a hard-line policy against Communist oppression.

Pope John Paul II, as former cardinal archbishop of Cracow, knows communism intimately and has been its resilient enemy. It is too early to know how he will deal with the relationship between the Church and Communist nations.[17] But it is certain that the "Church of Silence" will find in him a stanch advocate who will use his office to alleviate religious persecution and to promote religious freedom. It will be a formidable test of strength.

II. The Background of Future Candidates

It may seem odd to discuss the characteristics of future papal candidates when we are now at the start of a new pontificate, and when it is unlikely that the Church will be electing another Pope for many years. Nevertheless, I have written this section because

---

17 There are an estimated four million Catholics in Cuba and some five million in Asian countries under Communist control.

I believe that it is beneficial to evaluate the factors influencing the choice of a Pope. So my remarks are not directed specifically to the present Pope—who in fact seems to meet admirably the more decisive criteria I have listed—but rather to suggest some elements that may be significant in the election of his successors. I shall treat four items, not all of them of equal importance: age, nationality, experience, and spirituality.

A. Age

The contemporary emphasis on youth and its correlative, prejudice against the old, does not apply to the papacy. Popes are generally elected at an age when most people begin their retirement. Only one of the seven Popes elected in this century was below the age of sixty at the time of his election. John XXIII was seventy-six, and Paul VI and John Paul I were both sixty-five. The one exception is John Paul II, who at fifty-eight is the youngest Pope to be elected in 132 years—that is, since the election of Pius IX (1846–78), who was fifty-four.

The usual argument given for the practice of electing older men to the papacy is that wisdom comes with age. An older candidate has had a variety and depth of life experiences, has developed an integrated spiritual, intellectual, and psychological maturity, and has proven himself competent and successful. The cardinal electors know his ability and have some idea of how he would act as Pope. Although this does not rule out the unexpected—John XXIII, the *papa di passaggio,* was the notable exception—the probability is that an older man will act the way he has in the past.

A more subtle and compelling reason for the practice of electing older Popes is the uneasiness of the electors over the prospect of a very long papacy. They are generally reluctant to choose someone in his forties who could conceivably rule the Church for as long as forty years. In view of that possibility, older is better.

Future electors, which should include representatives—both clerical and lay—from the entire Church, should consider the alternatives we discussed earlier: an age limit or a set term of office for the Pope. If such a practice were adopted, it would allow younger men to be elected who might better be able to cope with the physical demands of the office and who would bring to it a fresh approach. It would also allay the fears of an extended pontificate. If the Church does not move in that direction, then most likely future Popes will continue to be chosen from the ranks of the older cardinals.

Incidentally, another biological aspect, other than that of age, would be the sex of the papal candidate. To some this item may appear to be irrelevant, since the ordination of women to the priesthood is still prohibited by the Roman Catholic Church, and in the past only males have been elected Popes. For many, however, it is a serious question rooted in justice. It may be argued that if the papacy is a sacramental-sacerdotal reality, then the possibility of a woman Pope is simply a corollary to the debate over the ordination of women to the priesthood. If the Church decides to ordain women priests, there would be no theological reason to exclude women from the office of bishop and Pope.

In 1976, Rome issued a formal declaration that reaffirmed the exclusion of women from the priesthood.[18] It called the example of Christ and the unbroken tradition of both the East and the West as normative and expressive of God's will for the Church. It further argued that since a priest acts in the person of Christ and as his image, only men can be ordained. Reaction to the Declaration was swift and generally negative.[19] For example, a report submitted to the Catholic Theological Society of America in 1978 presented a detailed analysis of the arguments from Scripture, tradition, theology, and anthropology. It concluded that it "does not, in sum, find that the arguments adduced on the question present any serious grounds to justify the exclusion of women from ordi-

---

[18] *Inter insigniores, Acta apostolicae sedis,* 69 (1977), 98–116. The Declaration is dated October 15, 1976. It was approved by Paul VI, who ordered its publication. English translation: *Declaration on the Question of the Admission of Women to the Ministerial Priesthood* (Washington, D.C.: USCC, 1977).

[19] See L. Swidler and A. Swidler, eds., *Women Priests: A Catholic Commentary on the Vatican Declaration* (New York: Paulist, 1977).

nation to pastoral office in the Catholic Church."[20] The debate continues, but until it is resolved in favor of women's ordination, there will be no possibility of a woman exercising the Petrine ministry.

B. Nationality

The papacy is open to any nationality, but over 200 of the 264 successors of St. Peter have been Italian. During the past 1,000 years, only 22 of the 125 Popes have been non-Italians. Twelve of them were French, four German, two Spanish, one English, one Portuguese, one Dutch, and, finally, one Polish Pope, John Paul II, the first non-Italian to be named Bishop of Rome in 455 years—since the Dutch Pope Adrian VI (1522–23). The latter's pontificate of twenty months was a turbulent one at the beginning of the Protestant Reformation. We can have some idea of what the Romans thought of him, since after his death they honored the physician who failed to save his life.

The election of John Paul II is a significant event in recent papal history. By breaking a long-standing precedent, it dramatizes the international and universal character of Roman Catholicism and symbolizes the transnational breadth of the faith. This change from the provincial image of the papacy owing to its Italian associations goes a long way in meeting a typical Protestant objection: "There is no possibility that the papal office could ever become acceptable to the Reformed churches unless it were clearly and radically freed from its almost exclusively Italian character."[21] The present Pope begins his pontificate with a decided ecumenical advantage.

[20] *A Report on the Status of Women in Church and Society: Considered in Light of the Question of Women's Ordination,* ed. S. Butler (Bronx, N.Y.: Catholic Theological Society of America, 1978), p. 47.
[21] Ross Mackenzie, "The Reformed Tradition and the Papacy," *Journal of Ecumenical Studies,* 13 (1976), 366.

C. Experience

A Pope, it should be noted, is above all else the servant of the Church. As such he participates uniquely in the Church's mission, which is, according to Vatican II, "to make God the Father and His incarnate Son present and in a sense visible."[22] In selecting a Pope who can communicate Christ to the world, the electors must carefully evaluate a candidate's background in their search for one with broad pastoral, academic, and administrative experience.

The pastoral requirement is clearly needed if someone is to be an effective minister to all believers. The papal candidate should be one who has experienced personally the joys, sufferings, and triumphs of the People of God, who has developed a deep concern for all that is human, and who has actively worked for an extended period of time in the parochial mission of the Church. Such an involvement would provide the future Pope with a firsthand awareness of the urgent needs of Christians and would foster a sense of compassion for those struggling to live according to Christian ideals. More pertinently, what a future Pope has learned in his own pastoral ministry will be reflected in the way he exercises the Petrine apostolate. A residential bishop, therefore, is a more preferable candidate than a curial official who has spent most of his priestly life in administrative tasks.

Several criteria can be used to judge a candidate's pastoral background. First, his zeal for evangelization. Does he speak with clarity and conviction about the Gospel and relate it realistically to contemporary needs? Second, his co-operation with other Christians. Is he autocratic or does he welcome advice and consultation not only with clergy and religious, but also with the laity? Third, his ecumenical spirit. Does he show a deep desire for Christian unity? Fourth, his social awareness. Is he sensitive to the needs of the oppressed, the dehumanization in modern culture, and the dangers of industrial technology?

[22] *The Pastoral Constitution on the Church in the Modern World* (*Gaudium et spes*), Art. 21.

The academic qualifications of a future Pope will include a sound theological training and a continuing interest in current issues. This does not mean that he need be a professional theologian, but he should be well read theologically, have a familiarity with contemporary thought, and recognize the value of theological research and debate. A grasp of the history of theology and some knowledge of the social sciences will enable a future Pope to contextualize reform movements and not be threatened by the prospect of change. The candidate should be a cultured and intelligent person who wears his learning lightly but who is able to assess critically the state of the Church and its priorities. He should be able and willing to engage in the widest possible kind of consultation before issuing any major doctrinal or disciplinary statement.

The administrative background of a Pope to be, although less important than his pastoral or academic experience, is hardly insignificant. Granting that the reformed papacy will be less bureaucratic and more collegial, there will still be many administrative decisions to be made, from formulation of policies and programs to the appointment and supervision of personnel, not to mention the inevitable crises that beset any international organization. In evaluating a candidate's administrative experience, the electors should inquire about his ability to work with others in a collegial manner and his willingness to delegate authority. Is he a true spiritual leader or simply an efficient executive?

An excellent summary of the kind of background a future Pope should have is found in the "Provisional Plan for Choosing Bishops in the United States," prepared by the Canon Law Society of America in 1971:

> In selecting a bishop the Church should consider carefully a man's previous experience. Sound and deep theological learning are indispensable. But theological wisdom and awareness, administrative skill, and secular knowledge are only developed through varied experience. Such competence should be demonstrated before a man is chosen to be a bishop; but skills and experience are not the full measure of a bishop. He must visibly share the basic concerns of his people if he is to share with them his own insight into the Christian message. Therefore, he

will need to be straightforward in his motivation, sponta-
neous in his way of speaking to and responding to men's
real concerns, and tireless in his wish to know and heal
human weakness. Such personal dynamism, rooted in the
priesthood of Jesus Christ, is a guarantee that the authority conferred in the episcopacy will grow into trustworthy
leadership.[23]

D. Spirituality

The spiritual quality of a papal candidate is much more important than any consideration of age, nationality, or experience.
Micah 6:8 succinctly formulates the basic criteria of holiness:
"This is what Yahweh asks of you: only this, to act justly, to love
tenderly, and to walk humbly with your God." A well-qualified
Pope who fulfills this mandate cannot help but have a successful
pontificate—at least in the eyes of the Lord. Each Pope, of course,
will have his idiosyncrasies and failings; papal temperaments and
styles will differ. Nevertheless, there is a spiritual ideal that,
though appropriated in different ways, still remains a constant re-
minder of what is demanded of the successor of St. Peter. Let us
consider two aspects of this ideal: personal holiness and spiritual
leadership.

As a spiritual person, the Pope should be deeply committed
to the Christian life with a positive and confident view of the
power of the Spirit at work in the world. By his words and actions he should convey true holiness, not superficial piety. His
faith should be strong enough to recognize the Spirit in freedom
but sensitive enough to have experienced the struggle to believe
and the utter dependence on God's healing grace. As a humbly
reflective person, he should realize his own weaknesses and those
of others and see himself in solidarity with all humanity. His
hope should be resolute in the face of opposition, because it is
rooted in Christ. Avoiding both presumption and despair, the
Pope should communicate his trust in God's promised help and in

[23] *Procedure for the Selection of Bishops in the United States* (Canon
Law Society of America, 1973), p. 21.

the indestructibility of the Church. Finally, his love should radiate the love of the Lord for his people. The Pope will be judged ultimately not as a theologian, diplomat, or administrator, but as a man of God. A thematic question throughout his pontificate will be: "Simon, son of John, do you love me?" (Jn. 21:15).

The Christian community needs a Pope who is not aloof but with whom they can identify. He should be a good and prayerful person who does not conceal his own humanity, who can act with a warmth that shows he cares, and who can inspire others to imitate the example of Jesus. In a word, he should be someone who is moved by the Spirit and who from the Spirit has received "love, joy, peace, patience, kindness, goodness, truthfulness, gentleness, and self-control" (Ga. 5:22).

As a pastoral leader, the Pope should recognize that the papal office is one of ministry and not of domination; one of service and not of control. His prime concern should be with people and not with institutions. By calmness and confidence, he should strive to foster a lively faith among his followers. This means that as a leader he must have a certain ego strength and sense of self-worth that will enable him to give encouragement and creative orientation to others. A trusting, open, and dialogic leadership will help him avoid the dangers of suspicion, inflexibility, and rule by fiat. The Pope should be able to take advice and not be trapped by his advisers. Tradition and continuity will be important to him, but he will also recognize that tradition must grow in response to needs. Moreover, he should have the courage to reverse decisions after careful thought and prayer, admit his mistakes, and abandon outdated positions. The Pope should be prudent but not vacillating, firm but not dictatorial. Finally, the Pope should possess or pray for the charism of discernment—the gift of detecting the movement of the Spirit and of responding to his guidance.

In concluding the spiritual profile of a Pope, I turn to St. Benedict who, in speaking of the qualities the abbot of a monastery ought to possess, gives a superb description of the kind of leadership that characterizes the head of the universal Church. In

Chapter 64 of his Rule, written in the sixth century, St. Benedict advises:

> Once he has been constituted, let the abbot always bear in mind what a burden he has undertaken and to whom he will have to give an account of his stewardship, and let him know that his duty is rather to profit his brethren than to preside over them. He must therefore be learned in the divine law, that he may have a treasure of knowledge from which to bring forth new things and old. He must be chaste, sober, and merciful. Let him exalt mercy above judgment, that he himself may obtain mercy. He should hate vices; he should love the brethren. . . . In his commands let him be prudent and considerate; and whether the work he enjoins concerns God or the world, let him be discreet and moderate, bearing in mind the discretion of holy Jacob, who said, "If I cause my flocks to be overdriven, they will all die in one day" (Gn. 33:13). Taking this, then, and other examples of discretion, the mother of virtues, let him so temper all things that the strong may have something to strive after, and the weak may not fall back in dismay.[24]

In the last analysis, the papacy—exalted institution that it may be—is the man. True, it is a man so graced and circumstanced that, during his reign, he is unique among men, but still a man. The ancient title "Vicar of Christ" is no longer theologically popular; it is thought to suggest a divinization of the Pope and to inspire an absolutism harmful to Catholics and repugnant to non-Catholics. Yet, on the other hand, the Pope cannot be called the vicar of the faithful. He is not their vicar, but their leader, albeit a collegial and pastoral one. Political and symbolic functions do not adequately characterize one who has been directly empowered by God with ruling the universal Church.

Nevertheless, the Pope remains a man, limited by his natural

[24] St. Benedict's Rule for Monasteries, trans. L. J. Doyle (Collegeville, Minn.: St. John's Abbey Press, 1948), pp. 83–84. A similar description is found in the Constitution of the Society of Jesus written by St. Ignatius of Loyola: Pt. IX, Chap. 2, "The Kind of Person the Superior General Should Be" (The Constitutions of the Society of Jesus, trans. G. E. Ganss [St. Louis: The Institute of Jesuit Sources, 1970], pp. 309–11).

gifts, education, and experience and by his geographical, social, and cultural milieu. He needs the prayers of all to help him respond to the graces of his supreme office, for whatever hopes we have for a renewed Church crucially involve this man who has been placed by Divine Providence upon the Chair of Peter. But in that very dependence on one frail man, the Church has unswerving confidence in the divine help promised him, for as Christ said to Peter: "I have prayed for you, that your faith may not fail and you, being once converted, confirm your brethren" (Lk. 22:32). Christ did not build his Church upon the strength of any man, but on the grace of God, so that the Pope can do all things in him who strengthens him. The full fruition of this papal power, however, requires the prayers and co-operation of the faithful, who must never forget that the Pope, like Moses in the wilderness, is a man chosen by God to lead them into the promised land, but that he can lead them there only if they are willing to be led and not stiff-necked and stubborn, lusting after false gods. Only if the Pope and the People of God work together in faith will Christ bring his whole body into glory. Christ does this with infinite wisdom and embracing love through that miracle of nature and grace, the papacy ever in transition.

A LIST OF THE POPES

The following catalogue of the Popes and the principal antipopes is based on the 1979 edition of the *Annuario Pontificio* and the standard historical works on the papacy. A Roman numeral in parentheses after a Pope's name indicates a lack of clarity in the historical evidence. I have listed the Popes in numerical order, but it should be noted that the legitimacy of certain Popes (for example, Dioscorus [530], Stephen [752], Leo VIII [963–65], Benedict V [964], and others) is still controverted. The dates for the first two hundred years are not always reliable.

NAME	NATIONALITY	LENGTH OF PONTIFICATE
1. St. Peter	Palestinian	?–67
2. St. Linus	Italian	67–76
3. St. Anacletus (Cletus)	Roman	76–88
4. St. Clement I	Roman	88–97
5. St. Evaristus	Greek	97–105
6. St. Alexander I	Roman	105–15
7. St. Sixtus I	Roman	115–25
8. St. Telesphorus	Greek	125–36
9. St. Hyginus	Greek	136–40
10. St. Pius I	Italian	140–55
11. St. Anicetus	Syrian	155–66
12. St. Soter	Italian	166–75
13. St. Eleutherius	Greek	175–89

14.	St. Victor I	African	189–99
15.	St. Zephyrinus	Roman	199–217
16.	St. Callistus I	Roman	217–22
	St. Hippolytus	Roman	217–35 Antipope
17.	St. Urban I	Roman	222–30
18.	St. Pontian	Roman	July 21, 230–Sept. 28, 235
19.	St. Anterus	Greek	Nov. 21, 235–Jan. 3, 236
20.	St. Fabian	Roman	Jan. 10, 236–Jan. 20, 250
21.	St. Cornelius	Roman	Mar. 251–June 253
	Novatian	Roman	251 Antipope
22.	St. Lucius I	Roman	June 25, 253–Mar. 5, 254
23.	St. Stephen I	Roman	May 12, 254–Aug. 2, 257
24.	St. Sixtus II	Greek	Aug. 30, 257–Aug. 6, 258
25.	St. Dionysius	Unknown	July 22, 259–Dec. 26, 268
26.	St. Felix I	Roman	Jan. 5, 269–Dec. 30, 274
27.	St. Eutychian	Italian	Jan. 4, 275–Dec. 7, 283
28.	St. Gaius	Dalmatian	Dec. 17, 283–Apr. 22, 296
29.	St. Marcellinus	Roman	June 30, 296–Oct. 25, 304
30.	St. Marcellus I	Roman	May 27, 308–Jan. 16, 309
31.	St. Eusebius	Greek	Apr. 18, 309–Aug. 17, 309
32.	St. Miltiades	African	July 2, 311–Jan. 11, 314
33.	St. Sylvester I	Roman	Jan. 31, 314–Dec. 31, 335
34.	St. Mark	Roman	Jan. 18, 336–Oct. 7, 336
35.	St. Julius I	Roman	Feb. 6, 337–Apr. 12, 352
36.	Liberius	Roman	May 17, 352–Sept. 24, 366
	Felix II	Roman	355–Nov. 22, 365 Antipope
37.	St. Damasus I	Spanish	Oct. 1, 366–Dec. 11, 384
	Ursinus	Roman	366–67 Antipope
38.	St. Siricius	Roman	Dec. 15, 384–Nov. 26, 399
39.	St. Anastasius I	Roman	Nov. 27, 399–Dec. 19, 401
40.	St. Innocent I	Italian	Dec. 22, 401–Mar. 12, 417
41.	St. Zosimus	Greek	Mar. 18, 417–Dec. 26, 418
42.	St. Boniface I	Roman	Dec. 28, 418–Sept. 4, 422
	Eulalius	Roman	418–19 Antipope
43.	St. Celestine I	Italian	Sept. 10, 422–July 27, 432
44.	St. Sixtus III	Roman	July 31, 432–Aug. 19, 440
45.	St. Leo I, the Great	Italian	Sept. 29, 440–Nov. 10, 461
46.	St. Hilary	Sardinian	Nov. 19, 461–Feb. 29, 468
47.	St. Simplicius	Italian	Mar. 3, 468–Mar. 10, 483
48.	St. Felix III (II)	Roman	Mar. 13, 483–Mar. 1, 492
49.	St. Gelasius I	African	Mar. 1, 492–Nov. 21, 496
50.	Anastasius II	Roman	Nov. 24, 496–Nov. 19, 498
51.	St. Symmachus	Sardinian	Nov. 22, 498–July 19, 514
	Lawrence	Roman	498; 501–5 Antipope
52.	St. Hormisdas	Italian	July 20, 514–Aug. 6, 523
53.	St. John I	Italian	Aug. 13, 523–May 18, 526
54.	St. Felix IV (III)	Italian	July 12, 526–Sept. 22, 530

NAME	NATIONALITY	LENGTH OF PONTIFICATE
55. Boniface II	Roman	Sept. 22, 530–Oct. 17, 532
Dioscorus	Alexandrian	Sept. 22, 530–Oct. 14, 530 Antipope
56. John II	Roman	Jan. 2, 533–May 8, 535
57. St. Agapitus I	Roman	May 13, 535–Apr. 22, 536
58. St. Silverius	Italian	June 1, 536–Nov. 11, 537
59. Vigilius	Roman	Mar. 29, 537–June 7, 555
60. Pelagius I	Roman	Apr. 16, 556–Mar. 4, 561
61. John III	Roman	July 17, 561–July 13, 574
62. Benedict I	Roman	June 2, 575–July 30, 579
63. Pelagius II	Roman	Nov. 26, 579–Feb. 7, 590
64. St. Gregory I, the Great	Roman	Sept. 3, 590–Mar. 12, 604
65. Sabinian	Italian	Sept. 13, 604–Feb. 22, 606
66. Boniface III	Roman	Feb. 19–Nov. 12, 607
67. St. Boniface IV	Italian	Aug. 25, 608–May 8, 615
68. St. Deusdedit I (Adeodatus)	Roman	Oct. 19, 615–Nov. 8, 618
69. Boniface V	Italian	Dec. 23, 619–Oct. 25, 625
70. Honorius I	Italian	Oct. 27, 625–Oct. 12, 638
71. Severinus	Roman	May 28–Aug. 7, 640
72. John IV	Dalmatian	Dec. 24, 640–Oct. 12, 642
73. Theodore I	Greek	Nov. 24, 642–May 14, 649
74. St. Martin I	Italian	July 649–Sept. 16, 655
75. St. Eugene I	Roman	Aug. 10, 654–June 2, 657
76. St. Vitalian	Italian	July 30, 657–Jan. 27, 672
77. Deusdedit II (Adeodatus)	Roman	Apr. 11, 672–June 17, 676
78. Donus	Roman	Nov. 2, 676–Apr. 11, 678
79. St. Agatho	Sicilian	June 27, 678–Jan. 10, 681
80. St. Leo II	Sicilian	Aug. 17, 682–July 3, 683
81. St. Benedict II	Roman	June 26, 684–May 8, 685
82. John V	Syrian	July 23, 685–Aug. 2, 686
83. Conon	Unknown	Oct. 21, 686–Sept. 21, 687
Theodore	Roman	687 Antipope
Paschal	Roman	687 Antipope
84. St. Sergius I	Syrian	Dec. 15, 687–Sept. 8, 701
85. John VI	Greek	Oct. 30, 701–Jan. 11, 705
86. John VII	Greek	Mar. 1, 705–Oct. 18, 707
87. Sisinnius	Syrian	Jan. 15, 708–Feb. 4, 708
88. Constantine	Syrian	Mar. 25, 708–Apr. 9, 715
89. St. Gregory II	Roman	May 19, 715–Feb. 11, 731
90. St. Gregory III	Syrian	Mar. 18, 731–Nov. 741
91. St. Zachary	Greek	Dec. 10, 741–Mar. 22, 752
92. Stephen (II)	Roman	Mar. 23–25, 752
93. Stephen II (III)	Roman	Mar. 26, 752–Apr. 26, 757

94.	St. Paul I	Roman	Apr. 29, 757–June 28, 767
	Constantine II	Italian	June 28, 767–69 Antipope
	Philip	Roman	768 Antipope
95.	Stephen III (IV)	Sicilian	Aug. 1, 768–Jan. 24, 772
96.	Adrian I	Roman	Feb. 1, 772–Dec. 25, 795
97.	St. Leo III	Roman	Dec. 26, 795–June 12, 816
98.	Stephen IV (V)	Roman	June 22, 816–Jan. 24, 817
99.	St. Paschal I	Roman	Jan. 25, 817–Feb. 11, 824
100.	Eugene II	Roman	Feb. 824–Aug. 827
101.	Valentine	Roman	Aug.–Sept. 827
102.	Gregory IV	Roman	827–Jan. 844
	John	Roman	Jan. 844 Antipope
103.	Sergius II	Roman	Jan. 844–Jan. 27, 847
104.	St. Leo IV	Roman	Jan. 847–July 17, 855
105.	Benedict III	Roman	July 855–Apr. 17, 858
	Anastasius	Roman	Aug.–Sept. 855 Antipope
106.	St. Nicholas I, the Great	Roman	Apr. 24, 858–Nov. 13, 867
107.	Adrian II	Roman	Dec. 14, 867–Dec. 14, 872
108.	John VIII	Roman	Dec. 14, 872–Dec. 16, 882
109.	Marinus I	Italian	Dec. 16, 882–May 15, 884
110.	St. Adrian III	Roman	May 17, 884–Sept. 885
111.	Stephen V (VI)	Roman	Sept. 885–Sept. 14, 891
112.	Formosus	Italian	Oct. 6, 891–Apr. 4, 896
113.	Boniface VI	Roman	Apr. 896
114.	Stephen VI (VII)	Roman	May 896–Aug. 897
115.	Romanus	Italian	Aug.–Nov. 897
116.	Theodore II	Roman	Dec. 897
117.	John IX	Italian	Jan. 898–Jan. 900
118.	Benedict IV	Roman	Jan. 900–July 903
119.	Leo V	Italian	July–Sept. 903
	Christopher	Roman	July 903–Jan. 904 Antipope
120.	Sergius III	Roman	Jan. 29, 904–Apr. 14, 911
121.	Anastasius III	Roman	Apr. 911–June 913
122.	Lando	Italian	July 913–Feb. 914
123.	John X	Italian	Mar. 914–May 928
124.	Leo VI	Roman	May–Dec. 928
125.	Stephen VII (VIII)	Roman	Dec. 928–Feb. 931
126.	John XI	Roman	Feb. 931–Dec. 935
127.	Leo VII	Roman	Jan. 3, 936–July 13, 939
128.	Stephen VIII (IX)	Roman	July 14, 939–Oct. 942
129.	Marinus II	Roman	Oct. 30, 942–May 946
130.	Agapetus II	Roman	May 10, 946–Dec. 955
131.	John XII	Roman	Dec. 16, 955–May 14, 964

NAME	NATIONALITY	LENGTH OF PONTIFICATE
132. Leo VIII	Roman	Dec. 4, 963–Mar. 1, 965
133. Benedict V	Roman	May 22–June 23, 964
134. John XIII	Roman	Oct. 1, 965–Sept. 6, 972
135. Benedict VI	Roman	Jan. 19, 973–June 974
Boniface VII	Roman	June–July 974; Antipope Aug. 984–July 985
136. Benedict VII	Roman	Oct. 974–July 10, 983
137. John XIV	Italian	Dec. 983–Aug. 20, 984
138. John XV	Roman	Aug. 985–Mar. 996
139. Gregory V	German	May 3, 996–Feb. 18, 999
John XVI	Greek	Apr. 997–Feb. 998 Antipope
140. Sylvester II	French	Apr. 2, 999–May 12, 1003
141. John XVII	Roman	June–Dec. 1003
142. John XVIII	Roman	Jan. 1004–July 1009
143. Sergius IV	Roman	July 31, 1009–May 12, 1012
144. Benedict VIII	Roman	May 18, 1012–Apr. 9, 1024
Gregory	Roman	1012 Antipope
145. John XIX	Roman	Apr. 1024–32
146. Benedict IX	Roman	1032–44; 1045; 1047–48
147. Sylvester III	Roman	Jan. 20–Feb. 10, 1045
148. Gregory VI	Roman	May 5, 1045–Dec. 20, 1046
149. Clement II	German	Dec. 24, 1046–Oct. 9, 1047
150. Damasus II	German	July 17–Aug. 9, 1048
151. St. Leo IX	German	Feb. 12, 1049–Apr. 19, 1054
152. Victor II	German	Apr. 16, 1055–July 28, 1057
153. Stephen IX (X)	German	Aug. 3, 1057–Mar. 29, 1058
Benedict X	Roman	Apr. 5, 1058–Jan. 1059 Antipope
154. Nicholas II	French	Jan. 24, 1059–July 27, 1061
155. Alexander II	Italian	Oct. 1, 1061–Apr. 21, 1073
Honorius II	Italian	Oct. 28, 1061–1072 Antipope
156. St. Gregory VII	Italian	Apr. 22, 1073–May 25, 1085
Clement III	Italian	June 26, 1080–Sept. 8, 1100 Antipope
157. Bl. Victor III	Italian	May 24, 1086–Sept. 16, 1087
158. Bl. Urban II	French	Mar. 12, 1088–July 29, 1099
159. Paschal II	Italian	Aug. 13, 1099–Jan. 21, 1118
Theodoric	Roman	1100 Antipope
Albert	Italian	1102 Antipope
Sylvester IV	Roman	Nov. 18, 1105–11 Antipope
160. Gelasius II	Italian	Jan. 24, 1118–Jan. 28, 1119
Gregory VIII	French	Mar. 8, 1118–21 Antipope
161. Callistus II	French	Feb. 2, 1119–Dec. 13, 1124
162. Honorius II	Italian	Dec. 15, 1124–Feb. 13, 1130
Celestine II	Roman	Dec. 1124 Antipope
163. Innocent II	Roman	Feb. 14, 1130–Jan. 25, 1143

	Anacletus II	Roman	Feb. 14, 1130–Jan. 25, 1138 Antipope
	Victor IV	Roman	Mar. 1138–May 29, 1138 Antipope
164.	Celestine II	Italian	Sept. 26, 1143–Mar. 8, 1144
165.	Lucius II	Italian	Mar. 12, 1144–Feb. 15, 1145
166.	Bl. Eugene III	Italian	Feb. 15, 1145–July 8, 1153
167.	Anastasius IV	Roman	July 12, 1153–Dec. 3, 1154
168.	Adrian IV	English	Dec. 4, 1154–Sept. 1, 1159
169.	Alexander III	Italian	Sept. 7, 1159–Aug. 30, 1181
	Victor IV	Roman	Sept. 7, 1159–Apr. 20, 1164 Antipope
	Paschal III	Italian	Apr. 22, 1164–Sept. 20, 1168 Antipope
	Callistus III	Hungarian	Sept. 1168–Aug. 29, 1178 Antipope
	Innocent III	Italian	Sept. 29, 1179–80 Antipope
170.	Lucius III	Italian	Sept. 1, 1181–Sept. 25, 1185
171.	Urban III	Italian	Nov. 25, 1185–Oct. 20, 1187
172.	Gregory VIII	Italian	Oct. 21–Dec. 17, 1187
173.	Clement III	Roman	Dec. 19, 1187–Mar. 1191
174.	Celestine III	Roman	Mar. 30, 1191–Jan. 8, 1198
175.	Innocent III	Italian	Jan. 8, 1198–July 16, 1216
176.	Honorius III	Roman	July 18, 1216–Mar. 18, 1227
177.	Gregory IX	Italian	Mar. 19, 1227–Aug. 22, 1241
178.	Celestine IV	Italian	Oct. 25–Nov. 10, 1241
179.	Innocent IV	Italian	June 25, 1243–Dec. 7, 1254
180.	Alexander IV	Italian	Dec. 12, 1254–May 25, 1261
181.	Urban IV	French	Aug. 29, 1261–Oct. 2, 1264
182.	Clement IV	French	Feb. 5, 1265–Nov. 29, 1268
183.	Bl. Gregory X	Italian	Sept. 1, 1271–Jan. 10, 1276
184.	Bl. Innocent V	French	Jan. 21–June 22, 1276
185.	Adrian V	Italian	July 11–Aug. 18, 1276
186.	John XXI	Portuguese	Sept. 8, 1276–May 20, 1277
187.	Nicholas III	Roman	Nov. 25, 1277–Aug. 22, 1280
188.	Martin IV	French	Feb. 22, 1281–Mar. 28, 1285
189.	Honorius IV	Roman	Apr. 2, 1285–Apr. 3, 1287
190.	Nicholas IV	Italian	Feb. 22, 1288–Apr. 4, 1292
191.	St. Celestine V	Italian	July 5–Dec. 13, 1294
192.	Boniface VIII	Italian	Dec. 24, 1294–Oct. 11, 1303
193.	Bl. Benedict XI	Italian	Oct. 22, 1303–July 7, 1304
194.	Clement V	French	June 5, 1305–Apr. 20, 1314
195.	John XXII	French	Aug. 7, 1316–Dec. 4, 1334
	Nicholas V	Italian	May 12, 1328–Aug. 25, 1330 Antipope
196.	Benedict XII	French	Dec. 20, 1334–Apr. 25, 1342
197.	Clement VI	French	May 7, 1342–Dec. 6, 1352
198.	Innocent VI	French	Dec. 18, 1352–Sept. 12, 1362
199.	Bl. Urban V	French	Sept. 28, 1362–Dec. 19, 1370
200.	Gregory XI	French	Dec. 30, 1370–Mar. 26, 1378

NAME	NATIONALITY	LENGTH OF PONTIFICATE
201. Urban VI	Italian	Apr. 8, 1378–Oct. 15, 1389
202. Boniface IX	Italian	Nov. 2, 1389–Oct. 1, 1404
203. Innocent VII	Italian	Oct. 17, 1404–Nov. 6, 1406
204. Gregory XII	Italian	Nov. 30, 1406–July 4, 1415
Clement VII	French	Sept. 20, 1378–Sept. 16, 1394 Avignon Claimant
Benedict XIII	Spanish	Sept. 28, 1394–May 23, 1423 Avignon Claimant
Alexander V	Greek	June 26, 1409–May 3, 1410 Pisan Claimant
John XXIII	Italian	May 17, 1410–May 29, 1415 Pisan Claimant
205. Martin V	Roman	Nov. 11, 1417–Feb. 20, 1431
206. Eugene IV	Italian	Mar. 3, 1431–Feb. 23, 1447
Felix V	Italian	Nov. 5, 1439–Apr. 7, 1449 Antipope
207. Nicholas V	Italian	Mar. 6, 1447–Mar. 24, 1455
208. Callistus III	Spanish	Apr. 8, 1455–Aug. 6, 1458
209. Pius II	Italian	Aug. 19, 1458–Aug. 15, 1464
210. Paul II	Italian	Aug. 30, 1464–July 26, 1471
211. Sixtus IV	Italian	Aug. 9, 1471–Aug. 12, 1484
212. Innocent VIII	Italian	Aug. 29, 1484–July 25, 1492
213. Alexander VI	Spanish	Aug. 11, 1492–Aug. 18, 1503
214. Pius III	Italian	Sept. 22–Oct. 18, 1503
215. Julius II	Italian	Oct. 31, 1503–Feb. 21, 1513
216. Leo X	Italian	Mar. 9, 1513–Dec. 1, 1521
217. Adrian VI	Netherlands	Jan. 9, 1522–Sept. 14, 1523
218. Clement VII	Italian	Nov. 19, 1523–Sept. 25, 1534
219. Paul III	Roman	Oct. 13, 1534–Nov. 10, 1549
220. Julius III	Roman	Feb. 7, 1550–Mar. 23, 1555
221. Marcellus II	Italian	Apr. 9–May 1, 1555
222. Paul IV	Italian	May 23, 1555–Aug. 18, 1559
223. Pius IV	Italian	Dec. 25, 1559–Dec. 9, 1565
224. St. Pius V	Italian	Jan. 7, 1566–May 1, 1572
225. Gregory XIII	Italian	May 13, 1572–Apr. 10, 1585
226. Sixtus V	Italian	Apr. 24, 1585–Aug. 27, 1590
227. Urban VII	Roman	Sept. 15–Sept. 27, 1590
228. Gregory XIV	Italian	Dec. 5, 1590–Oct. 16, 1591
229. Innocent IX	Italian	Oct. 29–Dec. 30, 1591
230. Clement VIII	Italian	Jan. 30, 1592–Mar. 3, 1605
231. Leo XI	Italian	Apr. 1–Apr. 27, 1605
232. Paul V	Roman	May 16, 1605–Jan. 28, 1621
233. Gregory XV	Italian	Feb. 9, 1621–July 8, 1623
234. Urban VIII	Italian	Aug. 6, 1623–July 29, 1644
235. Innocent X	Roman	Sept. 15, 1644–Jan. 7, 1655
236. Alexander VII	Italian	Apr. 7, 1655–May 22, 1667
237. Clement IX	Italian	June 20, 1667–Dec. 9, 1669

238.	Clement X	Roman	Apr. 29, 1670–July 22, 1676
239.	Bl. Innocent XI	Italian	Sept. 21, 1676–Aug. 12, 1689
240.	Alexander VIII	Italian	Oct. 6, 1689–Feb. 1, 1691
241.	Innocent XII	Italian	July 12, 1691–Sept. 27, 1700
242.	Clement XI	Italian	Nov. 23, 1700–Mar. 19, 1721
243.	Innocent XIII	Roman	May 8, 1721–Mar. 7, 1724
244.	Benedict XIII	Italian	May 29, 1724–Feb. 21, 1730
245.	Clement XII	Italian	July 12, 1730–Feb. 6, 1740
246.	Benedict XIV	Italian	Aug. 17, 1740–May 3, 1758
247.	Clement XIII	Italian	July 6, 1758–Feb. 2, 1769
248.	Clement XIV	Italian	May 19, 1769–Sept. 22, 1774
249.	Pius VI	Italian	Feb. 15, 1775–Aug. 29, 1799
250.	Pius VII	Italian	Mar. 14, 1800–Aug. 20, 1823
251.	Leo XII	Italian	Sept. 28, 1823–Feb. 10, 1829
252.	Pius VIII	Italian	Mar. 31, 1829–Nov. 30, 1830
253.	Gregory XVI	Italian	Feb. 2, 1831–June 1, 1846
254.	Pius IX	Italian	June 16, 1846–Feb. 7, 1878
255.	Leo XIII	Italian	Feb. 20, 1878–July 20, 1903
256.	St. Pius X	Italian	Aug. 4, 1903–Aug. 20, 1914
257.	Benedict XV	Italian	Sept. 3, 1914–Jan. 22, 1922
258.	Pius XI	Italian	Feb. 6, 1922–Feb. 10, 1939
259.	Pius XII	Roman	Mar. 2, 1939–Oct. 9, 1958
260.	John XXIII	Italian	Oct. 28, 1958–June 3, 1963
261.	Paul VI	Italian	June 21, 1963–Aug. 6, 1978
262.	John Paul I	Italian	Aug. 26–Sept. 28, 1978
263.	John Paul II	Polish	Oct. 16, 1978–

APPENDIX II SELECTED BIBLIOGRAPHY

1. *The Papacy in Transition*

    (a)   *Lives of the Popes*

Caspar, E. *Geschichte des Papsttums von den Anfängen bis zur Höhe der Weltherrschaft*, 2 vols. Tübingen: J. C. B. Mohr, 1930–33.

Duchesne, L., ed. *Le liber pontificalis*, 2 vols., Paris: E. Thorin, 1886.

Falconi, C. *The Popes in the Twentieth Century*. Boston: Little, Brown, 1967.

Gontard, F. *The Popes*. London: Barrie and Rockliff, 1964.

Mann, H. K. *The Lives of the Popes in the Early Middle Ages*, 18 vols. London: Kegan Paul, Trench, Trübner, 1902–32.

Mollat, G. *The Popes at Avignon*. London: T. Nelson, 1963.

Pastor, L. von. *The History of the Papacy from the Close of the Middle Ages*, 40 vols. St. Louis: Herder, 1899–1933.

Seppelt, F. X. *Geschichte der Päpste von den Anfängen bis zur Mitte des zwansigsten Jahrhunderts*, 5 vols. Munich: Kösel, 1954–59.

Seppelt, F. X., and Schwaiger, G. *Geschichte der Päpste von Anfängen bis zur Gegenwart*. Munich: Kösel, 1964.

Sugrue, F. *Popes in the Modern World*. New York: T. Y. Crowell, 1961.

Weltin, E. G. *The Ancient Popes*. Westminster, Md.: Newman, 1964.

Other reliable sources of information are: New Catholic Encyclopedia, Encyclopaedia Britannica, Dictionnaire de théologie catholique, Dictionnaire d'histoire et de géographie ecclésiastiques, Dictionnaire d'archéologie chrétienne et de liturgie, Dictionnaire de droit canonique, and Lekicon für Theologie und Kirche.

(b) *Church Histories*

Bihlmeyer, K., and Tüchle, H. *Church History*, 3 vols. Westminster, Md.: Newman, 1958–66.

Cambridge Medieval History, esp. Vols. 5, 6, 7, and 8.

Denzler, G., ed. *Päpste und Papsttum*. Stuttgart: A. Hiersemann, 1971 ff.

D'Ormesson, W. *The Papacy*. New York: Hawthorn, 1959.

Fliche, A. and Martin, V. *Histoire de l'Église depuis les origines jusqu'à nos jours;* 21 vols. have so far appeared. Paris: Bloud & Gay, 1934– .

Haller, J. *Das Papsttum: Idee und Wirklichkeit*, 5 vols. 2nd ed. Basle: B. Schwabe, 1950–53.

Hefele, C. J. and Leclercq, H. *Histoire des conciles d'après des documents originaux*, 8 vols. Paris: Letouzey et Ané, 1907–21.

Hughes, P. *A History of the Church*, 3 vols. New York: Sheed & Ward, 1934–47.

Le Bras, G. *Histoire du droit et des institutions de l'Église en Occident*. Paris: Sirey, 1955 ff.

Winter, M. M. *Saint Peter and the Popes*. Baltimore: Helicon, 1960.

2. *The Case Against the Papacy*

(a) *Documentation*

Giles, E. *Documents Illustrating Papal Authority* A.D. 96–454. London: SPCK, 1952.

Mirbt, C. *Quellen zur Geschichte des Papsttums*, 4th ed. Tübingen: J. C. B. Mohr, 1934.

Shotwell, J. T. and Loomis, L. R. *The See of Peter*. New York: Columbia University Press, 1927.

(b) *New Testament and Early Church*

Batiffol, P. *Cathedra Petri. Études d'histoire ancienne de l'Église.* Paris: Cerf, 1938.

Brown, R. E.; Donfried, K. P.; and Reumann, J. *Peter in the New Testament.* Minneapolis: Augsburg; New York: Paulist, 1973. This study, part of the continuing Lutheran-Roman Catholic Dialogue, has an excellent bibliography on pp. 169–77.

Campenhausen, H. von. *Ecclesiastical Authority and Spiritual Power in the Church of the First Three Centuries.* Stanford: Stanford University Press, 1969.

Chapman, J. *Studies on the Early Papacy.* New York: Benziger, 1929.

Dix, G. *Jurisdiction in the Early Church: Episcopal and Papal.* London: The Church Literature Association, 1975.

Duchesne, L. *Early History of the Christian Church from Its Foundation to the End of the Third Century,* 3 vols., 4th ed. New York: Longmans Green & Todd, 1909–24.

———. *The Beginnings of the Temporal Sovereignty of the Popes* A.D. 754–1073. London: Kegan Paul, Trench, Trübner, 1908.

Hertling, L. *Communio: Church and Papacy in Early Christianity.* Chicago: Loyola University Press, 1972.

Jalland, T. G. *The Church and the Papacy.* London: SPCK, 1944.

McCue, J. F. "Roman Primacy in the Second Century and the Problem of the Development of Doctrine," *Theological Studies,* 25 (1964), 161–96.

———. "Roman Primacy in the First Three Centuries," in H. Küng, ed., *Papal Ministry in the Church, Concilium,* Vol. 64. New York: Herder and Herder (1971), 36–44.

———. "The Roman Primacy in the Patristic Era: The Beginnings Through Nicaea," in P. C. Empie and T. A. Murphy, eds., *Papal Primacy and the Universal Church.* Minneapolis: Augsburg, 1974, pp. 44–72.

Ullmann, W. "Leo I and the Theme of Papal Primacy," *The Journal of Theological Studies,* N.S. 11 (1960), 25–51.

3. *The Pope as Monarch*

(a) *The Medieval Papacy*

Barraclough, G. *The Medieval Papacy.* New York: Harcourt, Brace & World, 1968.

Carlyle, R. W. and A. J. *A History of Mediaeval Political Theory in the West*, 6 vols. New York: G. P. Putnam's Sons, 1903–36.

Congar, Y. *L'ecclésiologie du haut Moyen-Age*. Paris: Cerf, 1968.

Corti, G. *Il papa, vicario di Pietro. Contributo alla storia dell'idea papale*, 2nd ed. Brescia: Marcelliana, 1966.

Hull, R. *Medieval Theories of the Papacy*. London: Burns, Oates & Washbourne, 1934.

Kempf, F. "Die päpstliche Gewalt in der mitteralterlichen Welt," *Miscellanea historiae pontificiae*, 21 (1959), 117–69.

Maccarrone, M. *Vicarius Christi. Storia del titolo papale*. Rome: Facultas theologica pontificii athenaei lateranensis, 1952.

Markus, R. and John, E. *Pastors or Princes: A New Look at the Papacy and Hierarchy*. Washington, D.C.: Corpus, 1969.

Pacaut, M. *La théocratie. L'Église et le pouvoir au Moyen-Age*. Paris: Aubier, 1957.

Tierney, B. *Foundations of the Conciliar Theory*. Cambridge: Cambridge University Press, 1955.

Ullmann, W. *Medieval Papalism: The Political Theories of the Medieval Canonists*. London: Methuen, 1949.

——. *The Growth of Papal Government in the Middle Ages*, 3rd ed. London: Methuen, 1970.

——. *A Short History of the Papacy in the Middle Ages*. London: Methuen, 1972.

Watt, J. A. *The Theory of Papal Monarchy in the Thirteenth Century: The Contribution of the Canonists*. London: Burns & Oates, 1966.

(b) *Vatican I*

Aubert, R. *Vatican I*. Paris: L'Orante, 1964.

Betti, U. *La costituzione dommatica "Pastor aeternus" del concilio Vaticano I*. Rome: Antonianum, 1961.

Congar, Y., and Dupuy, B.-D., eds. *L'épiscopat et l'Église universelle, Unam Sanctam* 39. Paris: Cerf, 1962, esp. articles by G. Dejaifve, "Primauté et collégialité au premier concile du Vatican," 639–60; W. F. Dewan, " 'Potestas vere episcopalis' au premier concile du Vatican," 661–87; and G. Thils, "Potestas ordinaria," 689–707.

Dewan, W. F. "Preparation of the Vatican Council's Schema

on the Power and Nature of the Primacy," *Ephemerides theologicae lovanienses*, 36 (1960), 23–56.

Pottmeyer, H. J. *Unfehlbarkeit und Souveränität.* Mainz: M. Grünewald, 1975.

Thils, G. *La primauté pontificale. La doctrine de Vatican I. Les voies d'une révision.* Gembloux: Duculot, 1972.

Torrell, J.-P. *La théologie de l'épiscopat au premier concile du Vatican.* Paris: Cerf, 1961.

(c)   *Theological Discussion*

Bellarmine, R. *Omnia Opera, De controversiis christianae fidei,* I, *De romano pontifice,* Liber I. Naples: J. Giuliano, 1856.

Billot, L. *Tractatus de ecclesia Christi,* 5th ed., Vol. 1. Rome: Gregoriana, 1927.

Cajetan (Tommaso de Vio). *Scripta theologica,* Vol. I, *De comparatione auctoritatis papae et concilii cum apologia eiusdem tractatus,* ed. V. Pollet. Rome: Angelicum, 1936.

Journet, C. *The Church of the Word Incarnate,* Vol. 1. London: Sheed & Ward, 1955.

Murray, J. C. "St. Robert Bellarmine on the Indirect Power," *Theological Studies,* 9 (1948), 491–535.

Rahner, K. and Ratzinger, J. *The Episcopate and the Primacy.* New York: Herder and Herder, 1962.

Salaverri, I. *De ecclesia Christi* in *Sacrae theologiae summa.* Madrid: Biblioteca de autores cristianos, 1952.

4.   *The Pope as Fellow Bishop*

(a)   *Collegiality*

Acerbi, A. *Due ecclesiologie. Ecclesiologia giuridica ed ecclesiologia di communione nella "Lumen Gentium."* Bologna: Dehoniane, 1975.

Alberigo, G. *Lo sviluppo della dottrina sui poteri nella chiesa universale.* Rome: Herder, 1964.

Barauna, G., ed. *L'Église de Vatican II,* 2 vols. Paris: Cerf, 1966.

Bertrams, W. *The Papacy, the Episcopacy, and Collegiality.* Westminster, Md.: Newman, 1964.

Betti, U. *La dottrina sull'episcopato nel capitolo III costituzione dommatica Lumen Gentium.* Rome: Città nuova, 1968.

Butler, C. *The Theology of Vatican II.* London: Darton, Longman & Todd, 1967.

Colson, J. *L'épiscopat catholique: Collégialité et primauté dans les trois premiers siècles de l'Église.* Paris: Cerf, 1963.

Congar, Y. *Ministères et communion ecclésiale.* Paris: Cerf, 1971.

De Broucker, J. *The Suenens Dossier: The Case for Collegiality.* Notre Dame, Ind.: Fides, 1970.

Dejaifve, G. "First Among Bishops," *Eastern Churches Quarterly,* 14 (1961), 2–25.

Duprey, P. "Brief Reflections on the Title 'Primus inter pares,' " *One in Christ,* 10 (1974), 7–12.

McBrien, R. P. "Collegiality: The State of the Question," in J. A. Coriden, ed., *The Once and Future Church: A Communion of Freedom.* Staten Island, N.Y.: Alba House, 1971. Contains excellent bibliographical references.

Philips, G. *L'Église et son mystère au IIe Concile du Vatican,* 2 vols. Paris: Desclée, 1967–68.

Rahner, K. "On the Relationship Between the Pope and the College of Bishops," *Theological Investigations,* 10:50–70. New York: Seabury, 1977.

Stanley, D. M. "The New Testament Basis for the Concept of Collegiality," *Theological Studies,* 25 (1964), 197–216.

(b) *Ecumenical Councils*

Burns, P. J. "Communion, Councils, and Collegiality: Some Catholic Reflections," in P. C. Empie and T. A. Murphy, *Papal Primacy and the Universal Church,* 151–72. Minneapolis: Augsburg, 1974.

Congar, Y. "The Council as an Assembly and the Church as Essentially Conciliar," in H. Vorgrimler, ed., *One, Holy, Catholic and Apostolic.* London: Sheed & Ward, 1968, pp. 44–88.

——. "Church Structures and Councils in the Relations Between East and West," *One in Christ,* 11 (1975), 224–65.

De Vooght, P. *Les pouvoirs du concile et l'autorité du pape au concile de Constance, Unam Sanctam* 56. Paris: Cerf, 1965.

——. "Les controverses récentes sur les pouvoir du concile et l'autorité du pape au concile de Constance," *Revue théologique de Louvain,* 1 (1970), 45–75.

De Vries, W. *Orient et occident. Les structures ecclésiales vues dans l'histoire des sept premiers conciles oecumeniques.* Paris: Cerf, 1971.

——. "Das ökumenische Konzil und das Petrusamt," *Theologische-Praktische Quartalschrift,* 124 (1976), 24–70.

Duprey, P. "The Synodal Structure of the Church in Eastern Theology," *One in Christ*, 7 (1971), 152–82.

Eno, R. "Pope and Council: The Patristic Origins," *Science et esprit*, 28 (1976), 183–211.

Franzen, A., and Müller, W., eds. *Das Konzil von Konstanz*. Freiburg: Herder, 1964.

Hefele, C. J., and Leclercq, F. *Histoire des conciles d'après des documents originaux*, 8 vols. Paris: Letouzey et Ané, 1907–31.

Hughes, P. *The Church in Crisis: A History of the General Councils 325–1870*. Garden City, N.Y.: Hanover House, 1961.

Küng, H. *Structures of the Church*. New York: T. Nelson, 1964.

L'Huiller, P. "Le concile oecumenique comme autorité suprême de l'Église," *Analekta*, 24 (1975), 78–102.

Mühlen, H. "Modelle der Einigung, auf dem Weg zu einem universalem Konzil aller Christen," *Catholica*, 27 (1973), 111–34.

———. *Morgen wird Einheit sein. Das kommende Konzil aller Christen: Ziel der getrennten Kirchen*. Paderborn: F. Schöning, 1974.

Oakley, F. *Council over Pope?* New York: Herder and Herder, 1969.

Schwaiger, G. *Päpstlicher Primat und Autorität der Allgemeinen Konzilien im Spiegel der Geschichte*. Paderborn: F. Schöning, 1977.

Ullmann, W. *The Origins of the Great Schism*. London: Burns, Oates, and Washbourne, 1948.

(c) *Synod of Bishops*

Anton, A. *Primado y colegialidad. Sus relaciones a la luz del primer Sínodo extraordinario*. Madrid: Católica, 1970.

Congar, Y. "Synod episcopal, primauté et collégialité épiscopale," in *Ministères et communion ecclesiale*, pp. 187–227. Paris: Cerf, 1971.

Fagiolo, V. "Il synodus episcoporum: origine, natura, struttura, compiti," in V. Fagiolo and G. Concetti, eds., *La collegialità episcopale per il futuro della chiesa*. Florence: Vallecchi, 1969.

Fesquet, H. *Le synode et l'avenir de l'Église*. Paris: Centurion, 1972.

Gerhartz, J. G. "Keine Mitentscheidung von Laien auf der Synode? Erwägungen zum Beschluss der gemeinsamen der deutschen Bistümer," *Stimmen der Zeit*, 184 (1969), 145–59.

Laurentin, R. *Le synode permanent: Naissance et avenir*. Paris: Seuil, 1970.

5. The Pope as Ecumenical Pastor

(a) Documentation

Anglican-Roman Catholic International Commission, *The Venice Statement, Origins* (Jan. 27, 1977), Vol. 6, No. 32, 501–8. For an analysis of this text see C. Dumont, ibid., 509–15.

Lutheran-Roman Catholic Dialogue, *Peter in the New Testament* by R. E. Brown, K. P. Donfried, and J. Reumann. Minneapolis: Augsburg; New York: Paulist, 1973.

——. *Papal Primacy and the Universal Church*, ed. P. C. Empie and T. A. Murphy. Minneapolis: Augsburg, 1974.

——. "Teaching Authority and Infallibility in the Church," *Theological Studies*, 40 (1979), 113–66.

(b) Theological Discussion

Cullmann, O. *Peter: Disciple, Apostle, Martyr. A Historical and Theological Essay*, 2nd ed. Philadelphia: Westminster, 1962.

Dulles, A. "The Papacy: Bond or Barrier?" *Origins* (May 2, 1974), Vol. 3, No. 45, 705–12.

——. *The Resilient Church*. Garden City, N.Y.: Doubleday & Company, 1977, esp. Chap. 6, "Toward a Renewed Papacy," and Chap. 9, "Ecumenical Strategies for a Pluralistic Age."

Falconer, A. D. "Contemporary Attitudes to the Papacy: Protestant and Orthodox Perspective," *The Furrow*, 27 (1976), 3–19.

Felmy, K. C. "Petrusamt und Primat in der modernen orthodoxen Theologie," in H. J. Mund, ed., *Das Petrusamt in der gegenwärtigen theologischen Diskussion*. Paderborn: F. Schöning, 1976, pp. 85–99.

Grant, F. C. *Rome and Reunion*. New York: Oxford University Press, 1965.

Journet, C. *The Primacy of Peter from the Protestant and from the Catholic Point of View*. Westminster, Md.: Newman, 1954.

Karrer, O. *Peter and the Church: An Examination of Cull-mann's Thesis.* New York: Herder and Herder, 1963.

Lindbeck, G. A. "Lutherans and the Papacy," *Journal of Ecumenical Studies,* 13 (1976), 368–78.

McCord, P. J., ed. *A Pope for All Christians? An Inquiry into the Role of Peter in the Modern Church.* New York: Paulist, 1976.

Mackenzie, R. "The Reformed Tradition and the Papacy," *Journal of Ecumenical Studies,* 13 (1976), 359–67.

Meyendorff, J., et al. *The Primacy of Peter in the Orthodox Church.* Leighton Buzzard, Bedfordshire: The Faith Press, 1963.

Ryan, H. J., and Wright, J. R., eds. *Episcopalians and Roman Catholics: Can They Ever Get Together?* Denville, N.J.: Dimension Books, 1972.

Wright, J. R. "Anglicans and the Papacy," *Journal of Ecumenical Studies,* 13 (1976), 379–404.

(c)   *Ius Divinum and the Papacy*

Dulles, A. *"Ius Divinum* as an Ecumenical Problem," *Theological Studies,* 38 (1977), 681–708.

Lindbeck, G. A. "Papacy and *Ius Divinum:* A Lutheran View," in P. C. Empie and T. A. Murphy, eds., *Papal Primacy and the Universal Church,* pp. 193–208. Minneapolis: 1974.

Peter, C. J. "Dimensions of Jus Divinum in Roman Catholic Theology," *Theological Studies,* 34 (1973), 227–60.

Piepkorn, A. C. *"Ius Divinum* and *Adiaphoron* in Relation to Structural Problems in the Church: The Position of the Lutheran Symbolical Books," in *Papal Primacy and the Universal Church,* op. cit., pp. 119–27.

Rahner, K. "Reflections on the Concept of *Ius Divinum* in Catholic Thought," *Theological Investigations,* 5, 210–43. Baltimore: Helicon, 1960.

Schlink, E. "Zur Unterscheidung von *Ius divinum* und *Ius humanum,*" in M. Seckler, ed., *Begegnung—Festschrift H. Fries,* pp. 233–50. Graz: Styria, 1972.

(d)   *Infallibility*

Castelli, E., ed. *L'infallibilité: Son aspect philosophique et théologique.* Paris: Aubier, 1970.

Chirico, P. *Infallibility: The Crossroads of Doctrine.* Mission, Kans.: Sheed Andrews & McMeel, 1977.

Ford, J. T. "Infallibility: Who Won the Debate?" *Proceedings of the Catholic Theological Society of America,* 31 (1976), 179–92.

————. "Infallibility: A Review of Recent Studies," *Theological Studies,* 40 (1979), 273–305.

Kirvan, J., ed. *The Infallibility Debate.* New York: Paulist, 1971.

Küng, H. *Infallible? An Inquiry* (Garden City, N.Y.: Doubleday & Company, 1971).

Rousseau, O., et al. *L'infallibilité de l'Église.* Gembloux: Chevetogne, 1963.

Thils, G. *L'infallibilité pontificale.* Gembloux: J. Duculot, 1969.

Tierney, B. *Origins of Papal Infallibility 1150–1350.* Leiden: E. J. Brill, 1972.

6. *The Pope as Elected Leader*

Bertrams, W. "De missione divina et de consecratione episcopali tamquam constitutiva officii supremei ecclesiae pastoris," *Periodica de re morali canonica liturgica,* 65 (1976), 187–242.

Eno, R. "Shared Responsibility in the Early Church," *Chicago Studies,* 9 (1970), 129–41.

Granfield, P. *Ecclesial Cybernetics: A Study of Democracy in the Church.* New York: Macmillan, 1973.

————. "Consilium and Consensus: Decision-Making in Cyprian," *The Jurist,* 35 (1975), 397–408.

————. "Episcopal Elections in Cyprian: Clerical and Lay Participation," *Theological Studies,* 37 (1976), 41–52.

Greeley, A. M. *The Making of the Popes 1978: The Politics of Intrigue in the Vatican.* Mission, Kans.: Andrews and McMeel, 1979.

Hebblethwaite, P. *The Year of Three Popes.* Cleveland: W. Collins, 1979.

Hortal Sanchez, J. *De initio potestatis primatialis Romani Pontificis: Investigatio historico-iuridica a tempore S. Gregorii Magni usque ad tempus Clementis V.* Rome: Gregoriana, 1968.

Krause, H. "Das Papstwahldekret von 1059 und seine Rolle im Investiturseit," *Studi Gregoriani,* 7 (1960).

Legrand, H.-M. "Ministère romain et ministère universel du pape. Le problème de son élection," in G. Alberigo et al.,

Renouveau ecclésial et service papal à la fin du XXe siècle,
Concilium [French ed.], No. 108, 43–54. Paris: Beauchesne,
1975.

Lynch, J. E. "Co-responsibility in the First Five Centuries:
Presbyterial Colleges and the Election of Bishops," *The
Jurist,* 31 (1971), 14–53.

Ortolan, T. "Election des papes," Dictionnaire de théologie
catholique, IV: 2281–319.

Pope Paul VI. *Romano pontifici eligendo* (apostolic constitution that provides the current norms for the election of the
Pope), *Acta apostolicae sedis,* 67 (1975), 609–45.

Roland, E. "Élection des évêques," Dictionnaire de théologie
catholique, IV: 2256–81.

Swidler, L. and A., eds. *Bishops and People.* Philadelphia:
Westminster, 1970.

Thils, G. *Choisir les évêques? Élire le pape?* Paris: Lethielleux,
1970.

7. *The Loss of the Papacy*

(a) *Resignation*

Denifle, H. "Die Denkschriften der Colonna gegen Bonifaz
VIII und der Cardinale gegen die Colonna," *Archiv für
Litteratur-und Kirchengeschichte,* 56 (1889), 493–525.

Fink, K. A. "Die Wahl Martinus V," in *Das Konzil von Konstanz,* A. Franzen and W. Müller, eds. Freiburg: Herder,
1964, pp. 138–51.

Giles of Rome. *De renuntiatione papae* in J. T. Rocaberti, ed.,
Bibliotheca maxima pontificia. Rome: I. F. Buagni, 1698,
I, 1–64.

Godfrey of Fontaines. Quodlibetum XII, Quaestio IV in
J. Hoffmanns, ed., *Les Quodlibets XI–XIV de Godefroid de
Fontaines* in *Les philosophes Belges.* Louvain: Editions de
l'Institut Supérieur de Philosophie, 1932, V: 96–100.

Granfield, P. "Papal Resignation," *The Jurist,* 31 (1978), 118–
31.

John of Paris. *De potestate regia et papali* in J. Leclercq, *Jean
de Paris et l'ecclésiologie du XIIIe siècle.* Paris: J. Vrin,
1942, pp. 251–60.

Leclercq, J. "La rénonciation de Célestin V et l'opinion théologique en France du vivant de Boniface VIII," *Revue
d'histoire de l'Église de France,* 25 (1949), 183–92.

Peter John Olivi. *De renuntiatione papae* in P. L. Oliger, *Archivum franciscanum historicum,* 11 (1918), 366–73.

Ullmann, W. "Medieval Views on Papal Abdication," *Irish Ecclesiastical Record,* 71 (1949), 125–33.

(b)   *Deposition*

Küng, H. *Structures of the Church.* New York: T. Nelson, 1964, pp. 249–68.

McSorley, H. "Some Forgotten Truths About the Petrine Ministry," *Journal of Ecumenical Studies,* 11 (1974), 208–37.

Manselli, R. "Le cas du pape hérétique vu à travers les courants spirituels du XIVe siècle," in E. Castelli, ed., *L'infallibilité: Son aspect philosophique et théologique.* Paris: Aubier, 1970, pp. 113–30.

Mirus, J. A. "On the Deposition of the Pope for Heresy," *Archivum historiae pontificiae,* 13 (1975), 231–48.

Zimmermann, H. *Papstabsetzungen des Mittelalters.* Graz: H. Böhlaus, 1968.

8.   *The Pope of the Future*

Alberigo, G. et al., *Renouveau ecclésial et service papal à la fin du XXe siècle, Concilium* [French ed.], No. 108. Paris: Beauchesne, 1975.

Bradenburg, A. and Urban, H. J., eds. *Petrus und Papst.* Münster: Aschendorff, 1977.

Carra de Vaux, B. "Les images de la papauté au cours des siècles," *Lumière et vie,* 26 (1977), 37–69.

Denzler, G., ed. *Das Papsttum in der Diskussion.* Regensburg: F. Pustet, 1974.

———. *Papsttum heute und Morgen.* Regensburg: F. Pustet, 1975.

Dulles, A. "Toward a Renewed Papacy," in *The Resilient Church.* Garden City, N.Y.: Doubleday & Company, 1977, pp. 113–31.

Ernst, C. "The Primacy of Peter: Theology and Ideology," *New Blackfriars,* 50 (1969), 347–55 and 399–404.

Hebblethwaite, P. *The Runaway Church.* New York: Seabury, 1975.

Küng, H., ed. *Papal Ministry in the Church, Concilium,* Vol. 64. New York: Herder and Herder, 1971.

McBrien, R. P. *The Remaking of the Church.* New York: Harper & Row, 1973.

Misner, P. "Papal Primacy in a Pluriform Polity," *Journal of Ecumenical Studies,* 11 (1974), 239–61.

Mund, H. J., ed. *Das Petrusamt in der gegenwärtigen theologischen Diskussion.* Paderborn: F. Schöning, 1976.

Ohlig, K.-H. *Why We Need the Pope. The Necessity and Limitation of Papal Primacy.* St. Meinrad, Ind.: Abbey Press, 1975.

Spencer, A. "The Future of the Episcopal and Papal Roles," *IDOC International,* May 9, 1970, pp. 63–84.

Stirnimann, H. and Vischer, L., eds. *Papsttum und Petrusamt.* Frankfurt: O. Lembeck, 1975.

Tavard, G. "The Papacy and Christian Symbolism," *Journal of Ecumenical Studies,* 13 (1976), 345–58.

Theisen, J. "Models of Papal Ministry and Reliability," *American Benedictine Review,* 27 (1976), 270–84.

Tracy, D.; Küng, H.; and Metz, J. B., eds. *Toward Vatican III: The Work That Needs to Be Done.* New York: Seabury, 1978.

Zizola, G. *Quale papa?* Rome: Borla, 1977.

INDEX